Cinemas of the Other:
A Personal Journey with Film-makers from Central Asia

2nd Edition

Cinemas of the Other:
A Personal Journey with Film-makers from Central Asia

2nd Edition

by Gönül Dönmez-Colin

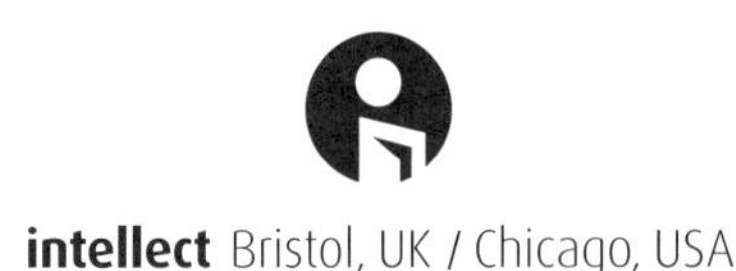

intellect Bristol, UK / Chicago, USA

First published in the UK in 2012 by
Intellect, The Mill, Parnall Road, Fishponds, Bristol, BS16 3JG, UK

First published in the USA in 2012 by
Intellect, The University of Chicago Press, 1427 E. 60th Street,
Chicago, IL 60637, USA

A catalogue record for this book is available from the
British Library.

Production manager: Jelena Stanovnik
Cover designer: Holly Rose
Copy-editor: MPS Technologies
Typesetting: John Teehan

ISBN 978-1-84150-549-7

Printed and bound by Hobbs the Printers Ltd, UK

Contents

Acknowledgements   ix

Introduction   1

KAZAKHSTAN

Ardak Amirkulov and Ermek Shinarbaev   15
A New Beginning   20
Being Young in Almaty   27

Serik Aprimov   34
The Last Stop is Aksuat   36
The Need for Hunters   43

Rachid Nugmanov   48
The Wild East, Rockers, Bikers and a New Life   50

KYRGYZSTAN

Chingiz Aitmatov   59
The Equivocal Marriage of Literature and Cinema   61

Aktan Arymkubat (Abdikalikov)   68
The Most Successful Kyrgyz Film-maker   71
Let There Be Light   77

Ernest Abdizhaparov   82
Minimalist World   84

Gennadi Bazarov   86
A Culture to Share with the Young   87

Tolomush Okeev   93
Searching for Lost Identity   93

TAJIKISTAN

Tachir Mukharovich Sabirov   105
More than a Generation Gap   105

TURKMENISTAN

Halmammet Kakabaev   115
Human Values in a World in Transition   115

UZBEKISTAN

Kamara Kamalova   123
The 'Grande Dame' Of Central Asian Cinema   124

Zulfikar Mussakov   129
Humour in the Absence of Hope and Laughter   129

Yusuf Razikov   136
The Unfair Battle of the Sexes   138

Film Credits   147

Selected Bibliography   169

for Maya, Inés and Phyllis

ACKNOWLEDGEMENTS

I would like to express my gratitude to all film-makers who participated in this project, which would not have been possible without the generous contribution of their time and sincere and open sharing of their work, ideas, feelings and dreams. Special thanks are due to film festivals that focus on the lesser-known cinemas of the world, making it possible to view films that are not otherwise available, particularly, *festival des 3 continents – Nantes*, Cottbus Film Festival, Rotterdam International Film Festival, Montreal World Film Festival, Locarno International Film Festival, Istanbul International Film Festival and Vesoul International Festival of Asian Cinemas.

INTRODUCTION

*C*inemas of the Other: A Personal Journey with Film-Makers from the Middle East and Central Asia* is a collection of interviews with film-makers, whose works are representative of the cinemas of their respective countries.

Cinema worldwide is dominated by the Hollywood film industry, which imposes its culture, values and cinematic gaze although its contribution is no more than a fraction of the annual production. National and regional cinemas/industries that cannot fight such an economically powerful giant have either withdrawn backstage or have begun to adopt the box-office success formula of the adversary. The 'other' in the title has a dual meaning: (1) the non-western nations of the Islamic Middle East and Central Asia that are commonly perceived from a Eurocentric point of view as a distinctly separate entity – remote, alien, mysterious, exotic, barbaric, savage and even threatening and dangerous and (2) the cinemas of these nations, which are committed to voice social and political issues of their peoples, and/or oppose, both in style and content, dominant mainstream cinemas, inside and outside the country.

To examine the cinemas of all countries that could be defined as 'the other' in this sense is beyond the scope of this book or my expertise. I have chosen Iran and Turkey from the Middle East, the two non-Arab Muslim countries in the region, which were never colonized and the Muslim Central Asian Republics of the former Soviet Union, Kazakhstan, Kyrgyzstan, Tajikistan, Turkmenistan and Uzbekistan that share several common traits – history, customs, traditions, languages and religious affiliation – with Iran and Turkey. For the second edition in paperback, we have decided to divide the two parts of the book into two separate volumes to make room for new additions and to provide easier access to readers with different interests. Hence, Volume One focuses on Iran and Turkey, whereas Volume Two concentrates on the Muslim Central Asian Republics of the former Soviet Union. Naturally, the list of distinguished film-makers from these regions is not confined to those included here. Several other film-makers have already taken their deserved place in some of my other books.

After the fall of the Soviet Union, Central Asian cinema drew attention of the film world when a new vitality was observed, particularly, in Kazakhstan. Its capital at the time, Alma Ata (presently called Almaty), was already the largest film centre of the USSR after Moscow, Leningrad (St Petersburg of today) and Kiev. Kazakhfilm Studio's origins go back to the 1930s. The first documentary was shot in 1925 and released in 1929 under the historical title *Pribytie Pervovo Poezda v Alma Atu/The Arrival of the First Train in Alma Ata*. Victor Turin's *Turksib/Stalnoi Put/The Steel Road*, about the building of the Turkish–Siberian railway, was also released the same year. Five years later, a documentary film studio was founded where newsreels, under the title *Soviet Kazakhstan*, documentaries and a few feature films were made. During the war, Mosfilm and Lenfilm were evacuated to Alma Ata, and Sergei Eisenstein shot two parts of *Ivan Grozyj/Ivan, the Terrible* there between 1943 and 1945. For the Kazakhs, national cinema began in 1954 with the first Kazakh fiction film, Shaken Aimanov's *A Love Poem*.

Central Asian cinema was already developed in the 1940s, but under the constraints of the Communist regime, it did not have much chance to flourish. From the time cinema was nationalized in 1919 by a Lenin decree, film production and distribution had been regulated by a government institution, the State Committee for Cinematography (Goskino), which gradually gained control, only to be dismantled with the arrival of *perestroika*, which opened new horizons for young film-makers who were mostly trained in VGIK (the All-Union State Institute of Cinematography) in Moscow and shared the same concerns and difficulties despite the diversity of their backgrounds.

Kazakhstan was perhaps the only Central Asian state, which was not seriously affected by the social, economic and ethnic turmoil that has swept the former republics after the fall of the Soviet Union. Under the liberal policies of President Nursultan Nazarbayev, the country moved to a free market economy smoothly, and banks and co-operatives took the opportunity to publicize through high-profile investments such as cinema. However, when investments did not show profit, the private sector withdrew and some investors were interrogated for laundering black money; film production has since fallen considerably.

When I met Rachid Nugmanov, one of the most prominent voices of the post-Soviet Kazakh *new wave*, in the summer of 1991 at the Kazakhfilm Studio, he told me the new movement was *post-perestroika*. 'It is about young generations everywhere, be they Kazakh, Russian, or any other – about new relationships and a new vitality. No restrictions'. No restrictions; not even commercial! Kazakh films could never make it to the commercial circuit. So, why worry?

Nugmanov's unreleased diploma film, *Ya-Ha* (1986), quickly became an underground cult classic. His first feature, *Igla/The Needle* (1988), starring a rock idol, sold 20 million tickets at the box office, but *Meist/Revenge/The Red Flute* (1990), by Ermek Shinarbaev, was shelved until invited to an independently promoted Festival of Unwanted Films. Turned down for foreign export by Moscow film officials the previous year, the film won the Grand Prix of that festival, which opened its door to Cannes and other prestigious festivals.

Serik Aprimov plunged into the socially and politically committed film genre right from the start. *Konechnaya Ostanovka/Qijan/The Last Stop* (1989), a pessimistic portrait of daily rural life, was praised by the critics but condemned by the villagers of Aksuat (the birthplace of the film-maker and the focus of the story) for exposing the naked truth on screen.

The golden period of the Kazakh cinema, which flourished with *perestroika*, gradually lost its momentum after the fall of the Soviet Empire and the transition to market economy. Private studios that had mushroomed following Independence have been obliged to re-evaluate their projects according to the dictates of the capitalist system.

Film-makers and producers began to think of the western markets while choosing scripts. Established names, even those who have received prizes at international film festivals, are unable to finance their projects unless backed by foreign financing. Some, such as Rachid Nugmanov, have settled in western countries. Darejan Omirbaev, or Serik Aprimov who had won the confidence of the West, are perhaps in a position to find foreign co-producers, but neither has made a film for a long time. The idea of a cinema with no restrictions, which Nugmanov had once advocated, is in the past.

Omirbaev's *Jol/The Road*, the only Kazakh film made in 2001 (produced with funds from France), sums up the situation of Kazakh cinema. Amir, a film-maker estranged from his roots, is obliged to return to his natal village to be on the side of his dying mother. While he is driving, the camera focuses on his troubled face, devoid of energy. Tradition is on the way out, but what is there to replace it? Memories are integrated. Past and present, real and imagined – all become one. His mind wanders to his editing room where the walls are decorated with posters of Serik Aprimov's *Aksuat* and Ardak Amirkulov's *Abai*. In an auditorium where his film is to premiere, Amir declares that a film is 'naked in front of an audience. No one judges a science project as good or bad. There is no objective way to evaluate a film' and concludes, 'the hardest job of all is to be a film-maker'. The projectionist mixes the reels and puts a karate film, which the audience prefer. A tribute to Kazakh film-makers, *The Road* is also a forceful statement on the condition of the film industry in Kazakhstan.

In terms of supporting Kazakh cinema, the government seems to favour mega-projects, which succeed in exalting national feelings. *Kosh Pendeler/Nomad,* the multi-million dollar epic directed by Sergei Bodrov (who is Russian by nationality but Kazakh by blood as he once told me); Talgat Temenov, Kazakh actor and film-maker (whose *Running Target* remains one of the classics of post-Soviet Kazakh cinema) and Ivan Passer, a Czech film-maker living in the US are good examples. Did Kazakhstan need *Nomad?* How many films could Serik Aprimov, who has since left his country for the US, have made with all that money? Regardless of these questions, some people were very happy with a film that reinforced national feelings and told their story using the accustomed and much enjoyed Hollywood blockbuster style. In 2004, when I was in Almaty, *Nomad* was the talk of the town and carpet sellers in the bazaar were selling 'authentic' *Nomad* carpets, the exact ones used on the set – such was the reputation of the homemade blockbuster!

The new obsession with Kazakh myths and legends (particularly in films funded by the government) was also evident during the X. Forum of the National Cinematographies of the ex-Soviet Union (21 to 27 April, 2006). *Svetoy Grech/Holy Sin* by Bolat Sharip, the story of a nomad girl who marries a very loving man but begins to resent him when she cannot have a child with him and finally gives way to temptation, which arrives as a virile young man, was a display of local jewellery and decorations rather than craftsmanship of narrative or character development. Women paraded in national costumes as in a fashion show, and the *yurt* of even the poorest nomad looked like the corner of an ethnography museum.

Films that are able to touch the hearts and minds of audiences who do not expect to be dazzled by flashy costumes or over-rated epics are still made by a handful of courageous film-makers from the younger generation who search for funds outside the borders. *Podarok Stalinu/The Gift to Stalin* by (2008) by Rustem Abdrashow is set in Kazakhstan in 1949, when minorities were forced to move from Russia to Central Asia. A Jewish boy called Sashka is being deported with his grandfather, who dies on the way. The title has a dual meaning: it refers to the nuclear test conducted for the 70th birthday of Stalin, which is considered the gift of death as many perished as a result of it; it is also about the dream of the little boy who believes that if he could give a birthday gift to Stalin, he would be able to see his parents again. The film was co-produced with partners from Russia, Poland, Israel and Kazakhstan, and is a good example of transnational cinema that has been established, particularly since the last decade, answering the demands of socio-political and economic changes in the world and at the same time challenging the old paradigm of 'national cinema' by carrying cinema beyond national borders.

According to what Gulnara Abikeyeva, the Kazakh film scholar and author has told me, Kazakh cinema gravitates towards Russia. Local spectators, especially in the urban milieu, watch Russian channels on television and Russian films in the cinemas, which makes the Russian market attractive to Kazakh film-makers. Starting with *Mongol* (2007) to *A Gift for Stalin,* including *Tulip* (S. Dvortsevoy, 2008), which was awarded at the Cannes Film Festival, Kazakh–Russian co-productions have become commonplace. In 2008, the State-owned Kazakhfilm studio systematically invited Russian film-makers to Kazakhstan, and in 2009, it became the official policy. Except for art-house films that receive recognition at international film festivals – such as Serik Aprimov's *The Hunter* or E. Tursynov's *Kelin* (2009) – most Kazakh films do not showcase national characteristics or Kazakh identity, which is unlike the cinemas of some of the other states, according to Abikeyeva. Although Kazakhstan's financial resources are favourable to developing Kazakh national cinema, a strategy in this direction is missing. Distribution of Kazakh films constitutes only 2.5%. In 2010, there were 170 theatres in Kazakhstan, 80 of which were in the major cities, mostly in Almaty. Multiplexes, which are all new and equipped with digital facilities, show Hollywood films because of agreements with the US. Piracy is widespread as in all of Central Asia.

Cinema arrived in Kyrgyzstan later than the other republics. Kyrgyzfilm Studio was founded in 1942. Between 1954 and 1960, Mosfilm Studio sent many talented film-makers to Frunze (Bishkek of today) to give a boost to the industry. Vasili Pronin's *Saltanat/Sovereignty* (1955) was produced there. The negative aspect of this policy was that Kyrgyz cinema did not have much chance to develop its identity.

Bolakbet Shamshiev and Tolumush Okeev are considered the founders of national cinema, but world-renowned writer Chingiz Airmatov and his works are responsible for feeding Kyrgyz cinema its artistic nourishment.

Aktan Alymkubat (formerly Abdikalikov) is the most successful Kyrgyz film-maker. *Beshkempir/The Adopted Son*, a sensitive story about cultural identity, was distributed in several countries through its French partner. Although it was not a favourite in its own country, the industry profited from its international success.

With political instability and economic difficulties, Kyrgyzstan is not in a position to develop a healthy film industry. Nourishing national cinema is not a priority for the government. Co-productions seem the only light at the end of the tunnel, but they may come with a price tag. Hollywood films are the most popular entertainment for those who can afford to go to the cinema. Political films directly dealing with the Soviet era are conspicuously absent. 'We got a good education studying there', comments Baktyr Karagulov, one of the prominent film-makers, 'Why should we offend them? Of course, we lost a little, but we always had our culture. Thanks to Khrushchev, we have Aitmatov'.

Before Independence, would-be film-makers had studied in Moscow. Hardly anyone with a Moscow education is working today. The Institute of Fine Arts in the capital Bishkek has a department of Film and Television, but only two or three films are made in Kyrgyzstan each year. In 2010, there were four modern theatres with a total of seven screens, but distribution is negligible for Kyrgyz films. Moscow has ceased to be the meeting point of film-makers from all parts of the Soviet Union. As Aitmatov ironically pointed out, 'we have to go to places like Cottbus (a small city in the former East Germany) to meet each other'!

In Tajikistan, the first documentary, about the arrival of the first train in the capital Dusbanbe, was made in 1929 by three Russian pioneers: Vasily Kuzin, Artem Pishevich and Nikolai Gexulin, and Tajikfilm Studio was established in 1930. The first significant feature film was *Pochetnoe Pravo/Honorary Right* (1934) by Kamil Yarmatov. Davlat Khudonazarov, a political activist, is an important representative of the new wave of 1960–1970, marked by a diversity of styles and themes. Tachir Sabirov made his most important film, *Margi Sudher/Death of an Extortionist* (1966), during this period.

Following Independence, a new 'new wave' similar to the one in Kazakhstan was aborted by civil war (1992–1997), which resulted in a wave of emigration from the republic. Many film-makers moved to Moscow or to western countries and began seeking foreign financing. Bakhtiyar Khudoynazarov, who has shown his talents starting with his first film *Bratan/Brothers* (1992), a black-and-white road movie that crosses the Pamirs with a steam engine and Jamseed Usmanov (*Little Angel, Make Me Happy*, 1992 and *Bihisht Faqat Barqi Murdagon/To Get To Heaven First You Have To Die*, 2006) are examples of successful Tajik film-makers who work outside the country and make transnational films.

In the last decade of the Soviet Union and early 1990s, video and audio cassettes became increasingly popular sources of entertainment as well as means of disseminating information outside government control. Today, films are shown in the Dushanbe theatres and in villages on an irregular basis. Depression and lack of prospects among the young generation formed the most prominent themes of short films screened during a retrospective on Tajik cinema held at the Cottbus Film Festival 2001.

Cinema tries to survive despite all odds. Budgets are allotted by the State according to priority and cinema is not a priority of the government. Furthermore, one needs a licence to make a film. As many specialists have left the country, competent teachers to educate the youth are lacking. But young people with ambitions are determined to make films even if it means mortgaging whatever they own to get a bank loan.

The first feature film after Independence, *A Statue of Love*, was made in 2003 by a young film-maker, Umedsho Mirzoshirinov, who does not come from the Soviet school. Since then, five to seven films are made each year, most of which are digital. However, Nosir Saidov's border story, *Ghiyame Rooz/True Noon* (2009), which garnered several international awards, was shot on 35 mm. General themes in these films are broken families with absent fathers/husbands who have either left the country to earn a living elsewhere or are involved in criminal activities. Children are often used as hopes for the future.

Tajik film-making has traditionally had closer ties with the Persian culture (the common Farsi language); particularly, Iranian cinema and Mohsen Makhmalbaf's efforts in recent years to support the Didor Film Festival and encourage young film-makers to make short films have been fruitful. Makhmalbaf shot his film *Sukut/Silence* (1998) in Dushanbe. But there are no distribution avenues inside the country for Tajik films.

Cinema in Turkmenistan began with the newsreels just like in the rest of the Soviet Union. In the 1920s, the first chroniclers recorded anniversary celebrations, inaugurations of Lenin monuments and similar events. During World War II, when Kiev Studio was moved to Ashkabad, war 'note-books' were made. The documentarians of the post-war period focused on socialist reconstruction, the reclaiming of the desert, newfound freedom of the Muslim women, etc. Feature film-making began in 1929, reaching its peak in the 1960s and 1970s. The most renowed Turkmen film-maker Khodzakuli Narliev made his best film, *Nevestka/The Daughter-in-Law*, in 1972. Some of the other prominent Turkmen film-makers are Biul-Biul Mamedov, Usman Saparov and Halmammet Kakabayev.

Turkmenian cinema after Independence has the most limited production of the Central Asian states. Caspian Sea offers Turkmenistan a 500-km coastline with numerous natural resources, including oil and fish, but is threatened by extreme levels of pollution as well as fluctuating water levels. Living standards dropped since 1991, although, Turkmenistan still maintains close bilateral economic and military ties with Russia. The government controls the media, and many talented film-makers from Narliev to Shugarev have found themselves in conflict with the regime and left the country when they could no longer make films. The isolationist policies of the government have been detrimental to the industry. The State studio Turkmenfilm in Ashgabad was closed in 1998, but re-instated by the president in 2007 with a new stature and a new name, Khan Oguz, to honour the legendary Turkmen ancestor. Three video feature films were made in 2008. Shooting 35-mm films is a dream of the past. There are only two theatres in the country, both of which are in Ashgabad.

Uzbekistan is proud to have the first known screening in Central Asia in its capital, Tashkent, in 1897. The first Uzbek documentary was shot there in 1923 and the first feature films, *Pakhta-Aral/Pahta Aral* (N. Scerbakov), *Minaret Smerti/The Minaret of the Dead* (Viatcheslav Viskovski) and *The Muslim Woman* (Dimitri Bassaligo) were made in 1925. Nabi Ganiev and Kamil Yarmatov are the founders of modern Uzbek cinema. During the 1960s, following the 'thaw' of Khrushchev and the New Wave in the West, Uzbek New Wave was born. Ali Khamraev is one of the important representatives of this movement. *Perestroika* opened the doors to talented young film-makers such as Jahangir Faiziev, Zulfikar Mussakov and Yusuf Razikov, but one must not forget the important contributions of Kamara Kamalova, the most prominent woman film-maker of Uzbekistan, if not Central Asia.

Uzbek films favour popular narratives. The genre and style vary from irony and farce to science fiction and period pieces. Melodramas, very similar to the *Yeşilçam* commercial cinema produced in Turkey, attract large audiences, with comedies coming second. The influence of Bollywood is very evident. Ninety-nine percent of the films distributed are Uzbek films, most of which are produced privately and very cheaply. The State finances six or seven films annually.

Uzbekistan is a country rich in natural gas, coal, oil, gold and other resources. Among all its Central Asian neighbours, its economy stands second to that of Kazakhstan. However, the market system has only accorded prosperity to a privileged few as the country tries to move away from the Stalinist heritage of cotton monoculture, which has brought tremendous environmental devastation. Although stronger and wealthier than either Tajikistan or Kyrgyzstan, Uzbekistan also faces deteriorating social and economic conditions. Formation of a new national identity, decolonization, Islamization, Turkification and de-Russification are some of the priorities. With daily life deteriorating in several areas, people blame the new capitalism for their sufferings, and Islamic fundamentalist movement is on the rise.

Just like in Kyrgyzstan and Turkmenistan, among recent productions, at least those that we see in the West, political films dealing with the issue of coming to terms with the Soviet period, or an analysis of the present situation, are absent among recent productions, at least those that we see in the West, just like in Kyrgyzstan and Turkmenistan. It has been reported in the western media that despite economic stability, there is still a lack of freedom, and journalists have been persecuted for their political stance. According to the constitution of 1992, media is free to cover any topic, but until 2002, the Chief Inspectorate of Secrets exercised strict pre-publication censorship. Abolished due to pressure from the international community, the pre-publication censorship works in other ways, warning editors that they would be held responsible for what is published, and many subjects stay taboo. Ali Khamraev, once hailed as the Godard of the East, offended the sentiments of traditional Uzbek society with his last fiction film, *Bo Ba Bu*, and now lives in Moscow.

Interviews I have conducted with film-makers from different generations point to the emergence of new cinema in the post-Independence Muslim Central Asian states, with young film-makers trying to find their path through a difficult transition period. In comparison to the Soviet regime, when the industry was under the tight control of Moscow, a certain amount of freedom is experienced. However, controversial political subjects are dealt with auto-censorship, if not State intervention. Hollywood films are the most popular. The largest drawback to the development of national cinema, however, is the lack of money. As the eminent Kyrgyz writer and philosopher Chingiz Aitmatov commented, 'The ideological censorship of the Soviet Union is now replaced with the censorship of money which is the reason behind the domination of the Western culture'.

A sampling of films from the younger generation during the X. Forum of the National Cinematographies of the ex-Soviet Union revealed that one of the pressing concerns was the borders that were sealed after the fall of the Soviet Union. Tajik, Kyrgyz and Kazakh films repeatedly focused on border issues that have affected people's lives. *Border*, a short film from Kyrgyzstan by Marat Azykulov, was about the futile attempts of a son to bury his father across the border, in a world where, as Hodzhakuli Narliev commented, 'tragedy is not respected anymore'.

Gulnara Abikeyeva asserts that post-Independence Kazakh cinema shows a desire to reach the global market by all means, including imitating western standards; Kyrgyz cinema searches for national identity; Tajik cinema reflects the internal situation of the country; Turkmen cinema tries to preserve the old culture and Uzbek cinema is occupied with beautiful lives. And in sum, Central Asian cinema is diverse in its messages.

While conducting interviews for both volumes, several interviewees from different countries expressed similar concerns regarding culture and cinema in the postmodern age. Erden Kıral and Ali Özgentürk from Turkey, Dariush Mehrjui from Iran, and Chingiz Aitmatov from Kyrgyzstan lamented the loss of values in consumer-oriented societies where intellectuals are either shunned or pushed to the margins. Kazakh Rachid Nugmanov and Iranian Abbas Kiarostami converged on the search for nothingness through Japanese *haiku* poetry. The future of cinema, which was one of the main topics of concern during its 100th birthday, is now linked to acceptance of new technologies, although with reservations. Several menaces were underlined as threatening national film industries: Hollywood dominance, economic limitations, State censorship, as well as the increasingly powerful network of film festivals and funding/distribution systems of the West that have begun to shape national products according to the tastes of western audiences, creating artificial products. The exotic quality of such films appeals to the West, and attracts foreign finance. Some are of exceptional quality, whereas others try to bank in on a tried-and-true formula and inadvertently reinforce the Orientalist point of view that assumes the East as the 'other' of the West – an 'othering' that reduces whole cultures to one dimension.

Despite the digital revolution that has offered economic advantages in addition to possibilities of free expression, national film industries faced with difficulties of funding, production and distribution have been relying on foreign monetary backing. It would be naïve to think that financial dependence would not determine the direction and destination of the end-product. The proliferation of film festivals plays a part in the abundance of films from the so-called third world or 'the South' that are supposed to be for a universal audience, but are in fact made for festival audiences with little to offer to the home audience.

The present project began in the early 1990s. To conduct the interviews, I have travelled from Kazakhstan to Canada via Iran, Turkey and several other countries along the way, participating in film events where it would be possible to screen the films and meet the film-makers. All interviewees, except one, are film-makers. I felt it necessary to include Chingiz Aitmatov, a novelist and screenwriter, who is considered the 'the heart and soul of Kyrgyz cinema'.

For the second edition, I have updated the bio/filmographies of the film-makers and have added more recent interviews, when possible. Unfortunately, two prominent film-makers of Central Asia, Tolomush Okeev from Kyrgyzstan and Tachir Mukharovich Sabirov from Tajikistan and the great writer, thinker and dear friend Chingiz Aitmatov have passed away. I hope that this work will do justice to their memories.

Each interview begins with direct questions discussing the film(s) screened most recently, leading to more general topics, such as the cinema of the country in question. In addition to artistic concerns, the integral part of the interview is to place the film-makers and their work within the socio-economic and political context of their environment. Personal questions are approached only if relevant to the work. In several cases, the precarious situation of the film-makers in their countries, their personal feelings and/or the government censorship and restrictions had to be considered before formulating questions.

I have tried to maintain a universal approach and a style that is not overly academic in order to widen the readership to include the general public interested in discovering less-known territories. To avoid redundancy, I have chosen to divert from a single pattern. Although my questions were prepared in advance with meticulous research, the circumstances and the atmosphere of the interview as well as the personality and the present mood of the interviewee often led to improvisations. Some interviews happened in a rather formal fashion, whereas others resembled conversations between old friends. In fact, several film-makers who participated have become friends over the years.

The interviews stretch over a decade, which I feel is enriching in terms of following trends, themes and overriding concerns from a chronological point of view. When the same film-maker is presented at intervals, it becomes more challenging to observe the evolution of the artist.

The book aims at familiarizing the readers – academicians, film studies students as well as laymen – with the cinemas of the region through first-hand accounts from the film-makers regarding historical and recent developments and trends, paying particular attention to political and cultural evolutions, with the eventual desired outcome of opening, without compromise, the 'otherness' of the 'other' to culminate in a better understanding that would overcome clichés, stereotypes and founded or imagined fears.

KAZAKHSTAN

ARDAK AMIRKULOV and ERMEK SHINARBAEV

Ardak Amirkulov and Ermek Shinarbaev are renowned film-makers of the Kazakh New Wave that gained prominence by the end of 1980s. Amirkulov was part of a workshop organized by the Russian film-maker Sergei Soloviev at the VGIK (All-Union State Institute of Cinematography) in Moscow in 1984, which is generally credited with the birth of a new movement that chose a new film language that favoured natural décor – night shots in public places, alleys or deserted roads – and non-professional actors. Abandoning the Soviet tradition for a more western outlook, the New Wave tried a sociological and psychological approach in the treatment of characters and in reflecting destabilized cultural roots.

Amirkulov and Shinarbaev have established their careers separately with remarkable films that are distinct in genre, narrative style and subject matter. Amirkulov's first film, *Ghibel Otrara/Otrar's Death* (1991), which took four years to make, is a historical epic about the ancient town of Otrar, the centre of nomadic civilization in Asia, which was destroyed under Chingiz Khan's orders. The fate of Otrar, a town so much divided by hatred and envy that it could not defend itself against the invaders, has been the subject of dispute among historians and ethnographers for many years. In this film, the events are seen from the point of view of a witness and participant in the battle, who exposes how the Mongol conquerors execute their military operations meticulously by recruiting local merchants, bribing enemies and torturing captives to obtain information while the Muslims of Samarkand, Bukhara and other ancient towns of Central Asia remain passive to the tragedy. The scriptwriters, Svetlana Karmalita and Alexei German, construct a historical fantasy with spectacular scenes of ancient times of flourishing towns, expanding trade, crafts and increasing military power. At the same time, they create an allegory for Russia and its political climate just before Hitler's invasion of 1941. The film stresses the importance of interconnecting people of different backgrounds with a warning that choosing personal ambitions over global concerns may endanger civilizations and humanity causing an entire way of life to disappear. The fact that Alexei German entrusted such a complex script to a student and a first-time film-maker is a confirmation of Amirkulov's talents.

Ermek Shinarbaev's first film, *Karalisulu/The Mourning Beauty* (1982), was a psychological drama about a young nomad woman who lost her husband prematurely. Its allusions to female sexual urges scandalized Alma Ata as well as Moscow. His first feature, *Sestra Moia Liussia/My Sister Lucy* (1985), partly based on the childhood of

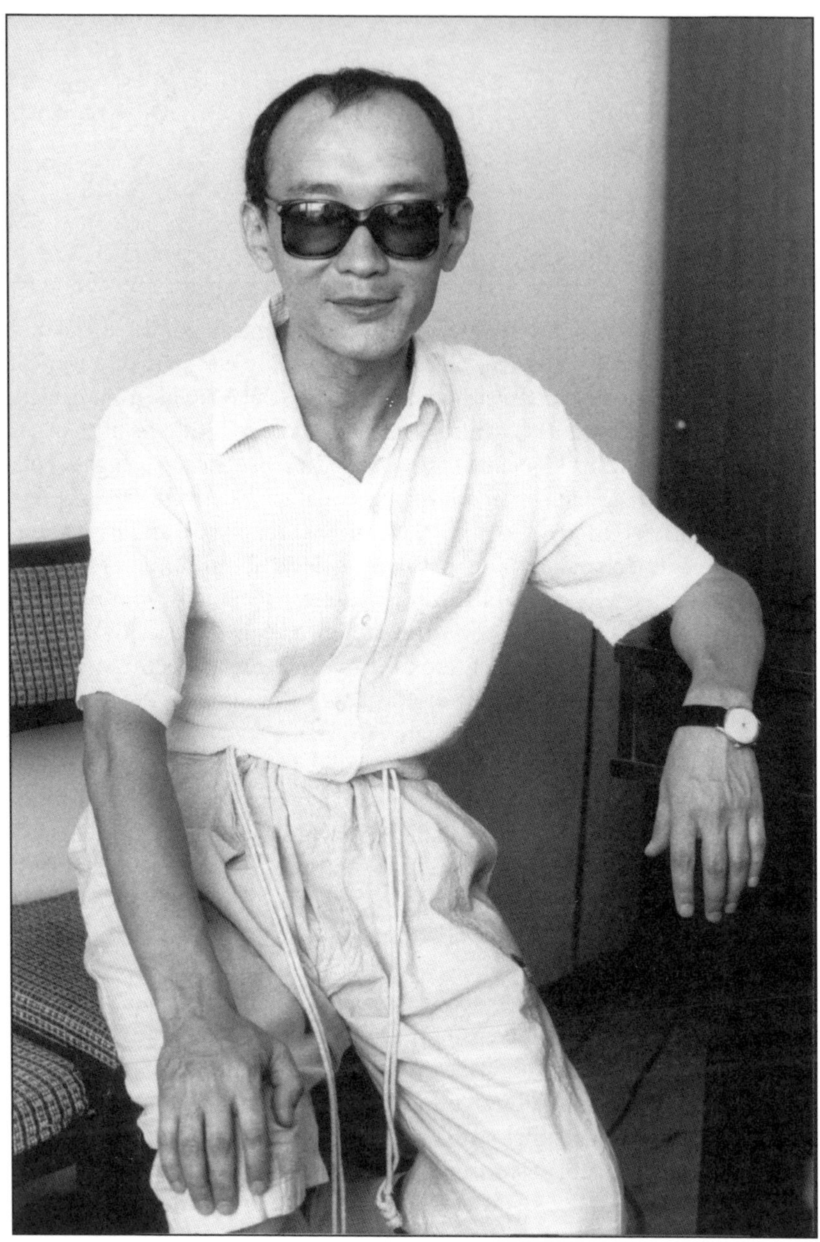

Ermek Shinarbaev

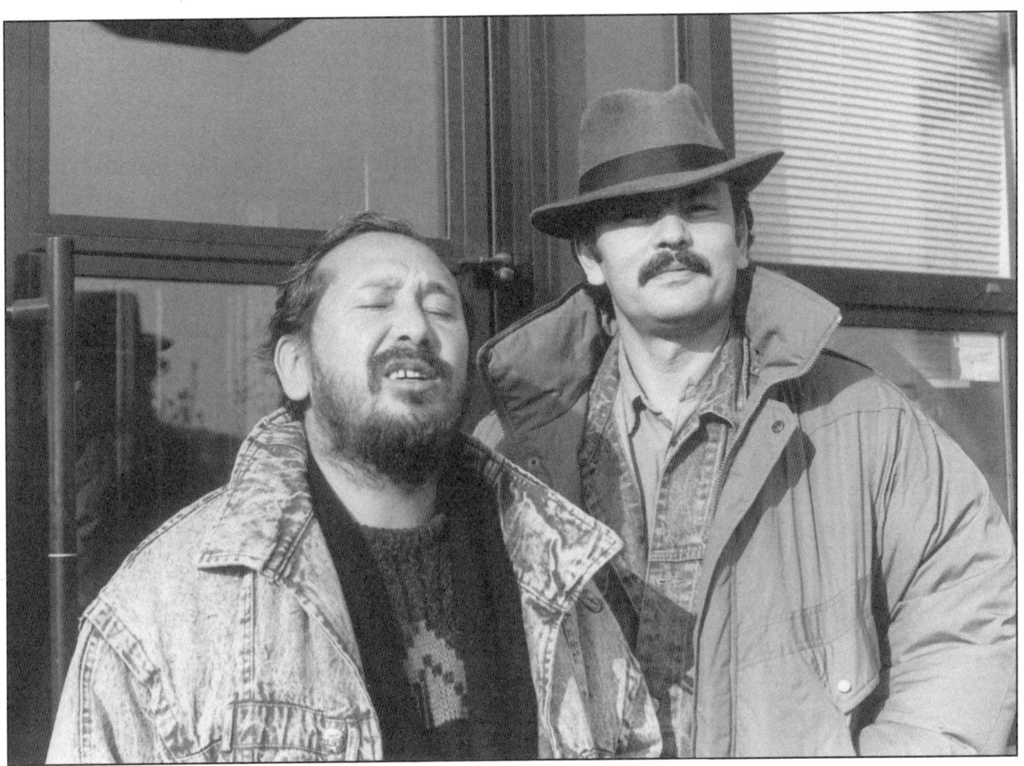

Ardak Amirkulov with Tungishpay Jamankulov,
actor from *Otrar's Death*. Nantes, 1991.

Anatoly Kim, the Korean novelist responsible for the script, explored similar themes within the story of a friendship between a Kazakh woman and a Russian one, both of them single mothers.

Meist/Revenge/The Reed Flute (1989) was another collaboration with Anatoly Kim. In this multi-layered and the deeply metaphorical film of seven novellas about life and death, the writer and the film-maker have gone beyond the concrete political reality of the tragic history of one million Koreans living in the Soviet Union to reflect on revenge that leads to degeneration and destruction, but the message, delivered by the poet protagonist, was concrete: 'True verses are not destined to appear in a world where revenge reigns'.

Azghyin Ushtykzyn' Azaby/The Place on the Tricone (1993), Shinarbaev's fourth feature film, a collaboration with a young Kazakh scriptwriter, Nikita Jhilkibaev, was on a contemporary subject and in that sense different from the other films written by Anatoly Kim. A psychological rather than sociological portrayal of youth in the former Soviet Union just before its demise, *The Place on the Tricone*, is realistic in reflecting the loss of morale. The film opens with two 20-year-old men rolling joints in a small flat in Alma Ata. Later, we see one of them in bed with a girlfriend. The mother wakes them up and lectures her son: 'You must work to make a living'. He replies, 'To live, you need courage' and returns to his room to spend his time listening to an Italian opera sung by Maria Callas that he plays on an old tape recorder. The film follows the lethargic young man through one summer: he meets friends, mainly women, and has important and trivial conversations until his experiments with drugs bring him face to face with death.

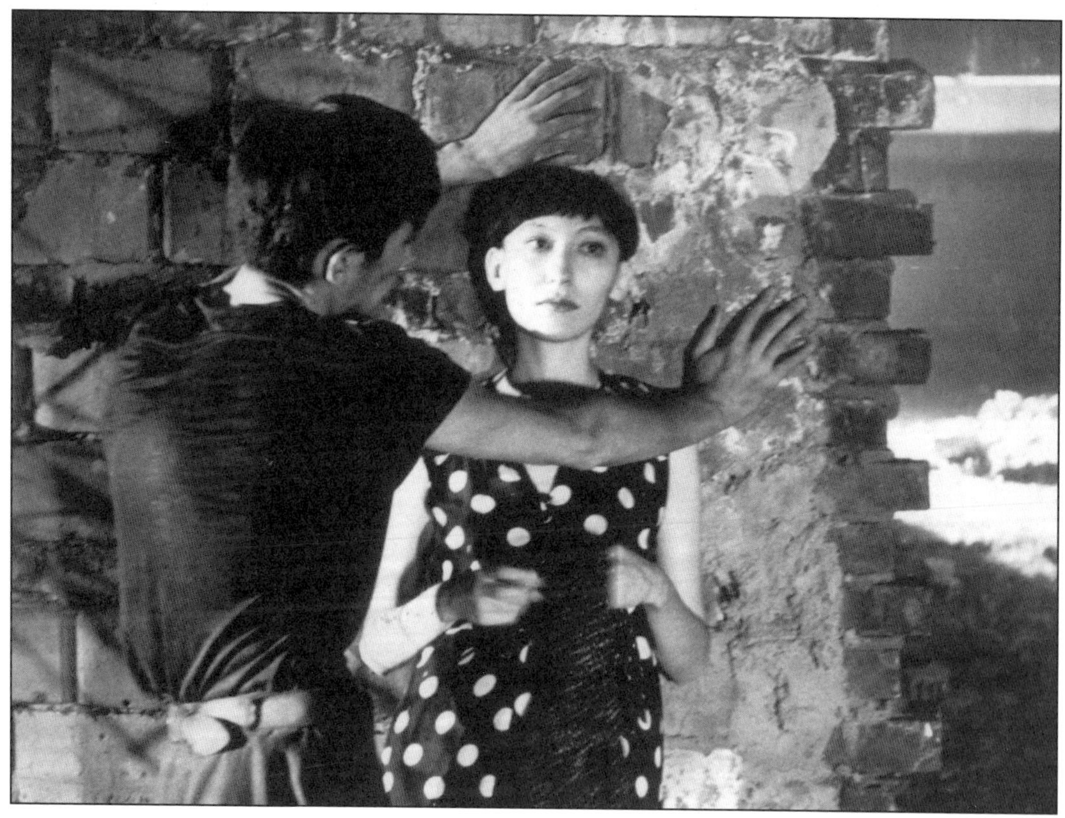

The Place on the Tricone

In 1997, Ermek and Ardak joined hands on a minimalist film about displaced youth, *1997 – Sapisi Rustema S Risunkami/1997 – Rustem's Notes with Drawings*, with Shinarbaev as producer Amirkulov as director. The focus of the film, the story of youth in a vacuum, is very different from Amirkulov's epic *Otrar's Death*, but perhaps closer to the heart of Shinarbaev, bringing to mind *The Place on the Tricone*. Nonetheless, the experimental genre is new to both. Shot with the participation of Ardak's students at the film school in Almaty, with neither professional actors nor a coherent narrative, *1997* offers the viewers a glimpse at characters that move in an out of the viewing range in a minimalist fashion. The protagonist, Rustem, is given a diary by his sister to record his thoughts, but he has nothing to write. So he draws. One day he meets a young delicate girl who also wanders

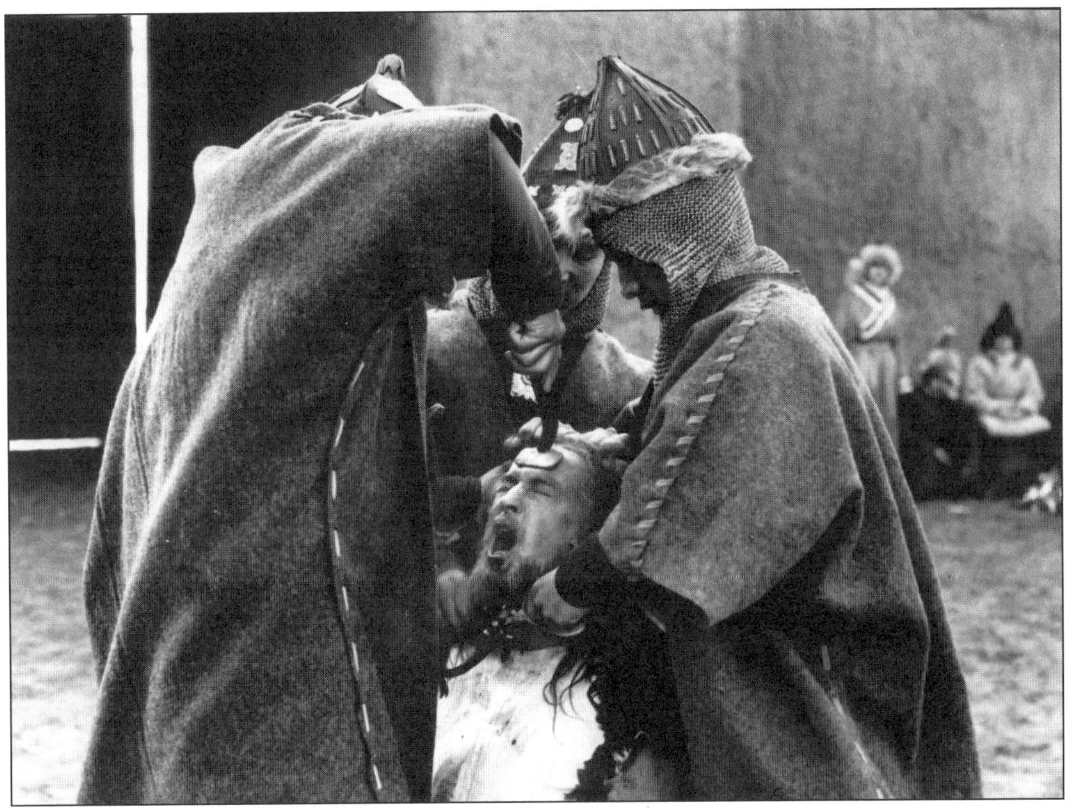

Otrar's Death

around the city aimlessly, but their relationship only goes in circles. The complete inertia that shrouds Almaty is likened to the insomnia suffered by the citizens of Makondo in Gabriel Garcia Marquez' novel *One Hundred Years of Solitude*, when exhaustion from lack of sleep causes amnesia.

It was an emotional moment to meet Ermek Shinarbaev and Ardak Amirkulov in 1998 in Berlin during the 49th International Berlin Film Festival, where they came to present *1997 – Rustem's Notes with Drawings*. Our last meeting was in 1993 in Montreal when Ardak's *Otrar's Death* was shown along with *Revenge* by Ermek. However, my first meeting with Ermek Shinarbaev goes back to Alma Ata (today's Almaty) during the summer of 1991, 22 July to be exact, only few months before the official declaration of Independence and in the middle of the drastic changes from one system to another. The first interview with Ermek took place in Alma Ata in 1991 in the Kazakhfilm Studio and the second with both film-makers in Berlin in 1998.

A NEW BEGINNING

Only some years ago practically no one had heard of Kazakh cinema and suddenly several important film festivals are organizing special programmes on the Kazakh New Wave. The films that were shown in Nantes in France during the Festival of 3 Continents last autumn drew large crowds. Amanjol Aituarov's first feature, *Kauchu Ikial/Light Touch*, a poetic rendition of the past lightly touching the present, as he explained to the enthusiastic audience, won an important award. In fact, most of us saw our first Kazakh films there. What is this New Wave and how did it start?

Fifty years of Kazakh cinema never interested others. During the last five years, a new situation arose with the arrival of the new wave. Creators of this new movement were a well-known Russian director, Sergei Soloviev, whose latest film, *Under the Sky Full of Stars*, will be shown at the Montreal World Film Festival next month and Murat Auezov, a Kazakh literary critic and the son of our famous novelist, Muhtar Auezov, the author of *Abai*. In the beginning of the 1980s, Sergei Soloviev organized a workshop for ten Kazakh young men who went to Moscow to study film at the VGIK. Five of them were directors, two were cameramen, two were designers and one was a scriptwriter. These students created the Kazakh New Wave. They all participated in Soloviev's film *Chuzhaya Belaya Iryaboi/The Wild Pigeon*, which received the Special Prize of the Jury at the Venice Film Festival in 1985. Murat became the chief, created a new atmosphere and ushered them into the world of culture. Before we existed as no one in nowhere; now we are part of the world culture. Rachid Nugmanov's diploma film, *Ya-Ha* (1986), produced at the VGIK, became an underground legend and won awards. Serik Aprimov's short film, *Two Men on a Motorbike*, won the first prize of All Union Film Festival in Baku in 1987. This summer, Moscow Film Festival organized a discussion on Young Kazakh Cinema and showed three feature films and a documentary.

When I asked Soloviev about the Kazakh New Wave, he said, 'There is a novel behind the story of each young man who attended the workshop, a novel that does not fit any formula'. And he added with his characteristic chuckle, '1984 was a strange year. The space rocket went up under Khrushchev and when it came down Brezhnev was greeting it. While we were filming (*The Wild Pigeon*), Soviet presidents were dying one by one. We started with Andropov in 1984, then Brezhnev and we finished with Gorbachev'.

The Wild Pigeon is based on an autobiographical novel by Boris Riakhovski, who was exiled to Kazakhstan in 1937. Kazakhstan was used as a prison for Soviet people, but many of them stayed after their terms, as their lives were not so bad.

According to Soloviev, Kazakh author Suleimanov was the Minister of Film-Making in Kazakhstan in 1984 but there were hardly any films made. He encouraged the project to propagate liberal Soviet policies to different nationalities with the condition that the film would be made in the Kazakh language and would show plenty of Kazakh scenery.

The film was shot in the Kazakh language and later dubbed into Russian.

The way Soloviev found his students was also very interesting. Those days students got into VGIK through connections. *Po blatu*, he called it. It must be a Russian word for 'uncle'. He decided to find the students himself and after three months of search in the scorching heat of an Alma Ata summer, he did find them: Rachid Nugmanov, Serik Aprimov…

Ardak Amirkulov, Amir Karakulov, Talgat Temenov … they went to Moscow to get their IDs and returned to Alma Ata to start work with Soloviev as his assistants.

Tell me about your training and your work.

I studied at the VGIK in Moscow twice, first to study acting under Boris Babochkin and then direction under Sergei Gerassimov. My diploma film, *Karalisu/The Mourning Beauty* (1982), was denounced as a *un-Kazakh* film by both Moscow and Alma Ata for breaking the taboos and showing that sexual urges existed for women as well. Kazakhs were scandalized because they did not like what they saw, but Moscow was equally scandalized because a Kazakh film was supposed to say nice things about Kazakhstan. *The Mourning Beauty* is based on a short story written in 1925 by Muhtar Auezov. When the film opens, nomads are moving to another village while an old woman tells a little girl a story: A young woman named Karagos meets a young man and they fall in love as they gaze at each other's eyes. They get married and have a son. Their marital bliss ends when, despite her forewarnings and implorations, he leaves home one night to fight in the war. When he is killed, she goes through an emotional upheaval. The changes in her moods exasperate her relatives. She refuses to marry someone else, runs to the woods, spends nights in the open and flogs herself as punishment for being alive. Natal'ya Arinbasarova, a famous Kazakh actress who also played in Kanchalovsky's *First Teacher* and won the Best Actress award at the Venice Film Festival, plays the nomad woman.

When did you start working with Anatoli Kim?

My collaboration with Anatoli Kim, a writer of Korean origin, began with *Sestra Moia Liussia/My Sister Lucy*, my first feature length film, which is partly based on his childhood in the south of Kazakhstan at the end of World War II. In the film, a pilot reminiscences his childhood through an imaginary letter to a girl he used to play with in 1947. There are two widows in the film: a Kazakh and a Russian. The Russian woman has a house where she lives with her daughter Lucy and she invites the Kazakh woman and her son to live with her. This film explores the psychological dimensions of the lives of young women who are forced to live alone, carrying the burden of widowhood and single parenthood while trying to deal with their natural urges.

You have created a remarkable balance with the two women characters. The Russian is an extrovert; she hides her sorrow by wearing a mask of joy and indulges in sex although this upsets her young daughter. The Kazakh is an introvert, tied to her customs and traditions. She internalizes her pain and even contemplates suicide. They both suffer. The agony of the death of a partner is two-fold: the loss of a loved one and the guilt of being alive. The scene that touched me the most in that film was the marketplace where widows go to sell, among other items, their dead husbands' overcoat, to have some money to buy bread or eggs to feed their children. You also use animals as symbols – a wounded bird on the beach, a big fish found in a little pond, a dog given to the boy by a strange woman. (Later on, in *Revenge*, the turtle is significant.) The tension of the times reaches a climax when a man is lynched by the crowd for stealing a cow.

In 1987, I made another feature film called *Go Out of the Forest into the Meadow*, which was a failure although I think it is my best film.

What about *Revenge*?

Revenge was made two years ago. It is a parable, an epic folk drama with philosophical dimensions and a mystical journey to the cultures of the Far East. The motive of water, as manifested by the boundlessness of the ocean, is pivotal to the film. It symbolizes *DAO*, the way or the flow, which is formlessness, emptiness and nothing-ness; it is also very dynamic and restless, its dynamism determining the development of life in the universe. The highest goal for an individual is to merge with *DAO*. That is why the turtle you see in the first scene crawls towards the sea and the women in the last scene have an unhurried conversation about a trip to the ocean, overcoming the fear of drowning because the vastness of the ocean cannot frighten them anymore.

This is another collaboration with Anatoli Kim.

The script is written in Russian by Anatoli Kim based on his recollections of the history of his people. I would have liked to shoot it in Korea but as USSR had no relations with South Korea, this was not possible and I refused to shoot it in the Communist North. The final scene was shot on the Sakhalin Island off the east coast of Siberia, an area from which native Koreans were expelled under Stalin during World War II and forcefully transported to Kazakhstan. The history of one million Koreans living in the Soviet Union has been a tragedy. Filming and photography had been forbidden on the island. Our cameras were the first. *Revenge* would never have seen the light save for an independently promoted Festival of Unwanted Films, organized in Podolsk, near Moscow, by the Union of Soviet Film-Makers in collaboration with several production studios across the Soviet Union. Turned down for foreign export by Moscow film officials the previous year, it won the Grand Prix of this festival. It was also shown at the Cannes Film Festival and it will be participating at several other international film festivals including Montreal, but it has not been released commercially here. All theatres belong to Goskino, whose main interest is money. Hollywood films dominate the market; Soviet films are not shown. Furthermore, Kazakh New Wave has refinement, which is difficult for the audiences.

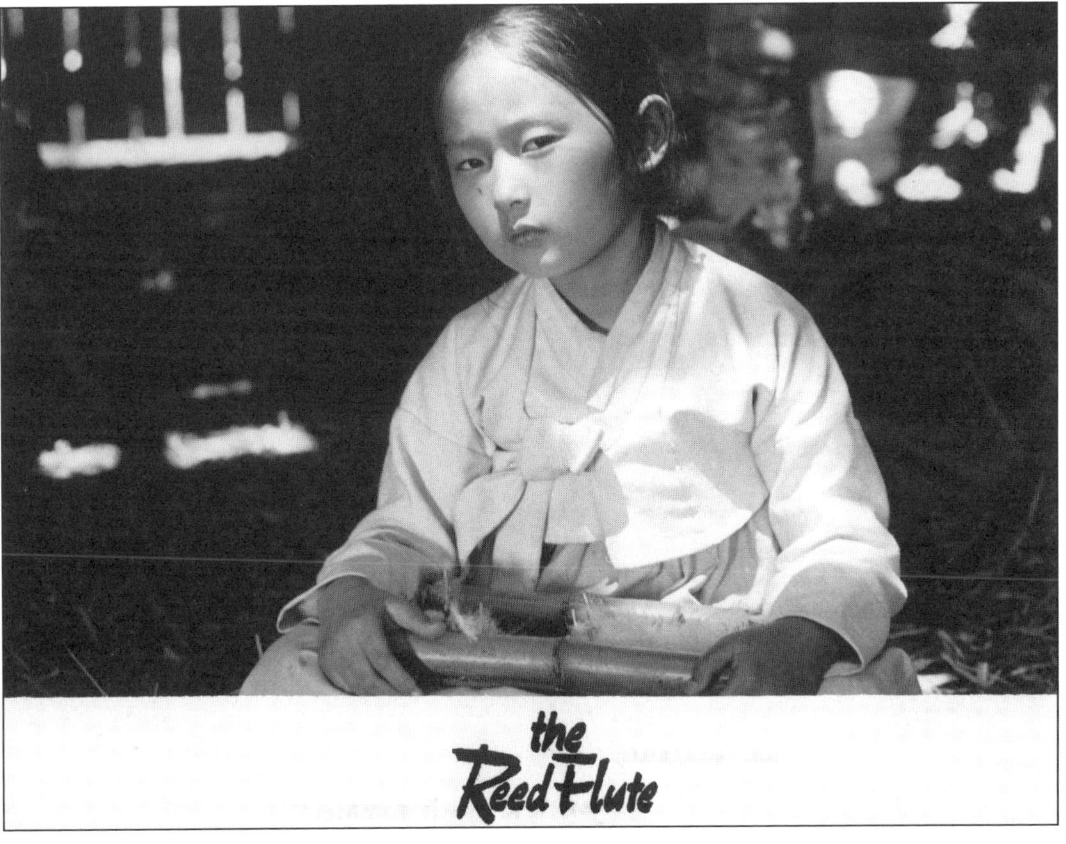

Revenge/The Reed Flute

You have mentioned Goskino, the State Committee for Cinematography. From the time cinema was nationalized in 1919 by a Lenin decree, film production and distribution had been regulated by Goskino, which gradually gained control of the film industry of the whole USSR. But in 1986, the Fifth Congress of Soviet Film-Makers Union challenged the authoritarian methods used by Goskino to control the arts and proposed the principles of free market as an alternative. It also assumed the responsibility of defending non-commercial cinema.

The idea was to shift the power to studios run by film-makers.

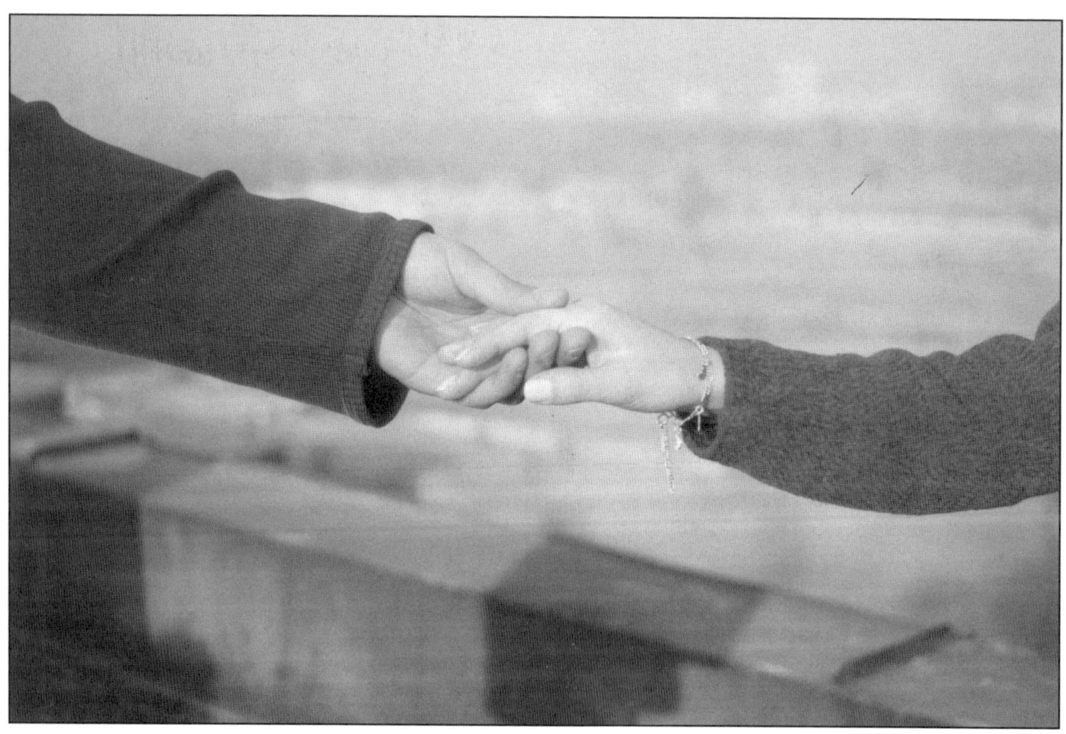

1997-Rustem's Notes With Drawings

A controversial film-maker like Elem Klimov, who had a long history of confrontations with Goskino concerning artistic freedom, was elected the First Secretary replacing Lev Kulidzhanov, who repressed the film-makers for two decades. This was already a revolution. Since then, Goskino lost its monopoly over the international market but, I understand, it still holds on to the domestic distribution. What are the most important changes during the transition period to Independence? How do you obtain funds to make films today? Could you also talk about the changes in censorship laws?

Funds are obtained from Goskino and the Kazakh Ministry of Culture. There is no system of distribution. Goskino has to distribute our films for a small percentage, but cannot. We need Goskino for finances but we have to be independent to choose our own topics. We need total freedom. Last summer, censorship was legally abolished except for State and military secrets, pornography and works that may ignite war or ethnic conflict. Films before *perestroika* were historical pieces stressing the communist aspects of history. You were not supposed to show the bad side of life. Formula films repeated the same love stories about a boy and a girl falling in love, having some conflicts and resolving it. Kazakh cinema today is interested in art films and in perfecting this genre. New Wave film-makers do not want to make propaganda films or commercial pieces. When you consider works such as Serik Aprimov's *The Last Stop*, you realize it was not possible to deal with such themes before. Rachid Nugmanov's *The Needle* had problems because it dealt with drug addiction, which was not supposed to exist in our society. We had to send our work print to Moscow and wait for their decision for months. Moscow decided how many copies we could make and which theatres we could show our films in. Some films had 15–20 copies and were never shown. Everything depended on their decision.

What role does Goskino play now?

Goskino's role is different now. The government gives us the money for new productions. We need the equipment that only Goskino can give us. We need government support. For instance, Mosfilm is now independent from Goskino as was declared during the Cannes Film Festival of 1990. The studio participated in the festival market for the first time as a private company. It does not depend on Goskino, but we do.

Kazakhfilm Studio has had a very long history. During World War II, Sergei Eisenstein shot two parts of *Ivan Grozyj/Ivan, the Terrible* there when some of the studios were relocated to Alma Ata. However, as you have pointed out, over the years, the propaganda films and formula love stories created a cinema that was of no interest to anyone. How does it operate today?

Under the Soviet system, Kazakhfilm Studio used to produce four feature films a year, four for television, five or six animation films and about 40 documentaries. Within the main studio, there are several other studios: *Alem/Universe*, created by Murat Auezov, who was the chief of the studio, is more sophisticated and has a universal approach, aiming at cinema 'with a new language'. He produced *Revenge. Miras/Heritage* gives precedence to history, national psychology, culture, etc. They are both State studios. Before *perestroika*, the head of *Miras* used to be an important person, but not anymore. There is also a documentary film studio called *Parallel. Kedam* is an independent organization for documentaries. This morning you have watched a documentary made recently, *Polygon*, by Oraz Rymzhanov and Vladimir Rerikh, which explores the nuclear exploitation of Kazakhstan during the Soviet regime. Interestingly, the film includes some military secrets that the government gave permission to be used. Andrei Sakharov actively took part in it, giving his final interview to the *Polygon* team.

Several independent studios have been formed beginning with the *perestroika*...
There are 15 independent studios in Alma Ata; the biggest is Catharsis, which produces short films, documentaries and features. Most co-operatives are independent studios making short films. The situation of the independent studios is very bad financially. Catharsis has made five or six feature films but, to my knowledge, none were released commercially. Independent studios buy foreign films, usually illegally, and make money releasing them in Kazakhstan. With this money, they make films. Things may change in the future.

What are the people from the Soloviev workshop doing now?
Rachid Nugmanov made money with his first feature film, *Igla/The Needle*, which was produced in 1988 by the Kazakhfilm Studio. Twenty million tickets were sold. He now formed his own studio called KINO. In 1989, only two Soviet films were on the top ten list and *The Needle* was one of them. It helped that he cast a famous rock star, Victor Tsoi, in the lead. He has no problem with money now but material and technical supplies are lacking. His new project has the storyline of *Seven Samurai*. It is a parody of film legends, Soviet and universal. After *The Touch*, Amanjol received one million from a bank to make a feature film, *Bilgisiz Yol*, about a group of hippies who go to Aral Lake, inside the military zone and are shot. Amir Karakulov made *Razluchniza/Between the Brothers* for Central TV and it will be shown (in Russian) in November. The film is based on a story by Jorge Lois Borges but is relevant to contemporary Kazakh life. It is about two brothers and a woman who belongs to the older brother, but the younger brother falls in love with her. She loves them both with the same force but with a different kind of love. There is no way out of this *ménage-a-trois*. They want her to decide but she cannot. The answer is death. I edited this film and did the soundtrack.

– Alma Ata, July 1991

BIO/FILMOGRAPHY
Ermek Shinarbaev was born on 25 January 1953. He studied at the VGIK twice, first acting with Boris Babochkin receiving his diploma in 1974 and then directing with Sergei Gerassimov, graduating in 1982 with a diploma film, the medium-length, *Karalisulu/*

Krassavitsa v traure/The Mourning Beauty. His first long feature, *Sestra Moia Liussia/ My Sister Lucy*, about two young single mothers trying to cope with psychological and economic problems following World War II, was shot in the classical trend of Soviet cinema. His second long feature, *Go Out of the Forest to the Meadow*, was a failure, although Shinarbaev considers it one of his best. He has also produced two films, *Abai* and *1997*, directed by Ardak Amirkulov. *Revenge* was restored in 2010 by the World Cinema Foundation at Cineteca di Bologna/L'Immagine Ritrovata Laboratory and shown at the Cannes Film Festival.

Feature films:
1985 *Sestra Moia Liussia/My Sister Lucy*
1987 *Go Out of the Forest to the Meadow*
1989 *Meist/Revenge*
1993 *Azghyin Ushtykzyn' Azaby/The Place on the Tricone*
1994 *Coeur fragile/Tender Heart*
2008 *Pisma Angelu/Letters to an Angel*

BEING YOUNG IN ALMATY

The first question that comes to mind about *1997 – Rustem's Notes with Drawings* is the title. Why 1997? This is not about Hong Kong!
Ardak Amirkulov: 1997 is a very special year for us as well. I had several ideas about the title, but finally decided on *1997*. This is my first film dealing with contemporary time; the first two were historical pieces. *1997* is an experimental film made with my students from the Film Workshop at the Almaty Film Institute. I thought it might be good for our memory to transfix a special time in history. Everything around us has been changing so fast that we wanted to make a film to mark this period in time to return one day to revive our memory. 1997 was also the year when it became clear that the political changes were now irreversible, the year when all monuments were replaced in Kazakhstan. While we were shooting, Lenin's monument was being changed with the monument of two young Kazakh girl soldiers who died during World War II. It is a pity that I did not have the possibility to shoot this event. At the same time, it was the 850th anniversary of Moscow, the return of Hong Kong to China and the death of Princess Diana. We wanted to mark all these events.

Why was the death of Diana so significant that this event is woven into the narrative as well?
A.A.: It is rare for a royal person to die in such a manner. Usually they die of natural causes. Diana's death was a world event. She was a remarkable woman and an attractive one. We thought that this was really an event for the whole world.

During an episode that takes place inside a theatre, we are told that *The Karamazov Brothers* is being staged, but suddenly we hear a dialogue about Princess Diana. The significance of this unexpected shift was not clear to me.

A.A.: The conversation was not about Diana but about love. Usually, this sort of conversation takes place in a cinema or theatre.

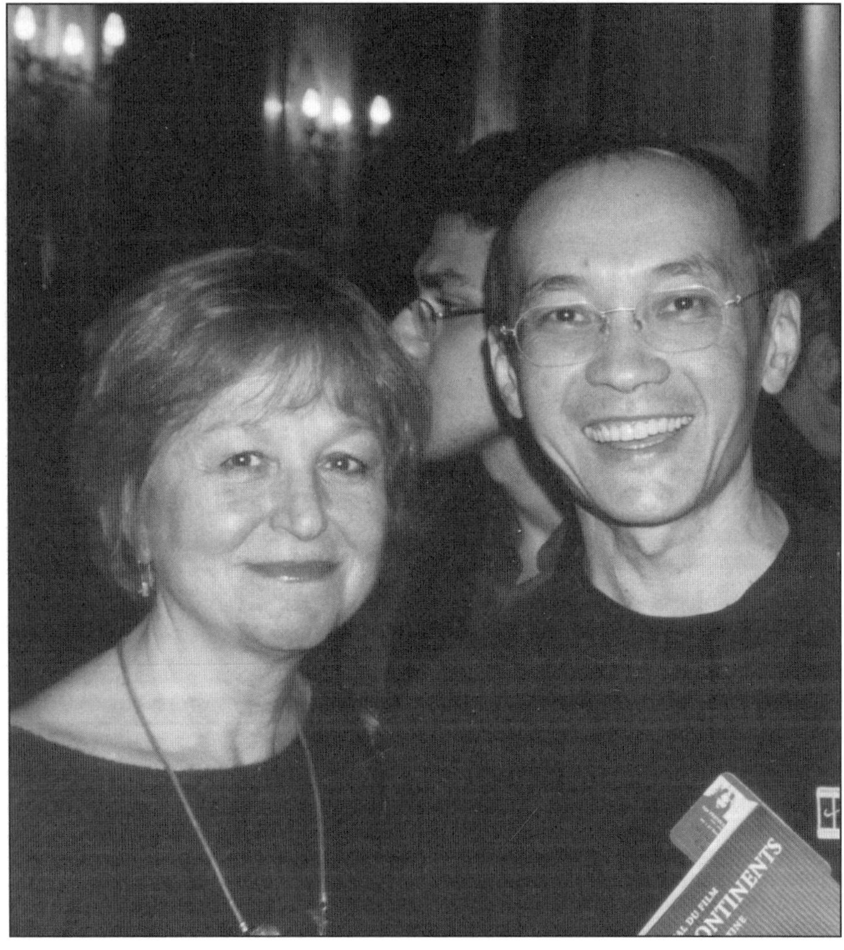

Author and Ermek Shinarbaev

Was the dialogue actually taken from the text of *The Karamazov Brothers* with a dialogue about the death of Princess Diana superimposed?

Ermek Shinarbaev: During the editing of the film, I also asked the same question to Ardak wondering why he wanted to put exactly this conversation at this place. He said, 'I don't know, but I want it'. When I watched the film on screen in Berlin, I said to myself, maybe he was right. The passage about the death of Diana marks the year and, at the same time, gives a certain intimacy to the conversation.

I found it very ambiguous as it arrived without any preparation for the audience. The only interpretation I could think of was perhaps an absurd play was being staged with dialogue about Diana superimposed on the dialogue from *The Karamazov Brothers*.

A.A.: Sort of. (*laughs*)

No one ever smiles in your film, not even once. Is this a reflection of the mood of the young in Kazakhstan today?

E.S.: It is a very good question. We have discussed this issue with Ardak. He remarked that the psychology of this generation was strange for us. One can call them a 'frozen generation'.

A.A.: I think young generations everywhere like to oppose authority. They are against everything in life. By the time they reach 20, they begin to be more flexible towards conforming to the rules of society. Then they begin to smile!

The films that came out during the first five years of Independence such as Talgat Temenov's *Byegushaya Mishen/The Running Target* (1991), Bolat Kalimbetov's *Ainalayin/Darling* (1991) and Darejan Omirbayev's *Kairat* (1991) are pessimistic portrayals of young people who have no hopes for the future. The generation in your film is equally unhappy. They are completely *blasé* about everything. There is nothing to do; nothing is interesting. They seem to be suffering from an existential boredom.

A.A.: Under the communist regime, we had faith in something. The new generation lost everything. They have no faith and this could be the reason for their indifference. The Soviet period was a global lie, not only for the youth but for the older generations as well. The lie has been exposed. That is why the young have no faith in the future. Now they have some other scale of values, the main one being money. If you have money, you are somebody.

The scenes you shot in front of the shops displaying fancy fashion clothes express this new value system very well. Such shops did not exist in 1991 when I visited Alma Ata. Also quite impressive was the last scene, when the girl kept turning round and round in the pond, an obvious image of a vicious circle.

A.A.: The vicious circle could represent the inability to express feelings. They are impotent in terms of their feelings.

Earlier, you talked about the teamwork with your students. Are all the actors non-professionals?

A.A.: All of them.

You have divided the film into chapters and marked the episodes by the use of silent-film-style cue cards. Why did you use this technique?

A.A.: The cue cards were necessary for the rhythm because the film does not have a classical dramaturgy. The episodes are like packages. Each new credit appears with the intention of drawing the attention of the spectator to a new chapter. I wanted to revive the interest of the audience and, at the same time, remind them that it was cinema.

This brings to mind another question. At the end of the film, you appear behind the camera, shooting. Is this a kind of a Brechtian distantiation device to remind the audience that it is only film?

A.A.: Yes.

Abbas Kiarostami appears in the last scene of *Taste of Cherry*, playing himself behind the camera. He has his explanation for this intrusion. Why was it necessary for you to have this scene?

A.A.: *1997* is a film full of problems, so we wanted to make it more optimistic at the end, just to remind the audience that nobody was dead and no one was killed.

A German critic told me today that your film reminded him of early Jim Jarmusch. What do you think?

E.S.: During the preparation for the film, the crew – Ardak and his students – made a point of watching new films by new generation film-makers, such as *La Haine/Hate* by Mathieu Kassavitz and *Trainspotting* by Danny Boyle. They wanted to be in the stream of such films. That could be the reason.

A.A.: We have also seen the *Dead Man* by Jim Jarmusch. As usual, Darejan (Omirbaev) brought the cassette to Almaty.

Ardak, between this film and *Otrar's Death*, which received the award of the Governor of Kazakhstan, brought you to the head of the Kazakhfilm Studio and won you the First Film Award of the City of Montreal in 1993; did you work on another project?

A.A.: After *Otrar*, I made another epic feature film called *Abai* (1995), the biography of an outstanding Kazakh poet. This film was commissioned and completely financed by the Kazakh government for the 150th anniversary of Abai, and I was nominated as the director.

Ermek, how did you get involved in *1997*?

E.S.: We began our collaboration with Ardak on his previous project *Abai*. When I saw the rushes of that film, I said to him, 'This is a big project, you must have a professional team'. I suggested a co-production with my French friends. We made a short visit to Paris and I presented him to my producers and to the editing team. They agreed to continue the editing, so we brought the whole team from Paris to Almaty. The final mix was made in Paris; we used the lab in Paris and made a copy there. I was somehow the Kazakh co-producer and it was a very fruitful experience. We were content with each other. When Ardak launched this new project, he proposed me to help him and his students. I agreed. We now have experience in production, and we should be producers ourselves.

Ermek, the last film I saw from you was *The Place on the Tricone*, which won the Golden Leopard in Locarno. I thought it was a radical departure from your previous films.

E.S.: For a long time, I wanted to make a film about contemporary life to explore the soul of the new generation, which is so different from mine. The outcome was *The Place on the Tricone*. Afterwards, I made another film with my French co-producers, *Tender Heart*, that I shot in Kazakh and later had it subtitled into French. I could show it nowhere except in Kazakhstan and France because I had neither the money nor the brains to do the English subtitles. I received many propositions to show it in the US and Europe, but it was blocked for lack of subtitles.

In the beginning of the Kazakh New Wave, the tendency was to make films in the native language, not only in Kazakhstan, but in the other Central Asian Republics as well, but now I see that Russian is coming back, at least in your country.

A.A.: The reality is that the young generation speaks Russian. To be open to this generation, the films should be made in Russian.

E.S.: Following our separation from Russia, we were so glad to be independent that we thought we should make our films for ourselves – Kazakh language for our dialogue with the Kazakh population. Soon, we had to realize that our connections with Russia were much deeper than just being a colony; we are related culturally as well. Besides, our population is only 16 million, which is not enough film audience. Russia is a big country with a big population and they did not lose interest in our cinema. Therefore, it makes sense to make films not only for the Kazakh population but also for our big neighbour. Even in Kazakhstan, only seven million of the population is Kazakh; 20% does not speak Kazakh at all.

Before Independence, Kazakhs used to comprise 40% of the population with around 30% Russian and then German, Ukrainian, Uzbek, Tatar and others.

E.S.: Now the percentage is higher for the Kazakh because of the exodus of the Russians, although there are still many Russians left. Our government made special efforts to keep the Russians. Kyrgyzstan has lost many Russians who immigrated to Russia and their industry is in shambles for lack of Russian engineers and workers. That is why the Kazakh government is trying to keep the population. During his last speech, President Nazarbaev openly said to the Russians, 'Please stay, it is your country, too'.

The eruption of Kazakh films in the international arena following the demise of the Soviet Union had lost its momentum by the middle of the 1990s, but recently, in addition to successful festival appearances, several Kazakh films have actually been playing in regular cinemas of Europe, which is unprecedented.

E.S.: Darejan Omirbaev's *Killer* (1998), as well as his previous films, *Kardiogramma/ Heartbeats* (1995) and *Kairat* (1992), have been very successful in Europe. Another Kazakh film, *Kozymnin Karasy/The Biography of a Young Accordionist* (1994) by Satimbaldi Narimbetov, funded by the European Union, will also be released in Paris soon. That will be the fourth Kazakh film released in regular cinemas in France. We have spoken to a French distributor regarding Ardak's film, *1997*, and it is almost certain that it will be released in January 2000 in France in the frame of a programme for the Arte television channel, roughly called *I Am Twenty Years Old*. The project is European; however, the distributor believes that it might be interesting to show a Kazakh film within this programme.

What does the Kazakh government do for film-makers? Does it give financial support?

E.S.: Because of the monetary crisis and the anticipation of a big crash like the one that happened in Russia, the government renewed the budget this year to cut all expenses. We are uncertain whether there will be some financing for cinema or not. At the end of the previous year, our government spent $2 million for the 1st International Film Festival, Eurasia. $2 million! It is incredible. Many film-makers complained. Darejan Omirbaev, in an interview given to a French newspaper, said that it was shameful to spend all that money for the festival instead of financing unfinished films. Last year, the government launched 12 projects, but only three were completed. The rest are waiting for money. I believe, for the Kazakh government, it seems to be more important to maintain the image of Kazakhstan than finance films.

The organizer, Gulnara Uzbakhanova, told me that there is no money to organize another festival.

E.S.: Yes and no. Our president, Nursultan Nazarbaev, may keep his promise and turn it into an annual event. The government now has a mega project for a feature film called *The Kazakhs* and they also launched another project, *Ablai-Khan*, about one of the main historical heroes, who founded the Kazakh state three centuries ago. Timur Nakmanbietov, a well-known Kazakh who lives in Russia and makes commercials, has already been appointed as the director for the second project, which has a budget on the Kazakh side of about $30 million! Nikita Mikhalkov is also involved. Right at the beginning of the presidential campaign, Mikhalkov paid a visit to Nazarbaev to give his support. They discussed big cinema projects. That is why I can say that our government does not support cinema but at the same time *does* support cinema. This is a contradiction. It is very transparent about the kind of films they are ready to finance. They do not care about Kazakh film-makers or new projects; they are not interested in supporting young talents. Large amounts of money are invested on prestigious projects collaborating with Mikhalkov. Mikhalkov's new film, *The Barber of Siberia*, premiered in Almaty as an act of support for Nazarbaev.[1]

For the film-makers who are not interested in glamorous films, is the only choice co-production with European countries?

E.S.: Darejan Omirbaev, Ardak and I have collaborated with France, Serik Aprimov and Amir Karakulov with Japan. This means that we are open to co-productions, but we cannot expect all our films to be supported by foreigners. The problem is there is no money for cinema in Kazakhstan. We are very poor. The average budget of a film is $300,000. It is very cheap, but it is impossible to find this money because it is not an investment; it is a gift. Who will give this gift? For many years, the State subsidized our films; now the State is very poor. In many villages, the population is hungry. It is very difficult for the government to finance cinema in such a situation, yet they are ready to finance prestigious projects. I do not understand why and how!

– Berlin, February 1998

Notes:

1. During my second visit to Almaty in October 2004 as a jury member for the second edition of Kazakh National Film Festival called *Shaken's Stars* to honour the first film-maker of Kazakh national cinema (as distinct from Soviet cinema in Kazakhstan), another mega project called *Nomad*, with a budget of $45 million, was being shot on the outskirts of Almaty, a co-production with the US and directed by Russian film-maker Sergei Bodrov.

BIO/FILMOGRAPHY

Ardak Amirkulov was born on 10 December 1955, in the village of Ak-Kul in Dshambul in Kazakhstan. He studied philology at the University of Almaty and graduated in 1980. In 1984, he attended the workshop of the Russian film-maker Sergei Soloviev along with other young Kazakh talents, who later came to be known as important voices of the Kazakh New Wave. Between 1994 and 1997, he was the President of the Kazakhfilm Studio. After a period of unemployment and sickness, he became a professor at the Almaty Film Institute.

Feature films:
1991 *Ghibel Otrara/Otrar's Death*
1995 *Abai*
1998 *1997 – Sapisi Rustema S Risunkami/1997 – Rustem's Dairy with Drawings*
2008 *Goodbye, Gulsary!*

SERIK APRIMOV

Serik Aprimov is one of the most important names of Kazakh cinema. *Konechnaya Ostanovka/The Last Stop* (1989), his graduation film, is considered a manifesto of the Kazakh New Wave, a movement that started when Soviet society was dismantling.

Aprimov was born in a small Kazakh village called Aksuat, which is the inspiration behind most of his films. After his military service, he began to work at the Kazakhfilm Studio in Alma Ata, first as a driver, then administrator and assistant director before becoming a film-maker. He was one of the students in the workshop Russian film-maker Sergei Soloviev organized, which led to the birth of the Kazakh New Wave. Aprimov graduated in 1984 and, in 1986, he made the short film *Dvoe Echali Na Motorsikle/Two Were Riding the Motorcycle*.

The Last Stop is the story of a young Kazakh man, Erken, who returns home to his demoralized village on the Kazakh plains after his military service. His friends are still where he left them, procrastinating in a state of despair and desolation, drowning the misery of their aimless existence in alcohol and petty crime. His girlfriend has married someone else. The pitiful lives of the people he once loved makes him decide to leave the steppes forever.

The film presents seemingly random episodes in a documentary fashion: Erken meets his childhood friends; watches his girlfriend get reprimanded by her tyrannical supervisor for stopping to talk to him while repairing an adobe; a wedding ceremony turns into a drunken brawl; an intoxicated man fires at the local police from a rooftop. The dismal portrait of the *aul* (the village), the centre of rural existence for centuries, is a testimony to the demise of the false dreams of socialism. The 'mythologized Soviet space' that Kazakh critic Bauyrzhan Nogerbek identifies 'with its beautiful landscapes, ethnographic costumes, national games, songs, and dances' is completely absent from this picture. 'Kazakh national space is not just ignored and squeezed out of the screen. It is also created new on the basis of the surrounding reality to which viewers have become accustomed, creating it in the style of "unrehearsed reality", of Vertov's "life caught unawares". … The cinematic *aul* is demythologized and, at the same time, assembled anew, but now there is no place in it for any moral–ethical norms of human conduct'.[1]

Aksuat (1997) is a visit to Aprimov's village ten years later. The older brother, who cut his ties with his roots, returns for a while to hide from his creditors. The one who stayed back falls in love with his brother's pregnant city wife but is unable to protect the family against the local mafia. Changes have taken place although the future is still uncertain.

Tri Brata/Three Brothers mixes realism with poetry in a story of the clash between the old and modern times. Three young brothers, living in a small village, hear a story from an old railway maintenance man about a wonderful lake where life is beautiful and women are available if you have the money. Their dreams turn to tragedy as they find out too late that the old trains are there for target practice for the rockets.

One may consider the three films a trilogy. At the centre of the three is the *aul*, which has lost its meaning both on national and personal levels as well as social and historical. According to Aprimov, the word Kazakh means 'the people who have wandered away from the centre'. Metaphorically speaking!

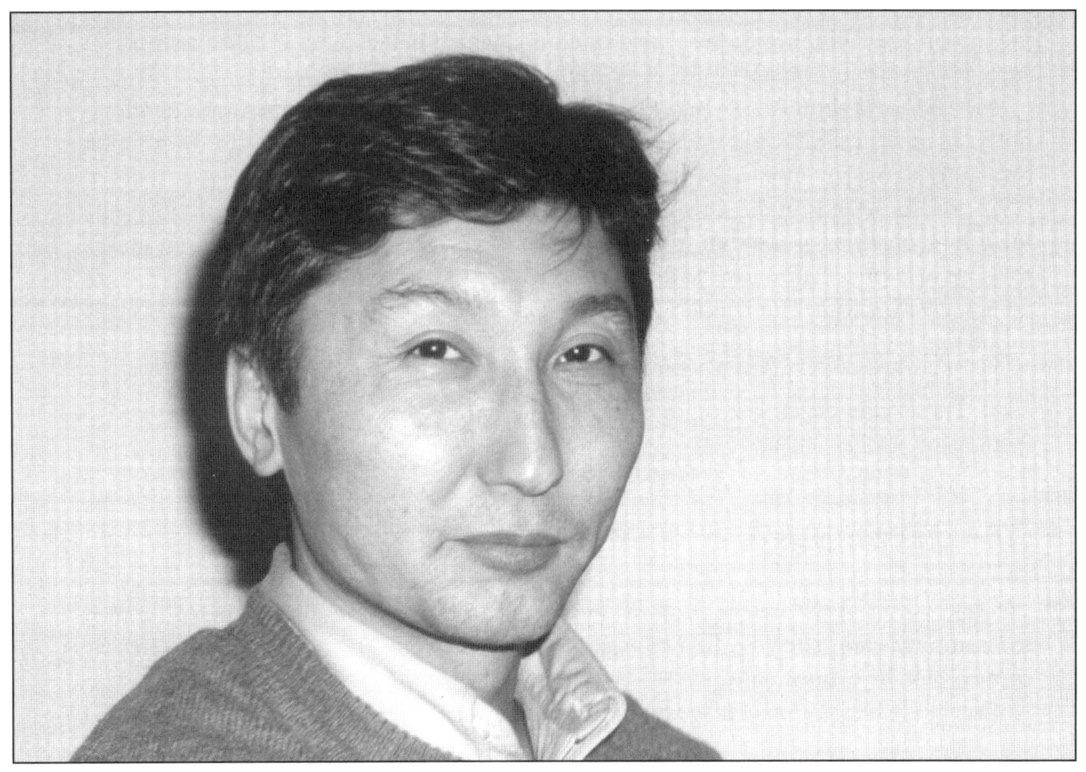

Serik Aprimov

In 2004, Serik was in Locarno presenting his most recent film, *Anshi/The Hunter*. Now a man in his 40s but still very much outside any film trend, local or global, he talked in riddles and proverbs. Over the years, he has polished this art along his cinematographic talents. He is like an *ak sakal* (white-bearded wise old man) from an Aitmatov story. In fact, *The Hunter* reminds one of early Aitmatov depicting the lives of the simple people of the steppes. It also follows the centuries-old Kazakh tradition of using stories as an indirect way to give advice, leaving the final decision up to the listener (viewer).

The Hunter is the most complete work of Aprimov to date. The rough, unfinished edge of his earlier films that had drawn the attention of the film elite of the West has rounded up into a more approachable film. The story is very straightforward. Brought up by a young, free-spirited and sexually liberal woman, the protagonist suffers from peer incrimination, which augments his adolescence pains in an environment that is cold, cruel and indifferent. He has a certain aversion towards a mysterious hunter, the lover of his surrogate mother. One night, while the couple are making love, he vents his anger by stealing the hunter's gun for a target practice at the local bar. The hunter bails him out of jail on the condition that he accompanies him on his journey. Hence begins the initiation of Erken into the world of adults, which brings with it certain emotions such as warmth for the opposite sex or for one's mother.

The Hunter is about the dying traditions of the Central Asian steppes, but the film is not a call to return to the old ways because this is no longer possible as Aprimov explains, but rather to incorporate the old ways into our modern life.

Certain loose ends in the script render the narrative somewhat confusing at times and the plastic qualities of the film (pressures from the producers perhaps) may not appeal to those who once fell in love with the rugged style of *Two on a Motorcycle* or *The Last Stop*. However, with *The Hunter*, Aprimov has created an epic film, which is also very intimate.

The first interview took place during the Rotterdam Film Festival, held in February 2000. The second began during the Locarno Film Festival in August 2004 and ended in Almaty in October 2004.

THE LAST STOP IS AKSUAT

Some essential themes or motives are found in all of your films. One of them is the country versus the city. In *The Last Stop*, the hero leaves his village, but when he comes back, he cannot cope, so he leaves again. In *Aksuat*, he decides to stay.

The village is not a real village but a place in my head. Sometimes people ask, 'Aren't you afraid that somebody else is going to make a film about Aksuat'? I say 'no' because that is the key, the Aksuat that I have.

The image of Aksuat in *The Last Stop* was so real that the villagers were offended. Western media reported that the people of Aksuat were unhappy to see the naked truth about their lives exposed.

Not the people of Aksuat, those were the government officials. The film was produced by Kazakhfilm as one of the five feature films that Goskino would annually finance. The situation in the Soviet Union was already very chaotic. Therefore, it was impossible for Moscow to control what was going on. The head of Kazakhfilm told me that if the film caused a scandal, he would not stand behind me. If I agreed to that, I could go ahead and do what I wanted to do. I had no problems during the production; the problems only started later. We wanted to have an *avant-premiere* in the village where the film was shot, but the authorities would not permit it. As the villagers insisted on seeing the film, a screening was organized at 3 a.m. When the film was released, the general prosecutor issued orders for the cinemas to be closed. The film was shelved for five years. However, it was distributed on video, mostly pirated. After a while, many people knew it by heart. People were not upset, and now eight years later, they tell me life is much worse than what I showed in my film.

In what sense?

Nobody has work and because of that crime is very high. Some years ago, crime was not an issue. When I was shooting *The Last Stop*, it was not so obvious to the people how desperate their situation was, but I felt it. Now, they also can see it. For the Kazakhs, *aul*, the village, is a holy place, the centre of one's life. When I returned to my native village after my military service, I realized that something had gone wrong. Among the three kids I used to play with when I was ten, one committed suicide, one was in jail and the third became an alcoholic. I realized the problem was the village itself. The Communist system destroyed the *aul*. The title of the film refers to the fact that there was no future. I did not want to use allegory. I wanted to hit directly with the truth. Something was bound to happen, and it did, three years later, with the fall of the Soviet Union. In a way, that film heralded the demise of the communist ideology.

Finding a new identity is another important issue in your films. Old times are lost and new times bring multiple problems of new identity.

Kazakh mentality is actually quite simple. We do not live in the past or the future. The future is the shadow of the past. We live in the present and take it as it comes.

Would you say that *Aksuat* was a commentary on the socio-economic situation of the country after 70 years of Soviet domination?

Not a commentary. I tried to avoid any kind of social commentary, but perhaps it is in the texture of the film.

It has been said that there is no political message in your work. I find all your films political.

I do not have such an aim but one way or another I seem to touch certain spheres.

Illusion and reality, as perceived by the old man and the boys, is the central theme in *Three Brothers*. Can one draw a parallel to the country?

There is an obvious parallel. After the break-up of the Soviet Union, the society has been divided into two major groups: the ones who still live with the memories of the communist time – there was nothing good about it, but they keep their memories – and the others, the young and aggressive, who want to make as much money as soon as possible. Neither of these groups can survive. The old cannot go on living dreaming about the past and the young want to achieve too fast. Only someone who lives day to day can survive.

'Miracles don't exist' seems to be the message.

If you want to survive, you have to take reality as it is. If you start dreaming, you begin to torture yourself. The old man was living with the dreams of the past and he died; the youngsters were living with the dreams of the future and they did not survive either. The little boy did not know anything about the past and did not know what the future would look like. He was just living from day to day and he was the one to survive.

Which means it is a matter of illusions and reality and dreams and tragedy. There seem to be no choice in your films. Dreams lead to tragedy; and there is no place for illusions.

Yes, it is all in one and they are so close to one another where I live.

In *Sergenden*, dreams create a monster.

Dreams force you into a cocoon and you are trapped. Since I am against illusions and dreams, I do not want to cheat the audience by giving them illusions. Encouraging someone to have illusions is like giving someone drugs. For a certain time, he will be excited and feel great but after a while, he will realize that it is temporary. (*He takes three matches and makes a triangle.*) If you ask what this is, most people will say a triangle. Actually, it is three matches; the triangle is a ready-made illusion. Illusion is a virus, which infects like a fatal disease. The old man in *Three Brothers* could be my own father who lived all his life with the illusion of communism. When the three children begin to believe the old man, they are eventually killed.

'The brothers' trope recurs in your films.

I have three brothers and they are completely different from me. They always say, 'Why don't you live like the rest of us'? They have their separate lives, so this is part of my experiences.

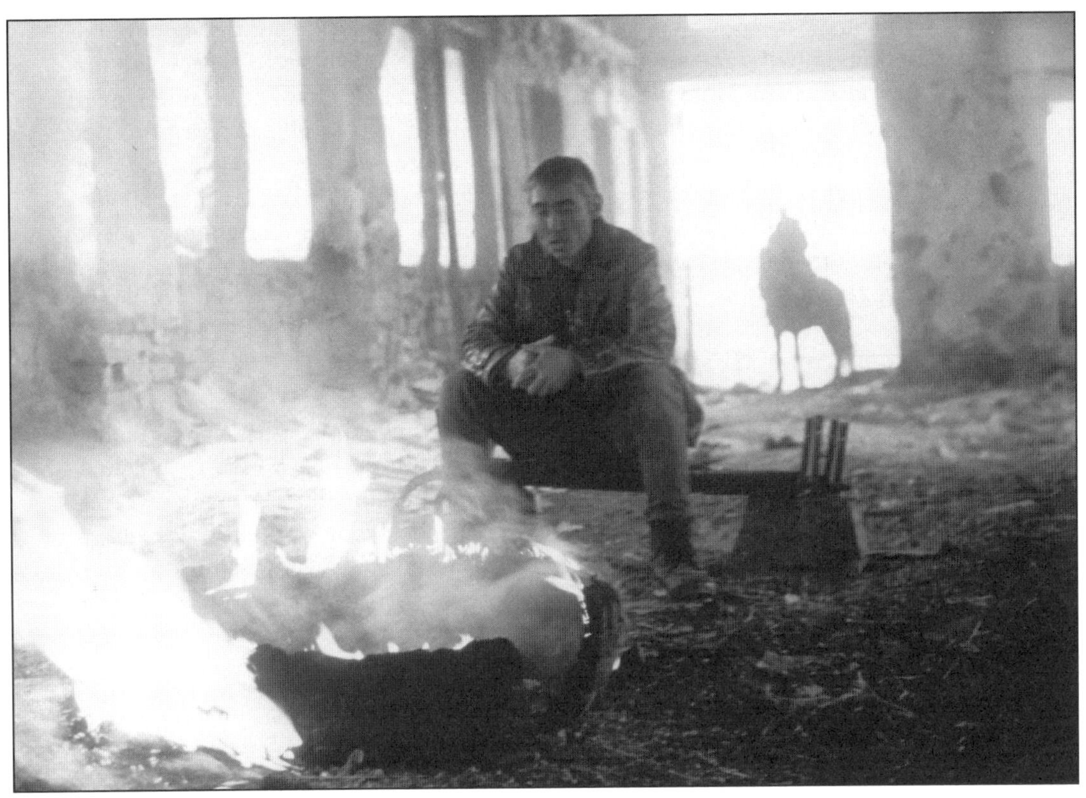

Aksuat

Actually, in *The Last Stop*, they were not brothers, but three friends.
At the time of *The Last Stop*, I was not in a conflict with my brothers.

Does the conflict now arise from ideology?
We have different values of life. They see life their way and I see in mine. The ideas of each one are representations of society.

How did the story of *Three Brothers* come about in the first place? How did you work with the children?
I had many ideas. I knew I wanted to make a film about children. Once I was chatting with an old drunkard who was talking about locomotives. The old man and locomotives was enough to give me an idea what the film would be about. I added

the military planes. The script had to be ready in four–five days. I got the money and started shooting. Usually, my script is not more than eight to twelve pages. First, I observed the way these children played. Then I explained to them what I wanted them to do, tried it three–four times and got the final shot. I do not give the script to the children or to any of the other players. Sometimes I even tell them to play something completely different because my aim is to find the right expression. When I get that, the dialogue becomes secondary. The most important thing is to find the right movement and expression of the face. *Aksuat* was shot in about 18 days and it took me a month to shoot *Three Brothers*.

Can you comment on the structure of *Three Brothers*, which is in three parts, and why you used divisions with pictures?

I told my wife, who is the executive producer, that I was not happy with it. She reminded me that I felt the same with *Aksuat* but it was OK after editing. *Three Brothers* was edited eight times. I was once visiting the artist working on the film and, accidentally, I saw some paintings in the house. He said he was doing sketches while working on the film. I thought I could use these in the film to divide it into episodes and, at the same time, they could represent the memories of the old man. There are two different periods while you are working on a film: in the beginning, when you are processing different ideas, and after it is shot when you have to look at it in a completely different way.

How do you procure the finances?

Kazakh film-makers cannot shoot a film unless there is a $400,000 budget. I have chosen another direction to make films that cost between $50,000 and $100,000. First, I figure out how much money I can get and find it, and based on the amount available, I formulate an idea for the film. Here is how we made *Aksuat*: After I made *The Last Stop* in 1991, I left film-making for a while and started to do all kinds of things. I wasn't even thinking of making another film. One day, a Japanese producer called me while I was lying down at home and said, 'Here is the money, make a film'. My first question was, 'How much money have you got'? '$50,000', he said. My wife said it is too little. But I thought that I was sitting around and doing nothing. I asked the Japanese what kind of film he wanted. He said, 'the style of *The Last Stop* and I will be happy'. By the time I made *Aksuat*, everyone knew that I could make films with a very small budget, so they told me to make another one. That is how I made *Three Brothers*. Everything is open, it is up to you to decide, like fishing – you wait and see if you catch something or not.

What would you do if they actually gave you $400,000 that you say other Kazakh film-makers expect?

I would make three films instead of one.

Aksuat and *Three Brothers* were made the same year, but there was an eight-year lapse between *The Last Stop* and *Aksuat* as you mentioned. What did you do during those eight years?

Everything except film-making. I was giving advice. And for two years, I worked at the press office of the president. There is almost no work there except chatting around. I used to sleep on the sofa but the guards of the president told me I was not allowed to sleep there. I found an old sofa that I took to the attic where I could stretch myself quietly and read books. They got me there, too, and told me I had to sit in the room and not sleep during the day.

Why do you appear in your films? I am sure Fellini was asked such a question innumerable times.

My reasons are purely practical. In *Three Brothers*, I needed the pilots but they were not allowed to act in the film. Within their work environment, it was not a problem, but not outside. My driver and I replaced them.

You also appear in *Sergenden*.

For a small role, I would not look for an actor, so it became a habit. Whenever there was a small role, people suggested me.

No one had heard of *Sergenden* before the screening here in Rotterdam. Why was it hidden for such a long time?

No one was hiding it except that after *The Last Stop*, people said *Sergenden* was not my style. It was not accepted the way the previous film was, so it was forgotten.

What is your opinion about the film?

All my other films were born of my experiences and feelings. *Sergenden* is purely the result of my imagination.

In 1991, when I visited the Kazakhfilm Studio, there seemed to be solidarity among the film-makers, particularly those from the Soloviev workshop that initiated the Kazakh New Wave. Does this solidarity continue or is each one following his individual path?

We see each other once a year and say 'hello'; that is all.

Ermek Shinarbaev produced two films of Ardak Amirkulov. They seem to enjoy working together. What about Talgat Temenov? Does he make films today?

Talgat made a film in 1998. I keep in touch with Amir Karakulov and Darejan Omirbaev.

I have heard that in Kazakhstan people do not go to the cinemas anymore. How much does the situation of cinema reflect the political situation of the country? What is the connection between Kazakh politics and Kazakh cinema today?

Now the government is fighting for oil and energy and is too busy to pay attention to cinema. For the moment, Kazakhstan is an industrially empty space, but this may change in the next five years. For instance, in Russia, big cinemas are opening now.

It seems that the government has money for cinema but wants to invest it on films about national awareness.

There was a try. Two films were made in such a mood, *Ablai Khan* by Timur Nakmanbietov and *The Kazakhs*, but they were both failures. The situation now is that each director tries to find an intermediate person to reach the government.

After Independence, what are the most important changes for Kazakh cinema – losses and gains?

During the time of the Soviet Union, every year we would produce six or seven films. But at that time, there was censorship. Now the government does not care at all but I cannot make the films that I want to make. When there was money, there was censorship. Now there is no censorship and no money.

I believe the audience has also changed.

Cinemas in Almaty closed one after another. Not even the American films are shown. In Kazakhstan, you don't see any films, not even the *Titanic*. The main problem is the television stations, which buy old American movies for about $1,000 and keep showing them year after year. I offered to show *Aksuat* free but they said, 'No. Life is hard enough without your films'.

During the Soviet period, your films were distributed by Goskino in Moscow. What is the situation now? Are film festivals the only way to see films like yours?

Distribution does not exist in Kazakhstan. I had an idea to invite my friends to see my film free, but someone said unless you send us an invitation to say that it is completely free, we won't come, which reminds me of a joke: Kazakh people have an ironic attitude towards religion. After the Soviet Union, there was a *mescit* (a small mosque) no one wanted to visit. The *mulla* kept saying you should come but everyone said, 'It is too much trouble. We have to take our shoes off, pray…' The *Mulla* said you don't have to do anything, just come. So they came and the *mulla* was promoted. When the new *mulla* arrived and saw all the chaos in the *mescit*, he asked for explanations. The first *mulla* said, 'My job was to bring them here, your job is to make order'. The same should apply to the Kazakh audience. First, you have to bring them to the cinemas. I don't worry about distribution. What happens after I make my film is not my business. I don't consider films a business. I am not trying to make a big fortune from my films. As a film director, what other choice do I have? There will always be some kind of money to make films, even less expensive films.

What about the language? After Independence, the tendency among film-makers from the former republics was to use the native language as opposed to Russian, which was used during the Soviet period.

Aksuat was about 70% in Kazakh, but *Three Brothers* is in Russian. I wanted to make the film in Russian because all children in Almaty speak Russian. I did not want to change the situation. It would not be true. I always work with the material that I have. Many Kazakhs do not know their language. When I grew up, my sister told me to speak Russian. Without speaking Russian, you could not get higher education. Now that everyone speaks Russian, there is another problem; we need to speak English.

You said *Three Brothers* came out of an idea about the trains, but it is also about the planes and it ends with the planes.

I felt that if there were an old negative force, there should be a new positive force. Locomotives are very old; there should be something modern. I like to work with binary opposites just like the good brother versus the bad brother. I think that when two opposites come together, something new can be born. Without that effect, nothing new can be born.

But planes can also be considered as a destructive force. Does that say something about progress?

My personal point of view is that progress leads to self-destruction.

– Rotterdam, February 2000

THE NEED FOR HUNTERS

For me, *The Hunter* is a film about closed spaces, the home and the *aul* (the village), and open spaces, namely, Nature. The former is locked in a present that has severed its ties with its heritage, an orphaned world like the protagonist who was found in the forest by the 'bad woman' of the village. The latter, Nature, is where past merges into the future, where babies are born to families living in *yurts* and are blessed by hunters as tradition demands, by spitting water on their faces. In Nature, man is free to run with the wolves, to make love without inhibitions, to live his life as it flows and to 'disappear' when the time comes. Do you feel nostalgic for the old Kazakh traditions?

I do not think we should (and can) go back to the old times. I come from the countryside but now live in the city. We have lost contact with nature. When I was a little boy and my uncle died, I saw my aunt crying and asked her why. Was it for him? She said, no, he would not come back. Was it for her difficult life? She said her life was not difficult. Why was she crying then? She said it was for the little red ball under the water. We lived as a community and we did not ask why. I would like to go back to that. We have a saying in

Kazakhstan, *asphalt young men*, the young who have lost connection with nature. They only know computer games and the cities. Computer games do not teach you how to deal with what you meet in nature.

Do we need more hunters?
The film-maker is like a hunter watching the world unknown to him and trying to understand. When I was young, we were living on the steppes and following the rules of our fathers, which were not to be broken. They were simple but they worked over the centuries. For instance, I was supposed to be respectful to older men, to get up even when someone one year older than me entered the room. Nowadays civilization proceeds so fast that the *asphalt young men* forget their traditional values. Our prisons are full of young men like the protagonist of the film.

Erken is an orphan, a common trope of the Stalinist tradition where biological parents were assumed to bear political, social and/or religious values of the past. Naturally, you reverse the tradition. But absence of the father and the search for a substitute (the hunter) is also a conventional trope of Soviet films, defining a condition of not belonging to a society that is different. What is the inspiration behind the script?
The script is original. The main reason I made the film is that in our traditions, mothers are not supposed to touch their boys or show any affection lest they become men. The first time my mother touched me on the forehead was when I was six years old and had a fever of 42°. We had to vomit our medicine to continue to be sick to be caressed by our mothers. When you are not caressed by your mother, you have problems later on.

The hunter takes onto himself the responsibility of initiating Erken into adulthood. A tacit understanding gradually develops between them although neither one is a man of much words, let alone emotions. Only after the death of the hunter, Erken discovers that the hunter kept the drawings he used to make as a child.
In our culture, men do not show their feelings. The hunter was a stern man, but he kept the drawings.

After the death of the hunter Erken realizes that the book he was reading was blank – although the audience is privy to this fact long before.
Knowledge is passed from father to son, etc. and not acquired from books.

Erken and the hunter meet a family living in a *yurt* on the steppes and the hunter blesses the newborn baby by spitting water on his face. The second time, when Erken as the mature hunter visits them, he only kisses the boy.
I used the old Kazakh tradition of spitting to emphasize the changes in modern times that have their repercussions in every aspect of life even in remote corners of the world.

Why did Erken have to pay the debts of the hunter after his death?

According to our tradition, a man cannot be buried before his debts are paid. Paying his debts, Erken fulfills his obligations towards the man who played an important part in his passage to adulthood.

Let us talk about women. The woman who mothers Erken is a young provocative village girl whose motivation for adopting the boy is a puzzle. She is presented right at the start of the film as a sexual being, like a playmate, whose maturity in the later episodes arrives as unexpected and even lacks credence. The woman the hunter indulges in sex on his horse is an unknown stranger who lets her hair down when she spots the hunter – a subtle sign that she is ready and willing. The third woman is married to an old man who allows her to have satisfaction riding a camel since he cannot make her 'happy'. While the men are busy doing whatever men must do, hunting or trading, women occupy themselves with sexual acts and/or thoughts. The only woman who is not presented as a sex playmate is the one who lives in a *yurt* with her husband and produces babies: she is like a shadow behind her husband. Furthermore, none of these women have a name.

I was reminded by a Dutch critic as well that none of my women characters has a name. It might be because I was not caressed by my mother as a kid as is the custom in Kazakhstan. Once you are brought up that way, it is hard to change into a nice man.

There is a good dose of exoticism in your film, not to mention eroticism, but it is still Aprimov to the core with your tongue-in-cheek sense of humour – the same Aprimov who showed love-making in a truck in *The Last Stop* while the woman had to keep her foot on the break pedal, follows the hunter practising every position of *Kama Sutra* and more on top of his horse with an unknown woman, while the animal is galloping at full speed over the Kazakh steppes. Is sex on the back of the horse part of the Kazakh traditions? What about the young woman with an old husband, who is allowed to satisfy herself on the camel? Some people may accuse you of using cheap tricks or resorting to sensationalism for commercial gains.

Tradition says we are free sexually. Communists came and said sex was bad, so we stopped being so free. When the woman let her hair down, it was a signal. The hunter did not speak to her. He sent the boy to see what was happing, then the boy said she let her hair down. This was a signal. He rode the horse well; he could also make love on the horse. We have a saying that if a man cannot make love on top of a horse, he is not sitting properly. Actually, the expression in Kazakh is 'to play on the ears of the horse'.

The cinematography is very sumptuous. The camera lingers on birds (especially the eagle, which appears twice), the wolf (an important character) and the endless steppes with almost an aura of sensuality. Tell me why the hunter says, 'I am the eagle, you are the wolf'?

I tried to stay away from symbols. We have a childhood habit of naming each other with animal names, the good ones as well as the bad ones. It is also believed that if a child is given the name of a good animal, his life will lead in a good direction.

Can you explain the breathing ritual?
In the Altai region in the East, where I come from, this is very traditional. We recognize two groups of animals: cold breathing such as the cow and the horse and warm breathing such as the dog and the sheep. When the hunter spends time with the cold animals, he goes to a shaman to have hot breathing. The one with cold breathing can never have any close contact with people.

The relationship between the hunter and the wolf continues until the wolf kills him.
We say the hunter does not die; the wolf comes and takes him away. When we are born, each one of us has his own wolf, and when we die, we go with the wolf. The hunter is a mysterious person. He just goes away. I left it at that. Nomadic life still exists. Soviets made us settle down and organize *kolkhoz* (agricultural farms). After they left, Kazakhs have gone back to living in the mountains and the steppes. A new generation of hunters appeared to kill the wolves that endanger lives. During the Soviet time, there was a law to kill 50,000 wolves each year. Now we don't do it, so there is a need to kill them. A new kind of wolf, the Red Wolf, appeared, which is very dangerous. Normally, they show themselves during the day and attack at night. Now they even attack during the day. Regarding this last episode, I had two versions: the first version had definite steps in the way western audiences would understand. The hunter runs, falls off the horse, is dragged and the wolf jumps on him. Then I tried to make it simple because for us, a person does not die; he just goes away. I had two options: either explain to the audience or show it the way it is in our culture. Nature does not explain a thunderstorm.

The fatal encounter between the hunter and the wolf is breathtakingly amazing considering the fact that you shot it live without resorting to some digital tricks. How did you manage this incredible scene with such a ferocious animal?
There is a certain manner to catch wolves. We give the wolf big pieces of meat and when its stomach is full, the hunter goes on the horse to catch him. It takes two hours. The wolf gets weaker and weaker because of vomiting. You have to be on one side all the time. It kicks its head because it watches the hunter. At the end, the hunter comes from the other side. The wolf runs in circles and is caught. Eight wolves were caught this way for our film. The wolf never looks at a man in the eye – it is the same with the camera. I would never like to repeat the scene of the wolf attacking the hunter.

The music in the film had a tone of nostalgia for the old ways. Is it an original composition or adapted from the traditional songs of the region?

I do not like the music to be composed by a composer. It gives a sentimental feeling and changes the way people accept the reality of the film. The music is in the picture. Nowadays, you choose to not only make films in colour, but add music, too. That is my compromise.

How did you recruit your actors?
The hunter is a colleague from the VGIK. He is the third hunter in his family and he spends most of his time in the mountains. I found Erken near Almaty. I try to find children outside the city. They are more natural and close to nature.

No Kazakh film is made without foreign aid. In fact, the film industry has come to a halt in Kazakhstan. Does the government have any plans to ameliorate the situation?
The president and the government want to make commercial films comparable to Hollywood. I cannot make commercial movies; I do not know how to make them. I said to the government, 'Why do you want to make Hollywood films? We do not make Boeing jets. You have to start making them first'. Once the government showed some commercial films to a German producer who said, 'When I want to drink Pepsi Cola, I don't drink Kazakh Pepsi Cola'. I am part of a small group of film-makers who make their own films. When we succeed in obtaining money from abroad, we bring the project to the Kazakhfilm Studio and ask them to add something.

One last question: why do children or adolescents play an important role in most of your films?
My strongest memories are from living in the *aul*. I want to preserve this memory. My father used to say that when he painted autumn, he did not paint the autumn as he saw it, but as he felt it. Now that I have spent 30 years in the city, the only emotions evoked in me are still from those first 12 years in the village.

– Locarno, August 2004 and Almaty October 2004

Notes:

1. Nogerbek, B. (trans. By Vladimir Padunov) (2004) 'Demythologizing and Reconstructing National Space in the Kazakh "New Wave" in *Kinocultura'* www.bris.ac.uk/kinocultura

BIO/FILMOGRAPHY
Serik Aprimov was born in 1960 in Aksuat in the Semipalatinsk region of Kazakhstan. In 1979, he completed a business course in Alma Ata. Between 1983 and 1988, he studied at the All Union State Institute of Cinematography (VGIK) in Moscow. He began working for Kazakhfilm Studios in 1988. After the short films, *Dvoe Echali Na Motosikle/ Two Were Riding a Motorcycle* (1986), *I Ljubov Mui Sochranim* (1987) (co-director) and

Gipnotozer (1988), he made his first feature, the graduation film, *Konechnaya Ostanovka/ The Last Stop,* which is considered a manifesto of the Kazakh New Wave.

Feature films:
1989 *Konechnaya Ostanovka/The Last Stop*
1993 *Sergelden/Dream in a Dream*
1997 *Akcyat/Aksuat*
2000 *Tri Brata/Three Brothers*
2004 *Anshi/The Hunter*

RACHID NUGMANOV

Rachid Nugmanov is one of the pioneers of Kazakh New Wave, which brought a new vitality to the Kazakh cinema. His diploma film, the 36-minute *Ya-Ha* (1986), an experimental documentary shot in the manner of an improvised diary, won the Tarkovsky prize at the Moscow International Film Festival. The underground rock scene in Leningrad just before *perestroika* when rock music officially did not exist was brought to screen perhaps for the first time. Many stars of the music scene appeared in the film, which features several of their hit songs. Although *Ya-Ha* was never distributed in the USSR, it became an underground cult classic.

Nugmanov's first feature, *Igla/The Needle* (1988), which exposed taboo subjects such as drug addiction, was seen by more than 9 million people during the first three months of its release in the Soviet Union. In this burlesque thriller, the protagonist, Moro, played by Viktor Tsoi (the leader of the popular rock band Kino, whose immature death created a James Dean-like cult), returns to Alma Ata to collect debts and discovers that his former girlfriend Dina has become a morphine addict. He decides to help her overcome the habit and to fight the local drug mafia responsible for her condition, but is confronted by the mafia head, 'the doctor' (played by the rock icon Pyotr Mamonov), who is exploiting Dina. The film does not delve into the background of Moro. We can only judge him by his actions. According to Anne Lawton there is no doubt that Moro is 'a positive hero, not in the socialist sense, but in the romantic sense of the word – free from all ties, material and psychological, a lone wanderer possessing innate dignity, honesty, an unerring sense of justice, and a mix of knightly might and kindness'.[1]

Several critics pointed out that perhaps a new romanticism was created by the New Wave, a romanticism that renders the pathos of the hero insignificant.

Following the success of *The Needle,* Nugmanov became the aesthetic voice of an emerging counterculture and a new generation in a dying empire, and was elected president of the Film-Makers' Union.

Diki Vostok/The Wild East (1993), a political allegory, was in production when the Soviet Empire collapsed. Hence, Nugmanov calls it *The Last Soviet Movie.* During

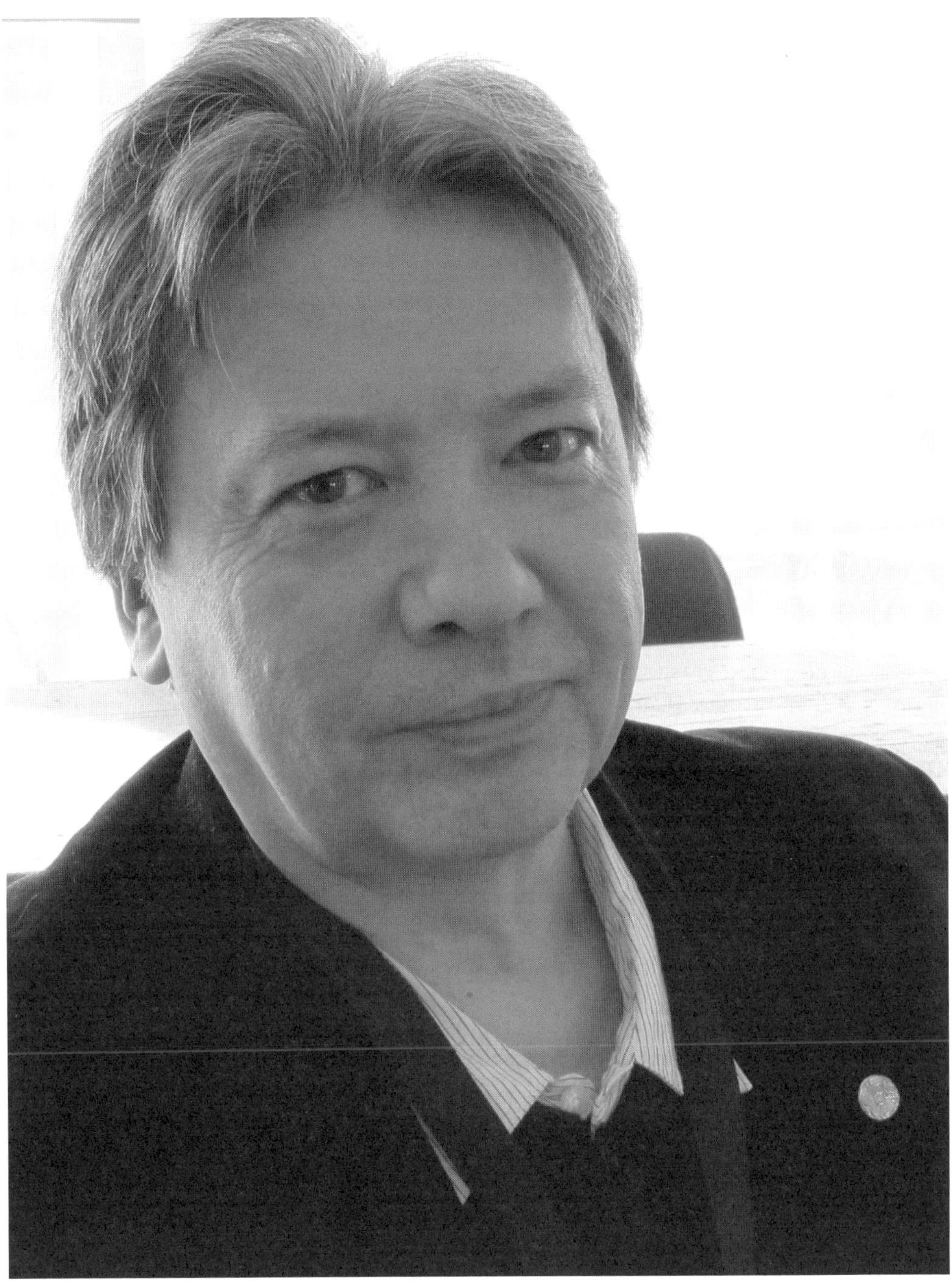

Rachid Nugmanov

the civil war in the ex-Soviet Empire, a troupe of midgets, called *The Children of the Sun*, escapes to the faraway Tian Shan Mountains in the east, where they have to deal with numerous gangs of racketing deserters. As the government does not control the situation, *The Children of the Sun* ask help from the vagabonds. Nugmanov parodies *The Seven Samurai* of Akira Kurosawa as well as the John Ford westerns in this offbeat story of bikers, rockers and midgets brought together in a landscape of burnt-out Red Army tanks and even the coffin of an Egyptian mummy. The film is shot in Kyrgyzstan by Nugmanov's brother Murat, who is responsible for the beautiful camerawork in several Kazakh films.

Nugmanov eventually settled in Tours, France, and has become a prominent voice of the Kazakh opposition government in exile.

The following interview took place in the Belgian city of Gand (Ghent) during the Flanders International Film Festival, 1994, but was finalized through numerous correspondence with Nugmanov over the years.

THE WILD EAST, ROCKERS, BIKERS AND A NEW LIFE

I met you for the first time in the summer of 1991 at the Kazakhfilm Studio in Alma Ata when you told me that the New Wave of Kazakh cinema was 'post-*perestroika*'. It was about young generations everywhere, be they Kazakh or Russian, or anyone else. It was about new relationships and a new mentality. No ideology, no politics. No restrictions. How did your career develop since *The Needle* (1988), which sold 20 million tickets at the box office and travelled to many prestigious festivals including Berlin?

Starting with the end of 1986, life was changing constantly in the Soviet Union. In 1989, everyone was enthusiastic about the future, thinking we would build the best country in the world in less than two years. In this fervour, I was elected the president of the Film-Makers Union when I was still a student. It seems like so long ago. I agreed because I also was not very serious. I thought, 'Good, I'll break the Guinness World of Records'. Since then, and especially after 1989, each year has been worse than the one before and all the enthusiasm has faded away. By 1990, everyone was concerned about the future. When I met you in Alma Ata, there was already a bad feeling about everything.

That was the year when many good films were made and *Variety* trade magazine called Alma Ata the 'Hollywood of Central Asia'. Alma Ata was the fourth largest film centre after Moscow, Leningrad and Kiev.

Those films probably were completed at that time but the concept was born in the 1980s. I was preparing *The Wild East* with Victor (Tsoi). When he died, I stopped the film. I did not know how to go on without him because it was written for him. I came back to the Film-Makers Union and for one year tried to think about the future of the Kazakh cinema. I was always for privatization. I understood even then that the government would not give us enough money. Perhaps it could give this year, but next year it would be lesser, and one day it would stop. Most people thought that we could not do anything without the government money. If one day the government betrays you, what do you do?

Are you talking about the Soviet government?
Soviet period was over at the end of 1991. It was clear then that if you could not become the owner of your own studio, eventually you would lose everything. Look at Mosfilm, which used to produce 50 or 60 films a year – what are they doing now? Six or seven films! In Kazakhstan, almost all financing has been cut. I do not know if you have heard this but all film production, except one, was stopped in the Kazakhfilm Studio this summer. The situation is very dangerous.

Right after Independence, under the liberal policies of President Nursultan Nazarbaev, Kazakhstan moved to free market economy faster than Russia and the banks and cooperatives did not miss the opportunity to publicize themselves through high-profile investments such as cinema.
They do it less and less because they lose money.

We hear about mafia money being washed. A certain company has been under fire.
I do not know who is mafia and who is not. They are responsible for themselves. I do not know where all the money they spend comes from and why they invest it in cinema. Some people want to wash dirty money and perhaps the company in question is involved in such an operation. At least they find some alternative. I, personally, believe we cannot survive alone. We may make some videos or half-amateurish stuff but not films like those that we used to make unless we go into international co-productions. New Wave was born at the end of the 1980s. It is still a child, but this child can die before it starts to walk.

The Kazakh films of the past few years are so pessimistic. Youth with no hope for the future, loss of morale and lament for dying traditions are some of the prominent themes.
This is a reflection of life. How can we make films that are not connected with life?

At the time that your first feature, *The Needle*, came out, the urban youth immersed in the culture of rock music, drugs, violence and shady deals was certainly an eye-opener, not only for us, westerners, but also for Soviet audiences from what I have read. And yet, you are quoted as saying that the film is not about drugs at all but about making a film with friends.
I agree that the film had a very strong feeling of realism and that is what I wanted to give to the audience. Scenes like Dina shooting up were real, but the film was not real. It

is something like the silent film era and Dziga Vertov's *kino pravda* (film truth), real in a playful sense.

All your films focus on sub-cultures, starting with *Ya-Ha*, your diploma film, but very few people outside the Soviet Union knew that subcultures existed.

Subcultures have always existed. Under the Soviet system, they took the form of an opposition to the communist ideology; now it is an independent movement of people who do not want to take part in commercial forms of art that are about selling yourself, your soul. What people call *subculture* is culture that does not have a big release and is not shown to the public because no one wants to invest in it. Nevertheless, these artists do not give up and they support each other. Subculture is all about being yourself. Sometimes being yourself can also lead to commercial success but this is very rare. Some become famous afterwards. Ninety-nine per cent of the time, they remain independent artists. They work for themselves to express their feelings. It is not a matter of being different as some people think. It is just being yourself, which is not easy in this world.

How much of your latest film, *The Wild East*, is related to that?

All of it. All actors are my friends from subculture. Most of them are from St Petersburg – musicians, artists, painters and the guys from the street, even the junkies. These people live together in their own cultural space. They understand each other very well. This is a very special world with its own values and prejudices, which was common in all republics even during the Soviet period. Stalin's definition of Social Realism dictated that art had to be national by form and socialist by content, which meant that a film from Kazakhstan was Kazakh only on the surface, in an ethnographic fashion, but Soviet by nature. The subculture, on the other hand, had no national form. It was international if anything, being influenced by trends such as rock 'n' roll and pop art. The content was anti-communist.

You have subtitled *The Wild East* as *The Last Soviet Film*. Apart from the fact that it was shot while the Soviet Union was disappearing, you seem to be anxious to close one chapter and open a new one. Your style is rather playful with nods to popular Soviet classics such as *Chapayev* (1934) and a tongue-in-cheek finale reminiscent of countless Social Realist films when the Solar Children pass the new grain from hand to hand. At times, *The Seven Samurai* of Akira Kurosawa takes over, but perhaps John Ford westerns are even closer to what you had in mind. The Lone Cowboy looks as if he was modelled after Clint Eastwood. Is the Wild East an answer to the Wild West of Hollywood?

Those days the Soviet Union was just like the Wild West of the last century – there were no laws or rules; the wild capitalism had arrived. 'East' does not refer to Asia but to 'communism', as 'West' is usually connected with 'capitalism'.

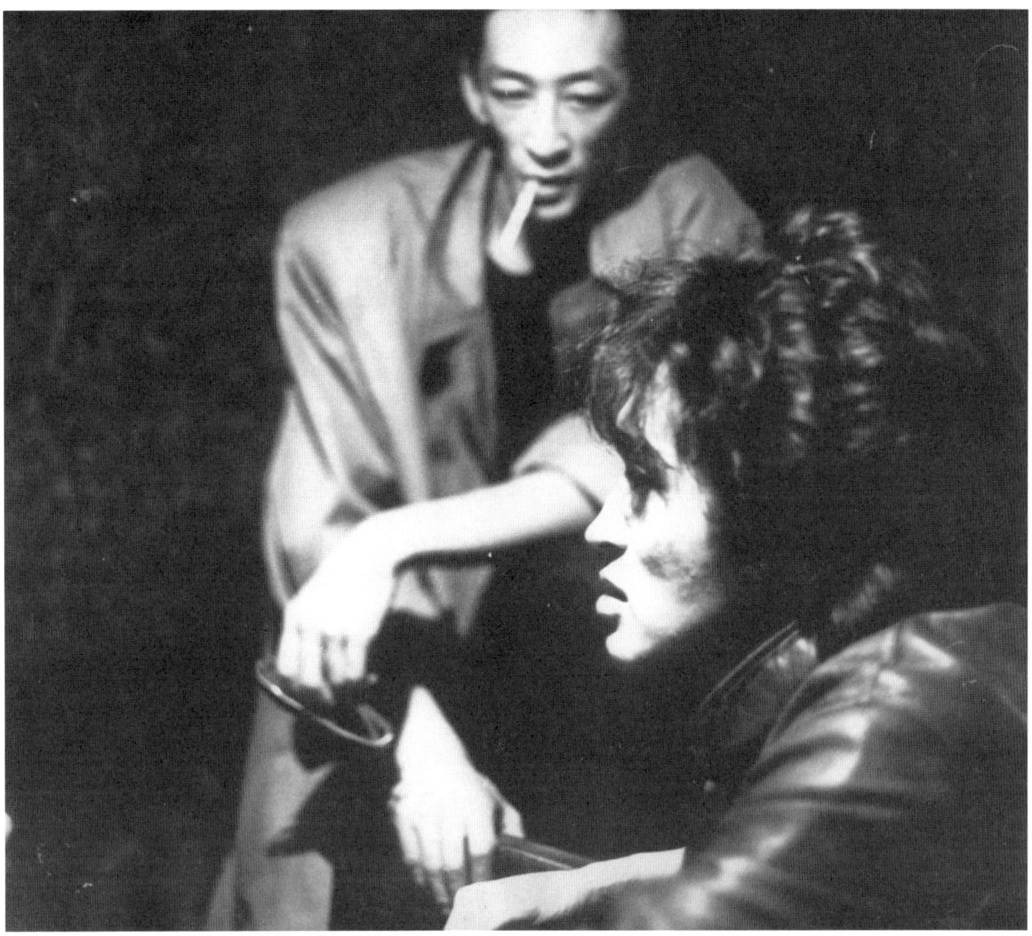

The Needle

What is the significance of the dwarfs?

It is quite easy to explain. In the original script, I had a tribe of nomads who were trying to escape from the civil war, not to take part in that bloodshed, which you could see everywhere in the former Soviet Union. They just wanted to live peacefully somewhere in the mountains. I decided to make them gypsies, what we call *ciganye* in Russian. When I looked up in the encyclopaedia, I found out that this word meant 'Children of the Sun'. Gypsies are generally quite strong and very courageous. I felt there was something wrong if they could not defend themselves, especially against the rock 'n' roll bikers, who are, basically, cowards. If one gypsy shouted at them, they would all run away. I thought perhaps they were very small, so I invited the midgets from the Moscow circus.

A British critic interpreted the midgets as representing 'restricted growth'.
I do not put symbols into my work. Later, when people discover many things, it is interesting. Initially, I try to stay away from symbols. I was in Kyoto once in the famous Stone Garden. There are no symbols there. It is so perfectly devoid of meaning that you can put so many meanings to it. I also was trying to be perfectly meaningless – without meaning, without philosophy, without symbols – an empty shell. Later, you can put as many symbols as you want. I do not know if I succeeded but that was my method of work. Every time I see the film (and I have seen it many times), I discover new things. Just like other people who have seen it several times tell me that each time it changes. One time, it may look like a stupid parody, at another a very complicated philosophical tale, then a good action movie or even a tasteless comedy.

What is your connection to rock music?
All main characters in this film are rock musicians.

Is 'rock' just a love for you or have you ever played in a band?
I always loved rock music. Beginning with the 1980s, many of my friends were rock musicians – Victor Tsoi and others. I was born the same year as rock 'n' roll. It has always had a great influence on me. I also worked with a rock band for two years in the mid-1970s. We wrote about 50 songs and made a record. Nothing was released, but the songs were passed around among friends.

Was there a rock culture in the Soviet Union just like in America?
Not like in America. Rock 'n' roll was forbidden in the Soviet Union. It was real underground. Officially, it did not exist. If you were a rock musician, you could not even call yourself as such because all those ideologists would say, 'Rock does not exist, you don't exist. Maybe you are a criminal. A parasite to society! A Punk'! I was always attracted to the artists. They loved to play; they were poets. They could not do anything else. If you are a poet, you have to take a pen and write verses. They say you are stupid; you cannot eat with that. What can you say? You go mad if you cannot write. Beginning with my first film *Ya-Ha* (1986), I was always working with these people. Not because they are rock musicians, but because I love them, and they happen to be rock musicians. An old guy in Moscow made a film called *Rock and Roll Tragedy* or something similar to that. He did not understand rock 'n' roll or the people involved. Why did he make such a film? Just because it was a popular idea! I never did it for that reason. I didn't even think of it as rock 'n' roll music. It does not matter to me.

Does *The Wild East* have distribution possibilities in Europe?

Many people liked it at the Festival of Action and Adventure Films in Valenciennes in France where it received the Jury Special Prize. However, I do not know how to sell myself to this kind of people. I talk to people like you at festivals, but I never visit film markets. The Japanese have bought it though. I have discovered that I have many friends in Japan. One letter I received from a woman says she has seen *The Needle* (also released in Japan) 21 times!

How does living outside your country reflect on your work?

Living far away from my country, I can look back and evaluate what is going on because when you live there, you are too close to understand. I could have made another film in Kazakhstan without major problems, but I decided to start from ground zero. In the West, who am I? I am a beginner. For the Kazakh New Wave, I am at the top; but it is nothing. I need challenge: to become nobody and to start from the scratch.

In your future films, do you think that you would be telling your own story, Kazakh or Soviet, or would you shift your focus to different characters and new lifestyles?

This does not concern me. I do not think much about Kazakhstan or the Soviet Union. I am trying to express myself, my understanding of people. From my first film to the last one, I have always worked with my friends in that kind of style. I never used professional actors. Even the cameraman, Murat, is my brother. I have always worked with people I loved and believed in. I knew that we could do beautiful things. Victor, who is now dead, became the most popular actor of the Soviet Union in 1989. Who could have imagined that a year before? All these talented people would never have gone on screen if I wouldn't take them there. I do not like the system of stars, the show business, the endless exposure, stars running from one film to another. I am bored with all that. We have film, we have camera, we have friends, we have energy; we are going to do it! It does not matter whether they are from Kazakhstan, Moscow, Hong Kong or London. If I know them, if I love them, I will work with them. Even while sitting here, I am preparing projects and, again, with people I know and love.

– Gand (Ghent), October 1994

Notes:

---

1.   Lawton, A. (1992) *Kinoglasnost: Soviet Cinema in Our Time*, Cambridge, Cambridge University Press.

BIO/FILMOGRAPHY

Rachid Nugmanov was born in 1954 in Alma Ata. In 1977, he graduated from the architecture institute. He entered the All-Union State Institute of Cinematography (VGIK) in Moscow in 1984 and was one of the students in the workshop Sergei Soloviev conducted. He graduated in 1987. His first film, *Igla/The Needle*, received the Grand Prix of the Festival of Nuremberg in 1990. Nugmanov has been living in France since 1993.

Feature films:
1988 *Igla/The Needle*
1993 *Diki Vostok/The Wild East*
2010 *The Needle Remix*

KYRGYZSTAN

CHINGIZ AITMATOV

Chingiz Aitmatov is one of the most well-known writers of Central Asia in the western world. His career flourished in the former Soviet Union where he told the tales of his people, the Kyrgyz of the steppes, from the turbulent years following the world wars to the establishment of the Soviet rule and its outcome, often employing the dominant language, Russian. His first novel, *Dzamilja/Cemila* (1958), was described by the French writer Aragon as 'the most beautiful love story of the world'. In 1963, he was awarded the Lenin Prize for literature. His relationship with the Soviet authorities, however, was not always so amiable. *Ak Keme/The White Boat* (1971), which exposed the moral destruction of the Kyrgyz peasants in the world of evil, was ostracized for its pessimistic ending – the suicide of the little boy. *The Dream of the Wolf* (1987) created a furore when god was printed with a capital 'G' for the first time in a Soviet publication but Aitmatov was already a world celebrity. His books were being translated into many languages and adaptations to screen by some of the best film-makers of the Soviet Union were winning awards at home and abroad.

It is not an exaggeration to say that the national cinema of Kyrgyzstan owes much of its history to its greatest writer. In addition to serving as president of the Cinematographer's Union for many years, Aitmatov has also given to cinema more than a dozen of his most important works, often scripting or co-scripting. Central Asian cinema has had a long tradition of adaptations from literature. However, the involvement of writers such as Aitmatov has been more direct and this has definitely influenced the themes, points of view and the aesthetic choices of the film-makers.

The works of Aitmatov attracted many film-makers from different parts of the USSR. There have also been collaborations with Turkey. The contributions of the non-Kyrgyz film-makers encouraged Kyrgyz cinema to establish a link between cinema and cultural traditions and brought a universal perspective to a cinema that by tradition is oriented towards national epics. Kyrgyz cinema also benefited vastly from the aesthetic climate created by Aitmatov and the way he pushed the limits and transgressed the national boundaries to present man as a universal being. Transpositions were not always successful, as the rich and complex nature of Aitmatov's work does not easily lend itself to the language of cinema. It has even been stated that Aitmatov sacrificed his talent for cinema and the cultural development of his people.

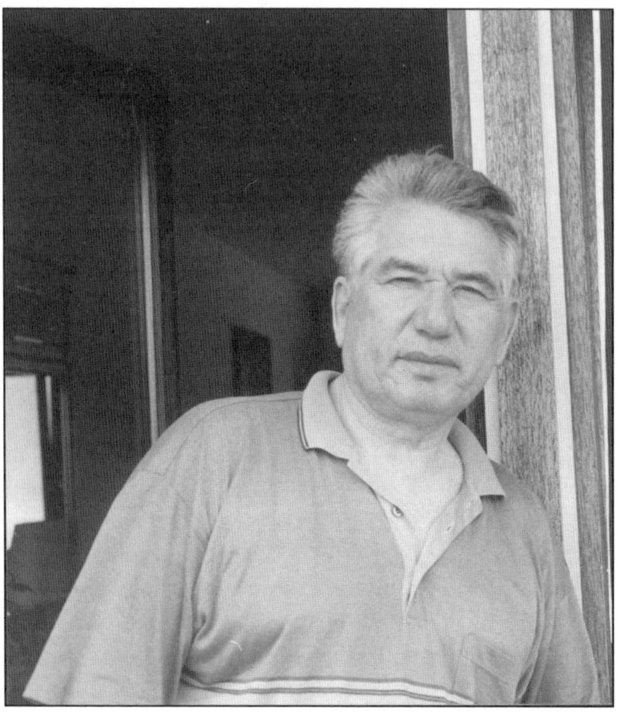

Chingiz Aitmatov

Chingiz Aitmatov was awarded the prestigious Berlinale Camera during the 46th International Berlin Film Festival in 1996 where a Kyrgyz film, Boranly Beket/Snowstormy Station (1995) by Bakyt Karagulov, was shown. Based on a famous Aitmatov novel, The Day that Is Longer than a Century, and the 13th Aitmatov work adapted to screen, the film tells the story of two former fishermen from the Kazakh region of Aral Lake who had spent World War II at a remote railway station in the Sary Ozek Steppe. When one of them dies, Soviet guards do not allow the other to bury him according to ancient Islamic rites and at a place sacred to Kazakhs, which is now a military rocket-testing zone. Memories of his friend, a teacher and a partisan, persecuted during the Stalin era for the diaries he kept, haunt the hero. Soviet totalitarianism that had threatened cultural and ethnic identities is linked in his mind with the Mankurts who, in ancient times, robbed conquerors of their memory by means of torture. Aitmatov, who also wrote the script, claims that the story of a writer persecuted by the regime is not based on personal experiences: 'numerous writers were oppressed by the State. It is a mirror of a period of crisis when the interests of the government were in conflict with the interests of the people particularly in regards to preservation of cultural roots'.

Critical of previous adaptations of his work to screen, Aitmatov was very pleased with this film, especially with 'the sensitivity of the filmmaker to the multi-layered symbolism of the original work – the incessant passing of the trains or the wheel that rolls down the dusty plains – that define the emotional ties of the characters to their cultural roots. Such abstract concepts are very difficult to capture on the screen. I had seen other works by Bakyt and I knew that he would understand this book'.

I met Chingiz Aitmatov for the first time in July 1994 in Luxembourg where he was serving as Kyrgyz ambassador. After several letters, faxes and telephone conversations, he invited me to his villa near the mountains where his daughter Shirin translated the interview from Russian to English. In 1996, in Berlin, although he was busy with jury duties, he gave me some time for an update. Our discussions continued informally wherever we had the chance to meet. In 2000, during the 10th anniversary of Cottbus Film Festival in the former East Germany, as the patron of the festival, Aitmatov led the delegation of Kyrgyz film-makers to present a comprehensive retrospective. A year later, again in Cottbus, in November 2001, we had a better chance to sit down for a longer conversation.

THE EQUIVOCAL MARRIAGE OF LITERATURE AND CINEMA

In the face of the present changes, the collapse of totalitarian regimes and the rise of the long oppressed nations with claims to their past and culture, an artist can no longer remain in his/her ivory tower. You were a Soviet citizen once and a Soviet ambassador during the *perestroika* years. You have even served as a Russian ambassador after the fall of the Soviet Union. Now you are Kyrgyzstan's ambassador. How do these changes affect you as an artist and as an individual?

I often ask this question myself. The global transformation can be examined from two points of view: personal and social. Naturally, you would see the interrelation when you analyse these two. I cannot separate myself from the mass that used to be called the 'Soviet citizens'. You may see in me a part that is used to the conservatism of the old times because I spent most of my life in that epoch. Living in a totalitarian regime was very difficult for everyone, but it was much worse for a writer. Nevertheless, I am proud that I have chosen a global role in my work and lived with it.

In the new architecture ensuing the fall of the Soviet Union, who are the winners and who are the losers?

I do not think there are any winners except perhaps the future generations. We have stepped from one level to another, which is one step closer to democracy. Our century is experiencing something that was not even possible theoretically. This touches not only the post-Soviet people, but also the world. *Perestroika* was initially seen as a process of reforms. History developed spontaneously with these reforms. We are now going through the repercussions of this spontaneous development of *perestroika*. The 'New East' is trying to find who he is. We look at Europe as a mirror. Do we copy the political liberalism, the dynamism and the productivity of the western market? We are not ready for these changes. We found a cruel reality in the capitalist world. Totalitarian ideology is now replaced by totalitarian monetarism. How long will this transition period take?

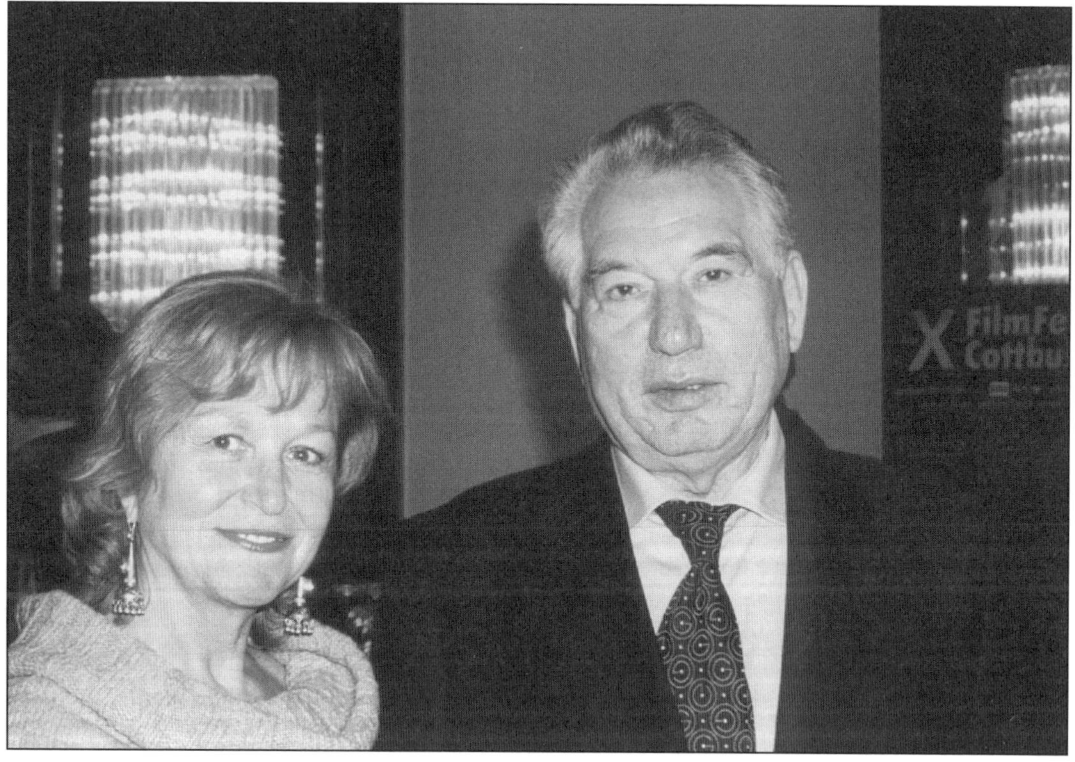

Chingiz Aitmatov and author at the
Cottbus Film Festival, 2000.

For a writer, film-maker and intellectual of the former USSR, Independence has brought certain gains such as freedom of expression; on the other hand, there are some losses.

Intellectuals form a part of society that takes everything to heart and suffers more than the others do. They see something attractive in a new society and in new constructions and feel obligated to fight for society and its liberation. However, the ideas of the intellectuals can also take a wrong turn, or they may not even be wanted. In the years of *perestroika*, we thought that everything would happen the way we wanted it to happen, but our ideas were exploited by other forces of society. Today intellectuals are not even on the path of history. The intellectual is a catalyst, the catalyst of historical movement and changes although these changes may not work well with his ideas. The important thing is the movement, the fight for the right cause. This is what develops culture.

In one of your plays, *Voshozdenie na Fudzijamu/The Ascent of Mount Fuji Yama* (1977), the hero, Sabur, is an intellectual who is alienated by his friends and society because his ideas were ahead of his time. Where would he be today?

I thank you for such a question. I have often thought of him myself. What would happen to Sabur today? Sabur is one of those spiritual relations of the dissidents, the intellectuals who fought against totalitarianism. He is a man with high goals. He would not be satisfied with the changes because if he did, he would not have his development as a person and as an individual. I could also say that I am satisfied with everything. We now have liberty – liberty of press, of expression. I can write what I want. If I decide to be satisfied with what I have, I would have no other goal in life. I must always find new problems and new challenges. The spirit of man is like space. It has no limits. The individual must fight for his own truth. If he has nothing to fight for, he does not exist anymore. A dialogue took place some years ago between the Japanese philosopher Daisuku Ikeda and me, which was later published in German, Russian and Japanese. Our first meeting was just before the Gulf War. We even tried to send a letter to Saddam Hussein to persuade him to leave Kuwait. Of course, it did not happen that way, but we tried. When we met again in Moscow after some years, we discovered that everything we had discussed earlier was still in front of us in a new way. This tells me that we should never stop. Democracy now exists in Russia, but democracy is not the highest possibility.

Now that we are in a completely new era, how should we treat our past? In *Fuji Yama*, the teacher asks, 'What for shall we come back to our past'? Bolat Shamshiev, who directed the film version, once commented that the film was 'an attempt to answer the question whether it is necessary to stir the past'.

Without a past, a present and some ideas about a future, life does not exist. The past holds us every hour. We have to measure the present with the happenings of the past. We often have a misconception that the future should always be bigger and better than the past. This is not always true. In art and literature, it is not true at all. I do not think modern music is as good as the music of the beginning of the century. We should analyse the past as a tool to know and to build the future.

You have always been very close to cinema, both as a scriptwriter and as the head of the Cinematographer's Union. Critics have referred to you as 'the heart and soul' of the Kyrgyz cinema. You have been on the juries of important festivals. Retrospectives of films based on your works have been held in *cinematheques* and specialized festivals.

I could not say that I am very close to cinema for the moment. During the last few years, politics and diplomatic work have completely separated me from cinema. Nevertheless, I have my own principles and I know what I want from cinema. I do not like those fashionable festivals such as Cannes. They have other goals, other aims. They represent well-developed countries. Festivals such as Berlin, Istanbul or the *festival des 3 continents* in Nantes, France, give a chance to the cinemas of other countries to have a voice.

What about Kyrgyz cinema after Independence?

Kyrgyz cinema, just like Kyrgyz theatre, is only a dry little branch. After losing government subsidies, it has gone through immense economic difficulties. However, artists still have a perspective. If they find subsidies, they can express themselves. There is no censorship now…

There is another kind of censorship. Economic problems determine the type of films to be made.

That is very true. We still have the illusion of liberty, not actual liberty.

It has been said that your work is much richer and more complex than adaptations to cinema. Do you agree that it is very difficult to film your work?

Certainly. Out of the 12 films that were made to date, only 2 are worth seeing: *Ak Keme/The White Boat* (1975) by Bolat Shamshiev and *Pegi Pios, Biegouchi Kraiem Moria/A Piebald Dog Running on the Edge of the Sea* (1990) by Karen Gevorkian.

***The White Boat* successfully balances the national legends and myths with the reality of daily life without sacrificing the poetry of the artistic structure and *A Piebald Dog Running on the Edge of the Sea* brings to screen, with visual poetry, the plight of a small ethnic minority on the Sakhalin Island who are threatened with cultural extinction. Shamshiev is Kyrgyz and Gevorkian is Armenian.**

Two very important Russian film-makers have also transposed my stories: Andrei Mikhalkov Konchalovsky with *Pervyj Ucitel/The First Teacher* (1965*)* and Larisa Shepit'ko with *Znoi/Heat* (1963), as well as some very talented Kyrgyz film-makers such as Okeev and Bazarov.

I find it a paradox that Kyrgyz cinema was first heard of in the West thanks to *The First Teacher*, a film made by a Russian. In fact, Konchalovksy started his career in Kyrgyzstan with this film. Larisa Shepit'ko was Ukrainian. She was supposed to direct *Heat*, based on your short story *The Eye of the Camel*, with Shamshiev as their diploma film to graduate from VGIK, but finished it alone, although Shamshiev played the leading role. The film won the Grand Prize of the Karlovy Vary Film Festival in 1964. *The First Teacher* is often referred to as the beginning of independent cinema although Konchalovksy was very much criticized for doing injustice to your novel of the same title and deviation from reality. Do you think that there should be a unity between the film and the book?

That is the idea, but it is not always so in reality.

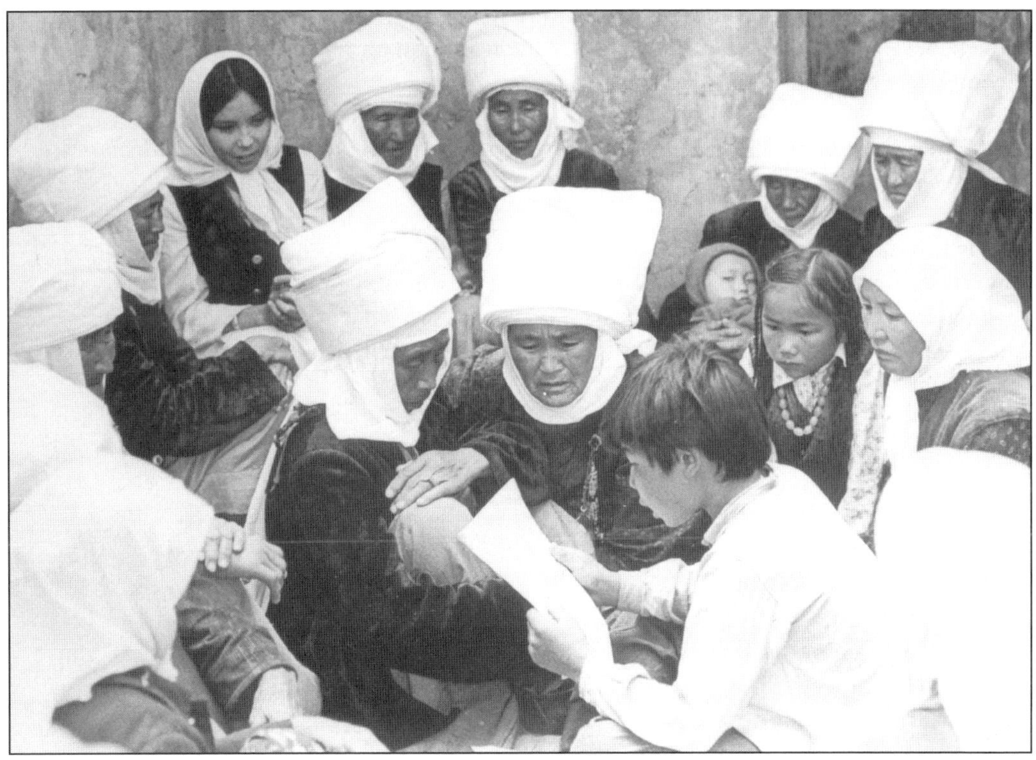

Cemila by Irina Poplavskaya

In your books, one can easily find a hero, usually a young one, who is fascinated with the magic of cinema – the little boy in *The White Boat* or the dead soldier's son in *The Soldier's Son*, for instance.

I have always loved cinema. In my childhood, there was no television. In the mountains, there was no electricity either. Films were shown by turning the handle of the projector manually. Naturally, the strongest boys got to do this job and, naturally, they would speed it up or slow it down as they pleased. There were so many fights!

What kind of films were those?

Russian films from end of the 1930s. National cinema only started in the 1950s.

In *The Soldier's Son*, the boy watches war films and thinks they are real.

Cinema is illusion. The little boy does not remember his father; he thinks someone on the screen is his father. For the boy, this is the reality.

For him, illusion is more real than reality.

Children are very sensitive and they were more so in the days before the advent of the television. Now they can sit in front of the television for 24 hours if they wish. It is a completely different world.

Could you tell me something about your last novel, *The Stamp of Cassandra*?

It is difficult to explain. It is very different from my traditional stories.

Is this difference connected with the global changes or internal, personal changes?

The two are interrelated. On the one hand is the issue of nationalism; on the other, the global view of the planet and the human race – a view, which does not depend on race or religion. The hero reflects about what is happening on earth from an interplanetary station in space. A new Cassandra!

– Luxemburg, 1994

* * *

Six years ago, we discussed the new world order after the fall of the Berlin Wall. Today we are in the former East Germany, now unified with the West, but bombs are falling not far from your country. You have told me that we have to change our perspective.

At this moment, it is very important to think about humanitarian values while talking about the world. Through the mass media, which has become more important and powerful, the danger of the absolutization of one or the other religion has entered our lives. Mass media must be aware of this danger. To be more concrete, in the past, when two countries were in conflict with each other, this conflict could not have repercussions on the rest of the world. Through the development of the mass media, which permits us to witness with our own eyes what happens in faraway places, we see that a conflict between two sides, regardless of which side we are on, can influence the world. This is the point, which has to be taken into account while talking about the war, and this point worries me.

The development of the mass media has become dangerous.

Mass media monopoly can be very dangerous. It can influence our minds and further development of the world. The responsibility of mass media has increased enormously because now it deals with global issues.

To turn our attention to cinema, you once told me that Kyrgyz cinema was like a baby learning to walk. At what stage is it now? The film industries of all former Soviet Republics have been negatively affected after Independence and the transition to market economy.

Kyrgyz cinema is not a baby anymore, but a youth, a teenager thrown out on the streets to find his way. I am quite sure that talented young directors like Aktan Abdikalikov will go an interesting way. I am not *Ak Sakal* (the wise old man with a white beard), but I will try to answer your questions. In the past, we used to meet our colleagues in Moscow but now our focus seems to have moved to Cottbus! The world changes and everything becomes history but these changes affect our creative development. National art including cinema was the invention of the Soviet era for us. I count myself among those who discovered national cinema tradition during the Soviet period. We achieved great things within the context of the Soviet cinema and language. We had our own cinema, our own directors and stars. I do not want to comment on national cinema today and I do not want to blame anyone for the present situation either. We are in a free space where we can work. Each country has the opportunity to prove what they can achieve and, in the end, life will prove what can be achieved. We have moved from one system with all its limitations that seemed to work for us to a different system of market economy. New tasks await us. The question is, are we going to survive? Many factors influence this outcome. The fact that Cottbus Film Festival has focused on Central Asia is very important. In the new social and cultural circumstances, such festivals give us psychological support. Naturally, film-making always offers alternatives. One of these is that we might move towards mass cinema. When I say 'mass cinema', I mean Hollywood. We can also try to preserve our identity and show it. This is not a problem for only Central Asia. For international cinema and culture also, it is important to maintain its diversity and originality, which find a voice in national representations. Our task is to keep pace with international film-making and show that national spiritual values are important and can contribute to interesting film-making. There are many international film festivals – Cannes, Berlin, Venice – and may they prosper in the future. In psychological terms, it is important for us to find our own place.

In the past, we were under the pressure of the totalitarian society, which created difficulties, but also some advantages. Now we are swimming in a large ocean; it will be seen whether we can keep our head above the water or swim. The potential is there. The subject of culture and art is infinite at this stage of our civilization and very important to talk about.

In the context of the recent events, we are facing a challenge of universal proportions – spiritual values against international terrorism. I am sure that cinema will participate in this struggle. To reflect on what happened in the past and what will happen in the future has become crucial. The current structure calls upon us to change our perspective if the human race is to survive at all.

– Cottbuss, November 2001

AKTAN ARYMKUBAT (ABDIKALIKOV)

Aktan Arymkubat's *Selkinchek/The Swing, Beshkempir/The Adopted Son* and *Maimyl/ The Chimp* constitute an autobiographical trilogy, a *bildungsroman*, one might say, which narrates in chronological order the film-maker's childhood, adolescence and passage to adulthood within the context of historical, social and political changes in Kyrgyzstan. The protagonist is interpreted by Arymkubat's son, Mirlan, in all three.

The Swing is almost a wordless film about a young boy, who spends his days with an old retarded man pushing a beautiful girl on a swing. The idyllic picture of childhood is disrupted with the arrival of a stranger. *Beshkempir/The Adopted Son* (1998) narrates the dramatic effects of the ancient custom of offering babies from large families to childless couples on a young village boy. One spring day, five women sitting on a colourful *kilim* in the village square pass a white bundle from hand to hand, pronouncing the words, 'It is not my son, but the son of the sky', and the newly weaned Azate acquires new parents. At the age of 13, when he finds out that he is adopted, he experiences a deep sense of loss. The death of his grandmother is very crucial as it marks Azate's passage to manhood. This is perhaps the first time Azate articulates his feelings. He will pay her debts if there are any, as according to custom, a person who owes cannot be buried. Ironically, he has to take care of his family at a moment when he discovers they are not his blood relatives.

The absence of the real father had been a regular trope for Soviet cinema, to emphasize the split, the exteriority between the hero and the laws of his society or social group, where the hero must exist within the socio-cultural models that are already determined. However, Arymkubat asserts that the character of Azate stems from his personal experiences as he also was adopted.

The emotional journey of the young rural hero moves to an urban environment with *Maimyl/The Chimp* and the common language is Russian. The protagonist is waiting to be drafted into the army. Once again, he is outside the society, a misfit among his

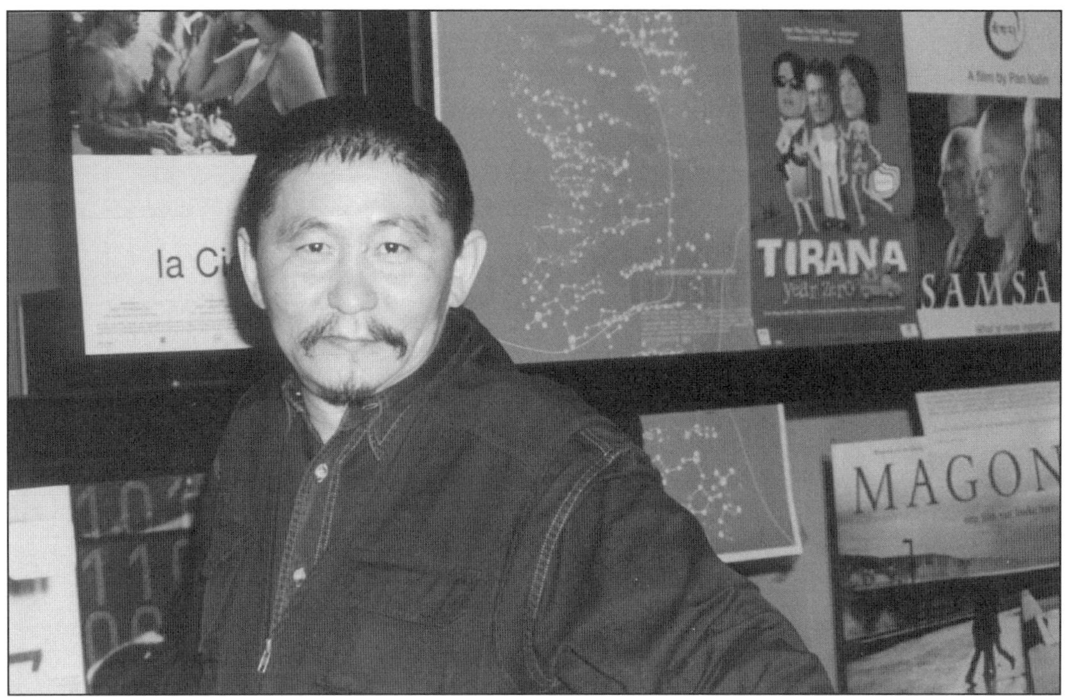

Aktan Abdikalikov

peers, this time because of his protruding ears. Extreme self-consciousness about his appearance augmented by family problems – alcohol dependency of his father and the departure of his mother – exacerbate his alienation. He does not have the confidence to approach the blonde-haired Russian girl, with whom he has fallen in love.

Nature is very important in Arymkubat's films as a part of daily life. Although Kyrgyzstan is theoretically an Islamic country, Animism is practised widely. Starting with the almost shamanistic ritual of the giving away of a baby boy to a childless couple, *The Adopted Son* opulently indulges in centuries-old beliefs that connect men to nature. Another example is different birds proclaiming different seasons in nature, which in turn connect with the emotional development of the protagonist.

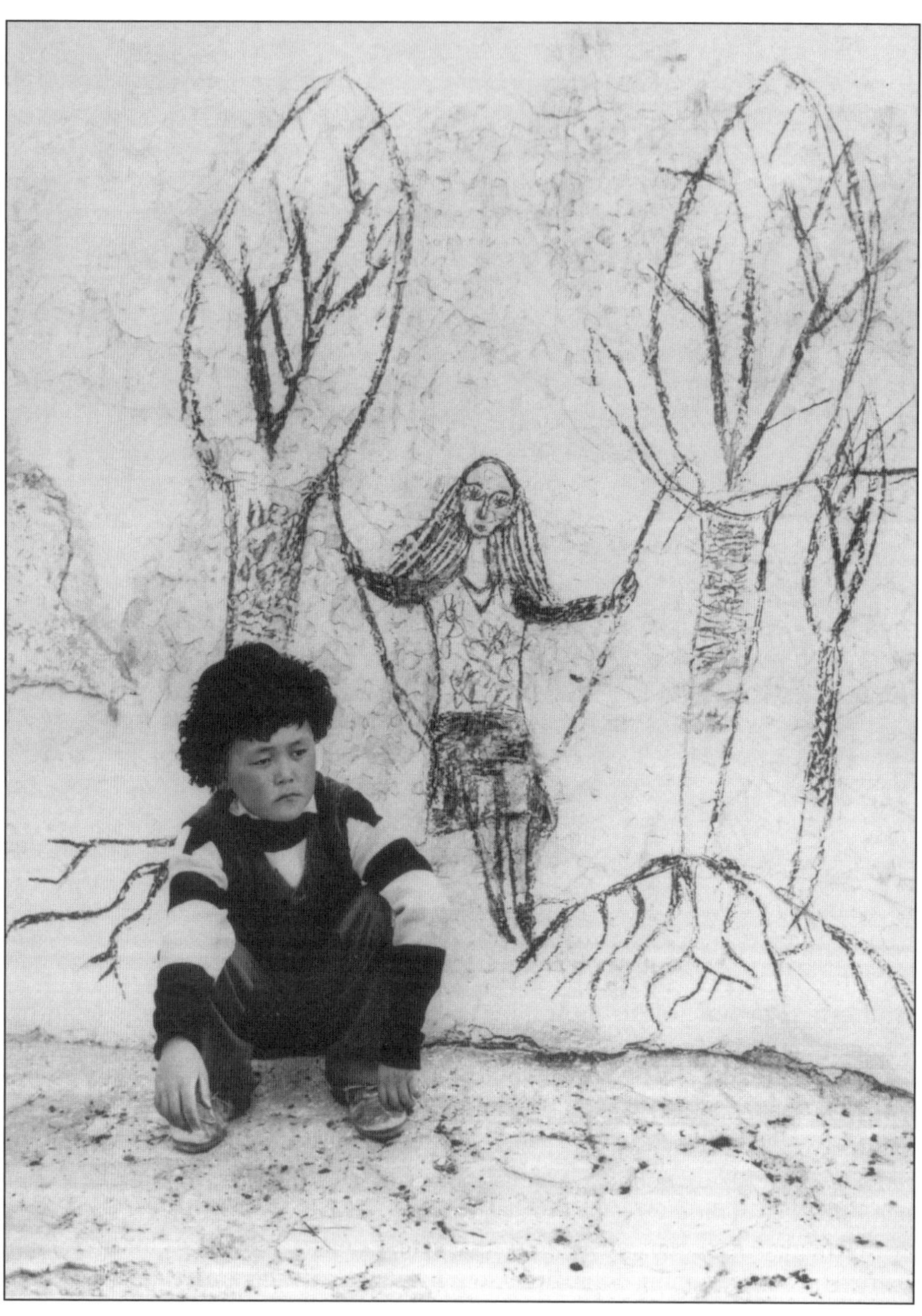

The Swing

The film is mostly in black and white with an economical use of colour. Abdikalikov, who was trained as a painter, experiments with tones and nuances in recreating a village life that undulates between sexual awakenings, fist fights, hopes, uncertainties, as well as fear and disappointment. He explains that all significant memories of youth were in colour for him, signifying emotional memory and meaning, and the rest in nebulous black and white. Colour, which is an integral part of the trilogy, also defines the interior and exterior landscape in *The Chimp* when the garish decoration of the disco and the dull grey landscape of the urban space are juxtaposed with the vivid hues of nature.

Arymkubat's *Svet-Ake/The Light Thief* (2010) is about an electrician who is called Mr Light (Svet-Ake) by his friends. He brings light to the inhabitants of a small city who have not lost the ability to love and laugh despite desperation in their daily lives. Naïvely, he strikes a bargain with a rich developer running for the local office to supply wind-generated electricity to the whole valley, but faces deep-rooted corruption in this simple tale of ordinary people who try to keep traditional values of solidarity and human decency in a rapidly changing harsh and unjust world.

The first interview took place during the Rotterdam Film Festival in January 2002 and the second in Locarno in 2010 terminating in Karlovy Vary in 2011

THE MOST SUCCESSFUL KYRGYZ FILM-MAKER

Many opinions have been expressed about your work: *The Swing, The Adopted Son* and *The Chimp*. Critics easily identify a trilogy. Is this what you originally had in mind, or is it a term used by journalists who like to compartmentalize?

Journalists started to speak about a trilogy after I emphasized it. I had the trilogy in mind when I made *The Swing* ten years ago. By the time I finished the second film, *The Adopted Son*, I knew that I needed a third film. It was like the periods of my life: childhood, adolescence and becoming an adult.

You mean the trilogy developed as it went and it was not fixed from the beginning.

That is right. By the second film, I knew I had to do it.

Why did you choose your son to play the lead role?

Because this is an autobiographical trilogy, I thought of someone closest to me to interpret my ideas, feelings and emotions, and I chose my son.

Your alter-ego?

Yes, yes.

Perhaps on your part, there was an innate wish for your son not to have the same kind of experiences that you had – a wish for a better future.

I did not choose this topic to illustrate that the son should not be like his father. I wanted to focus on the father and son experiences and disclose the differences between them. My aim was to mirror the good as well as the bad.

Is the trilogy autobiographical in terms of facts or feelings?

The plot is very autobiographical. The events of *The Swing* were drawn from direct experiences. I was an adopted son and I had the nickname *ape*, the chimp. Furthermore, when I was a young boy, I was in love with my 16-year-old neighbour and I followed her everywhere. However, some subplots are not autobiographical, but stem from my

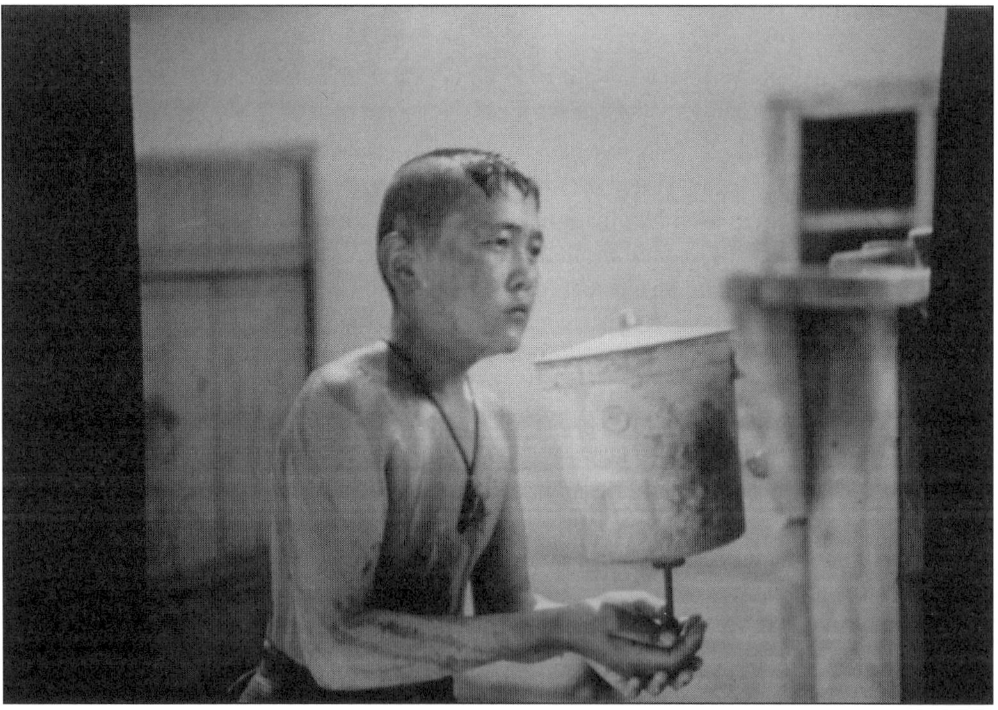

The Adopted Son

co-scriptwriter's suggestions or stuff I read somewhere. Emotions and feelings are autobiographical to the maximum. I don't know why I always feel the need to bare my soul. It must have something to do with the fact that in our daily lives, we repeatedly experience the disintegration of the original principles of ethics. In our chaotic world, to give a definition to truth has become very difficult. The only thing one is capable of is to try to be truthful to oneself. I am not a beautiful person, and this reality formed the foundation of my spiritual development. I know that appearance is not what counts, and it does not bother me anymore, but adolescence is the most vulnerable period of our lives when we long to be loved. Slowly, you begin to understand and try to be beautiful through thoughts and feelings. Another painful memory from my childhood that found its way to the film is growing up with an alcoholic father.

The character of the fat girl in *The Chimp* reminded me of Fellini's *8½*. Does this image come from life or from love of cinema?

I knew that I would repeat the same things that one could find elsewhere, but I had a neighbour exactly like this woman. I just took a real fact. This kind of woman exists in the childhood of all men.

Little bit real, little bit imaginary. Boys usually have big imaginations before actual experiences.

Fantasies.

You use several powerful images, one of which is the mirror. Once you said that the father in *The Chimp* puts the mirror down when he loses his soul.

I do the 'cinema of images', so I use all tools and all material available to achieve that goal. I put meaning to the surroundings, to the atmosphere and to the construction of the film. The mirror is the reflection of all our secrets. As we grow up, we keep gazing at the mirror. I can also recall several metaphors that connect the mirror to cinema or to mythology. For instance, the bad are not to be seen in the mirror. They have no reflection.

Is this from Kyrgyz mythology?

I don't remember but in Russian mythology, one always finds the image of the mirror that tells the truth. There is even a proverb about telling the truth, which is connected to the mirror. This is expressed in Kyrgyzstan with turning down the mirror. In that scene, the father starts to cry and turns down the mirror. To be more precise, I wanted to say he could no longer face himself. He was weak and he was afraid of himself. The reflection that is broken is like his faith that has been corrupted. The woman with a scar on her face looks at the mirror a little differently. Her faith is broken. On the other hand, the little mirror the boys hold to look under the skirts of the girls reflects the devilish nature of adolescent boys.

The last one is universal. Boys used to behave the same way in Turkey, too, when I was a young girl. It is good that in the film, we can recognize these experiences and laugh about them, but they also help us to reflect because the subject is very serious. To see young people with nothing to do, waiting to go to the army, is depressing. If they had something good to do, they would not think of going to the army. Is this a true reflection of the Kyrgyz youth today?

Yes, it is true and the period just before the army is a period of decision. You have to decide about your life.

This aspect can be applied to the country as well. For instance, in your short film *Ostanovka/Beket/Bus Stop*, which you co-directed with Ernest Abdizhaparov, people are waiting for the bus that never comes.

After the fall of the Soviet Union, there was a vacuum. Before people had faith to construct, to build communism. Now there is no faith, nothing to build. A vacuum has been created. In *Bus Stop*, people are waiting for some kind of a future to come, but they are just waiting and waiting.

Traditions were suppressed during the Soviet era. In *The Adopted Son*, they play an important role. The title *Beshkempir* signifies 'five women' in Kyrgyz. These women, who look like tribal heads of the village, perform an initiation ritual that declares the boy adopted. When the grandmother dies, the boy performs the ritual of settling her accounts and through this action enters the world of adulthood. How do people feel about traditions in modern Kyrgyzstan? Do the young want to search their roots or do they simply not care? It is rather significant that the protagonist is an adopted boy, a familiar motif of the Stalinist cinema although the purpose is reversed here.

After the break from the Soviet Union, we were eager to find our roots. In my earlier films, I gave prominence to Kyrgyz traditions for the people to remember. Along with cinema, political and cultural life was also actively involved in the revival of roots. Now we try to re-evaluate the role of traditions because the country should not isolate itself; it should integrate with the world. That is why I used people from different cultures in my last film, *The Chimp*. In the Soviet Union, different cultures and nationalities had lived together. In Kyrgyzstan, there are about 80 nationalities. This was a plus, so why ruin it? The nation itself, the people are not guilty. Politicians are. Now these issues are stabilizing. People reject the bad things and take the good ones to make decisions.

Does the government have control over arts?

Not at all! Absolutely not! And I am scared about that because control is order. You can avoid control. Things that are forbidden, you have to avoid, which means the artist has to be more concentrated to be more inventive. During the Soviet era, many films ended up on the shelves, but still films were made and these films were good. Perhaps it is easier to live in an authoritarian regime than in total freedom. Living in a free country, every individual needs to have a bigger chance, and I don't think our country is ready for that kind of freedom.

When Independence arrived, what were you doing, or thinking, and what was your reaction?

I was in the mountains trying to write the screenplay for *Gde tvoi dom, ulitka/Where Is Your House, Snail?* When I heard what happened, I was surprised. I went to the mountain with one regime and came back with another. But I still think that people did not understand what was happening. It is all the politicians. People could not make a conscious decision.

The film industry received a big setback. Many film-makers are not shooting at all. One of your eminent film-makers, Gennadi Bazarov, has not made a film since 1989.

It was as if people had more confidence in film-makers before Independence. I needed a kind of a stepping-back period to reflect because what we had was taken away from us and each individual was trying to survive as he could. Now it appears that I am the only one of the Kyrgyz cinema who survived. I know many very talented film-makers, perhaps more talented than I am, who could make good films, but they are sitting idle somewhere. Was a selection made and only the best survived? I do not think so. We were never told how to make different kind of films, how to work for money or how to finance projects. I cannot explain how I get the money. I was not ready for that myself. I was just shooting. I am still shooting.

You receive funds from the West because they have seen your films and liked them and they trust you. What are the dangers of making films with foreign funds? Any ramifications on your thinking or planning?

No. No remarks were made during the screenwriting, editing or shooting. When I say this, everyone is surprised. But this is the truth. I am the sole author of my films.

In the past, you had worked with Bazarov. When I met him in Nantes recently, he spoke highly of your work and told me that even those days one could already sense your curiosity and artistic creativity.

I was his assistant director and set designer.

What about Tolomush Okeev, who passed away recently? Didn't he produce *Where Is Your House, Snail*, a children's film?

Yes, my first film. Nobody knew about this film. The first screening was in Cottbus last autumn and the next was Nantes. The script of that film was ordered from Moscow. It is like a propaganda film. I was not allowed to change the script but I tried to adapt it to Kyrgyzstan.

Do you think that one can see a marked difference between a Kyrgyz film and a Kazakh film or an Uzbek film?

The Kyrgyz are perhaps closest to the Kazakhs. I think Kyrgyz films have a more melancholic but at the same time more brusque way of looking at life, which could be interpreted as typical of the mountain people. The Kazakhs are more introspective in their films reflecting the steppe mentality. Uzbek films are more extravagant, even kitsch. Cultural differences have become more pronounced within the film industries after the fall of the Soviet Union.

You are a self-made man. You did not go to film school and you were a painter before becoming a film-maker at the age of 33.

I studied painting.

Do you still paint?

No. I tried at the beginning, but the project is different in terms of the form. You have to change your mind. Now I express my thoughts successfully through cinema. If I fail, I will go back to painting.

Most people do not know much about Kyrgyz cinema. The most prevalent name is not a film-maker but a writer, Chingiz Aitmatov, who has been actively involved with the film industry in many ways. Do you feel the influence of his work on your artistic and intellectual development?

He was my favourite writer and he certainly influenced me. But I liked the earlier Aitmatov. I do not like the wise old Aitmatov. I think his thinking has become European and I think he is wrong.

Aitmatov told me he considers you the most important Kyrgyz director!

(*laughs*) I like the earlier Aitmatov more, such as *Dzamilja/Cemila*. I think Kyrgyz people need that kind of understanding of Kyrgyz mentality of looking at life. Books like *Cassandra's Stamp* – nobody needs such literature. His themes are very global. I think of Aitmatov that way because I want to remind myself not to step over this barrier: Don't shoot films about general global issues from somewhere in Paris! Aitmatov would not be mad at me for saying this, he would agree with me.

What kind of movies do you like to watch?

I watch very little. I am always thinking of my own way. I don't know if it is good or bad, but for me, it is more interesting to have some kind of an experience to create a personality. If I will be mistaken, it still would be an interesting road of the lonely stranger.

Are you starting another trilogy?

Not now, but everything starts very spontaneously. We don't know why we fall in love. Only afterwards, we can try to understand. I won't be surprised if I end up with another trilogy.

– Rotterdam, January 2002

LET THERE BE LIGHT

***The Light Thief* is a politically charged film that offers no hope. Is this how you see the future of your country?**
The political situation is very difficult and life is very hard. But I hope that things may change. *The Light Thief* ends with the wheels of the old bicycle turning although the rider is not seen.

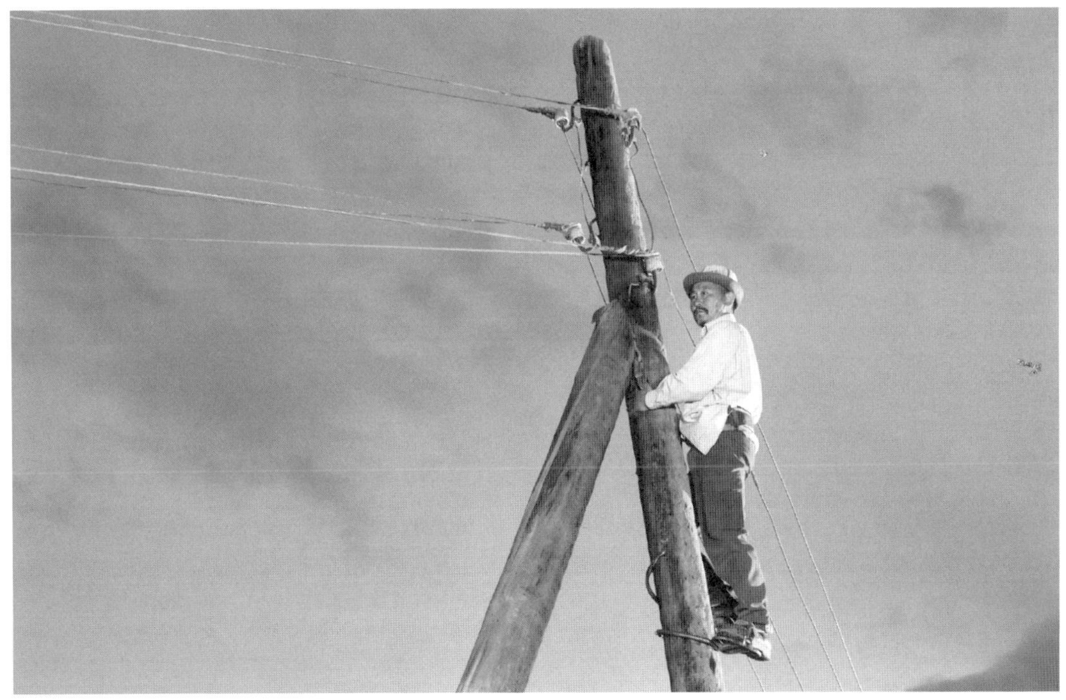

The Light Thief

With the collapse of the Soviet Union, capitalism has gained ground over most of the former republics including Kyrgyzstan.

We are between Russia and the US. Historically, we are inclined towards Russia. The latest uprisings in Kyrgyzstan were triggered by both pro-Russia and pro-USA elements. We have two political forces and two military bases. It is not clear which one is stronger.

What role does religion play?

The country is constitutionally secular. Religion has never been a strong element of our Kyrgyz mentality. Influence of Islam is felt and it was proposed to include religion in the new constitution, but it did not happen.

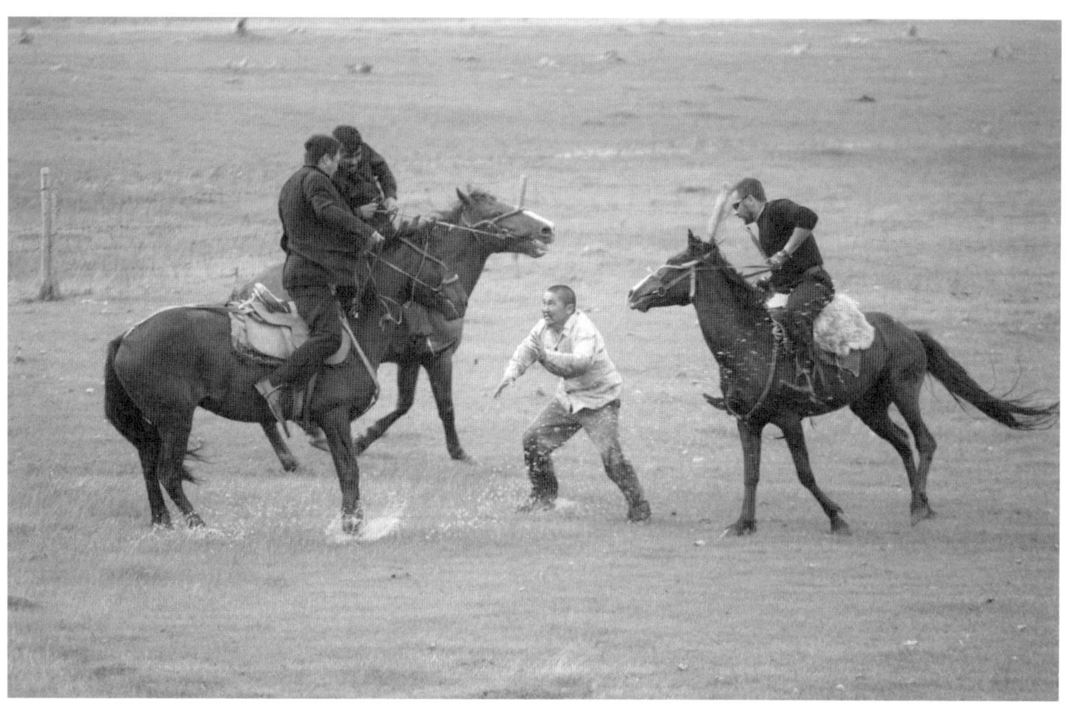

The Light Thief

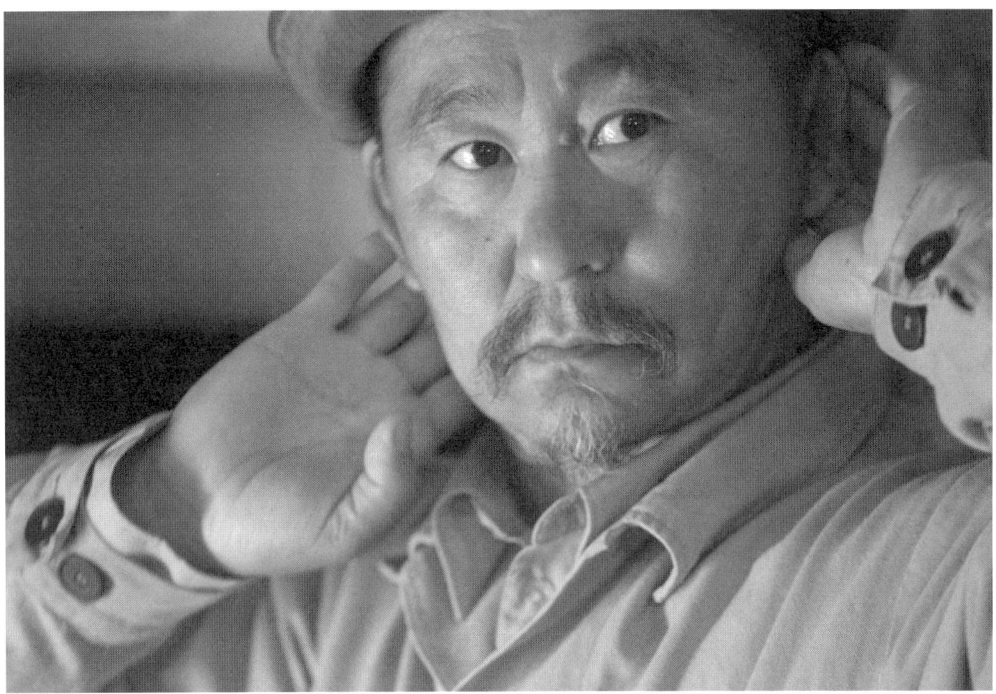

The Light Thief

In addition to the political and military influence of Russia and the US, do you feel the economic influence of China? In *The Light Thief,* you show a Chinese delegation coming to the Kyrgyz village to invest.

Historically, our relations with China have been complicated. We fear their physical presence. The Chinese market is very important economically.

In the film, the mayor of the village represents neo-capitalism. In comparison, the village council meeting was almost anachronistic.

The mentality of our people requires that the elderly have to be consulted in making important decisions. New ideas are present but the elderly are also very powerful.

In a significant episode, the light thief is told by his friend Assen that the world would be better if there were more people like him.

The purpose of the film was not to give a message but rather let the audience to formulate their own interpretations.

The landscape and the light seem to be crucial to most Central Asian movies. Your film perhaps has the added touch of a film-maker who was a painter.

For me, nature is part of human nature and is unavoidably present. I am also interested in impressionism and impressionist painters and feel their influence in my work.

You are a regular name at important film festivals.

In 1993, I won the Leopard of Tomorrow in Locarno with my medium-length film, *Swing*, and met my producer. *The Adopted Son* was also presented in Locarno. I was in Cannes twice, the first time with *The Chimp* and then with *The Light Thief*. This is my third time in Locarno.

Why did you choose European co-producers instead of Central Asian, for example Kazakh? What are the advantages and disadvantages?

With the dismantling of the Soviet Union, the ties between the former republics have broken. I have already made one film at the Kazakh Film Studios with Sergei Azimov, but not yet in Russia. Neither Russia, nor Kazakhstan is very familiar with art house cinema, its production and distribution. *Mother's Heaven* was made with Kazakh funds. It was easier to shoot but more difficult to produce. Our producers do not know the procedures. After the film is shot, its future is not clear. The film was completed two–three years ago but nothing has happened to it. *The Light Thief* will be released in Kyrgyzstan in September. The occident and organizations such as Fond Sud (South Founds) have shown interest in our cinemas. Obstacles exist. In Europe, the nationality of the film-maker plays a large role in funding art films. *The Chimp* and *The Adopted Son* benefited from the co-production treaty that had existed between the Soviet Union and France, but we could not apply for *The Light Thief* because Kyrgyzstan did not renew the treaty. The Minister of Culture had already been approached; however, cinema does not seem to be the priority of the government. A large part of the financing for the film came from Germany. The total budget was 1 million Euros, which did not include the lead actor, because I assumed this role. My company Oy-Art (the former Beshkempir studio) was the co-producer. One problem with foreign funding is the obligation to spend the money inside the benefactor country, which increases the budget. Also, this kind of film does not generate much interest, not even in France. After its premiere at the Directors' Fortnight section of the Cannes Film Festival, 2010, we have secured distribution rights in France, Germany, Switzerland, Canada, Brazil, and the Benelux countries, but very few distributors take a chance with the non-European films.

Are there any disadvantages to working with several European producers in terms of retaining the original project?

No one interfered with me, neither in the script, nor editing or casting. Mutual confidence is very important.

Why did you decide to play the main character?

When I had difficulties finding a lead actor, my crew suggested that I play the lead. I thought it was not a bad idea as I usually act out the scenes anyway to illustrate to non-professionals, who play in my films.

What advice would you give to young film-makers?

Do not take advantage of those who help you, or your friends, or profit from their emotions. Be truthful to yourself, believe in yourself and be close to yourself. Most importantly, make your films for brothers and sisters. This can be made without money.

– Locarno, August 2010

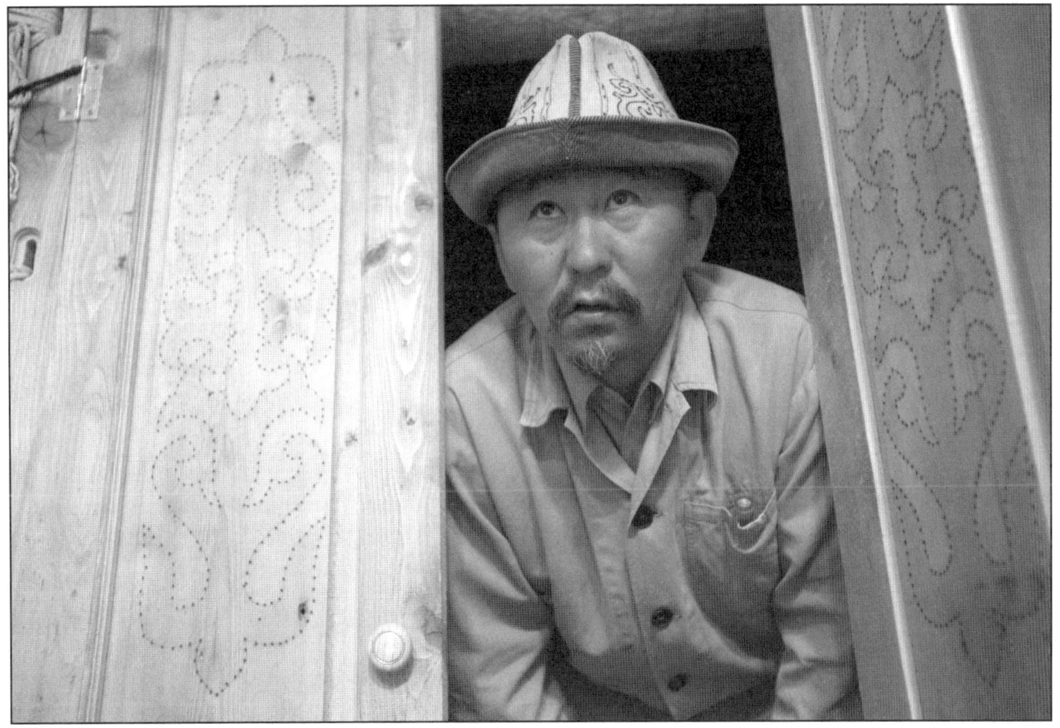

The Light Thief

BIO/FILMOGRAPHY

Aktan Artmkubat (Abdikalikov) was born in 1957 in the village of Kuntuu in Kyrgyzstan. He studied at the Art Institute and started to work as a set designer. He produced numerous short and feature films. In 1993, he entered the international film world with his medium-length film *Selkinchek/The Swing*.

Feature films:
1992 *Gde tvoi dom, ulitka/Where Is Your House, Snail?*
1993 *Selkinchek/The Swing* (mid-length film)
1998 *Beshkempir The Adopted Son*
2001 *Maimyl/The Chimp*
2009 *Raj dlja mamy/Mother's Heaven*
2010 *Svet-Ake/The Light Thief*

ERNEST ABDIZHAPAROV

Ernest Abdizhaparov excelled in short films before directing his feature film *Saratan* in 2004. *Beket/Bus Station*, a 22-minute black-and-white film is a visual poem that serves, in a minimalist manner, as a metaphor for the isolated situation of the country. Co-directed with Aktan Abdikalikov, the film shows people of different ages waiting for the bus. There is snow everywhere. We can almost hear the crisp snow and feel the cold and the feeling of waiting and desperation, thinking the bus will never come as vehicles keep going in the other direction. The characters are anonymous, like shadows. The camera is closer only once when the middle-aged man pushes the drunken intruder bothering the young woman.

Menim Pirim Almanbet/I Worship the Spirit of Almanbet (1993–2000) is about the Kyrgyz national epic, *Manas*, which is almost impossible to reduce to film. The focus here is on one of the storytellers who has had troubles in his life and has made mistakes. The film narrates his relationship to the epic – the way he looks at his life through *Manas* and tries to find his place in *Manas*.

Saratan/Village Authorities, his first feature, uses a small Kyrgyz town as a metaphor for the nation ten years after Independence. The film is an episodic comedy set in a contemporary village. Tragicomic tales of politics and religion, tradition and modernity, pride and honour are told using stock characters – a mystical healer, a Jehovah's Witness, a 'new Kyrgyz', an oppositionist–communist, a womanizing militiaman, a mullah who is late to prayers, a drunken father – that represent post-Soviet reality. Just as in *Bus Station*, Abdizhaparov keeps his distance except for the final scene when spring brings hope. The heroes of the film, according to Abdizhaparov, are the people of Kyrgyzstan who endure everything but finally find the right way.

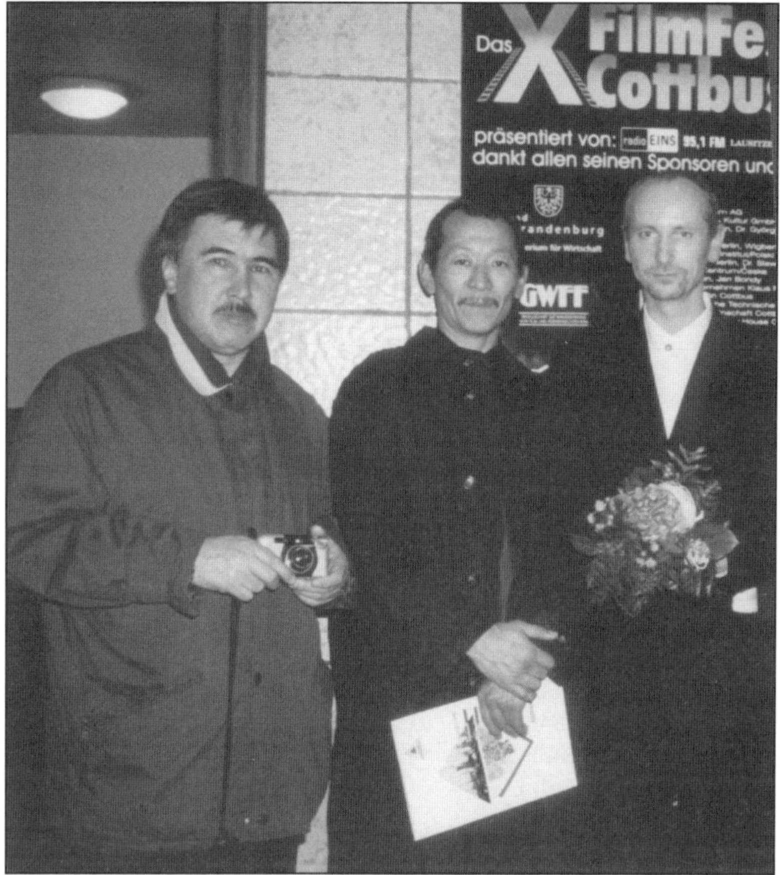

Ernest Abdishaparov with Tinay Ibrahimov,
Kyrgyzfilm Studio head (left) and Roland Rust,
director of Cottbus Film Festival (right), 2000.

Unlike so many Central Asian films that target festival audiences, the film has touched a chord with the local audiences and became a box office success in addition to receiving the Best Screenplay Prize at KinoShock and a special mention of the F.i.p.r.e.s.c.i at the Fribourg International Film Festival, 2005.

The following interview took place during the Cottbus Film Festival in former East Germany in October 2001.

MINIMALIST WORLD

As this is our first meeting, I would like to know about your background.

My film career began in Germany with the screening of *Beket/Bus Station* in Ausburg. The second screening is here in Cottbus. I am a self-taught man. I did not learn film-making at school. I began making films five years ago in the post-Soviet era. I made five short films to practise my trade, to learn about making films. Now I want to make feature films.

How did your collaboration with Aktan Abdikalikov in *Bus Station* happen?

Aktan offered me to write the screenplay, but he could not find the money to shoot the film. I offered him some money and suggested that we ask for equipment from the studio.

The characters in *Bus Station* are anonymous, almost 'faceless'. You seem to keep the audience at a distance intentionally.

I was afraid to show this film. Not everyone reads the film the way you did. Some find it very long. The film is about waiting. People have to experience the real feeling of waiting. Only distance can give this feeling. We wanted to eliminate the subjective character of the film-maker. From a distance, everything is objective.

The passengers waiting for the bus are from different age groups – old man, young boy, middle-aged people.

They represent Kyrgyz people after the break-up from the Soviet Union. They are near a big road, waiting – for what? Cars pass by, and they are still waiting.

***I Worship the Spirit of Almanbet* draws from Kyrgyz traditions. When Chinghiz Aitmatov introduced the film at the festival here, he said many storytellers try to connect *Manas* to some mystic and mysterious circumstances. One of the greatest storytellers once told him that while he was sleeping in the fields, he was awoken by the sound of running horses and an old man appeared and told him, 'You'll be the teller'. 'How it is possible to know by heart such a large amount of text'? Aitmatov said he often asks himself. 'The great storytellers were able to improvise. This short film has a mystic characteristic for me. It has a possibility to improvise'.**

In the retelling of the *Manas*, what is said is less important than how it is said. People are generally familiar with the story, especially through the works of Aitmatov. That is why I did not think it was necessary to subtitle the recitations. To hear the words is more impressive. The poetry of *Manas* is the inspiration for the Kyrgyz culture. *Manas* is like an encyclopaedia about Kyrgyz life.

What language is used in Kyrgyz films today?

Kyrgyz language; it used to be Russian during the Soviet Union.

What are the conditions for the film-makers?

The government is not in a position to help the film-makers. We want economic reforms to change our system and we understand it must be a difficult period. That is why we accept the problem as normal. Perhaps, after some years, the attention of the government will turn to us. In the meanwhile, we make videos to survive. In the Soviet era, Kyrgyzstan made three films per year. After *perestroika*, we made more because directors could find rich sponsors. In 1992, 12 long feature films were produced. But after that, it became gradually more difficult. Between 1995 and 1996, no films were made. Usually, it is one film in two years and this year two films have been completed: one by Aktan, produced with French money, and one by Marat Sarulu, *My Brother, the Silk Road*.

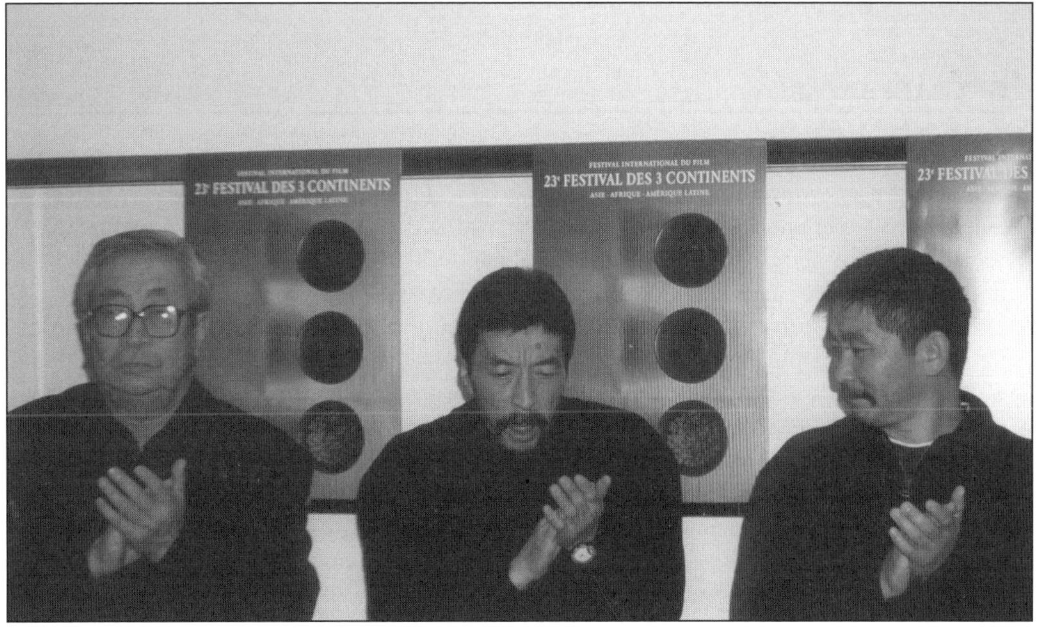

Gennadi Bazarov with Tolomush Okeev (left) and
Aktan Abdikalikov (right), Nantes, 2001.

Do you find the Kyrgyz tradition slowly eroding?

On the contrary, we are beginning to recover our lost traditions and parallel to that searching for the best tradition to adopt: to incorporate our traditions with the western civilisations. This is the best. In our theatres, American films are shown. Currently, only the young are working. Well-known film-makers of the older generation are no longer active. We understand that Kyrgyz film industry cannot produce commercial films and cannot compete with Hollywood. Firstly, there is not enough money and, secondly, it is not our mentality. We can only make our traditional Kyrgyz cinema and develop intellectual films. I think this is our way.

– Cottbus, October 2001

BIO/FILMOGRAPHY

Ernest Abdishaparov was born in Frunze (Bishkek today) in Kyrgyzstan in 1961. He studied Russian literature and worked as a teacher. In 1988, he started working at the Kyrgyzfilm Studio in various capacities. He made his first film, *Menim Pirim Almanbet/I Worship the Spirit of Almanbet* (a short film), in 1993.

Feature films:
2004 *Saratan/Village Authorities*

GENNADI BAZAROV

Gennadi Bazarov is one of the prominent film-makers of Kyrgyz cinema. His first feature *Samancynyn jolu/Materinskoe Pole/The Mother's Field* (1968) came at a time when Kyrgyz cinema was experiencing a golden period. Narrating the story of a strong woman who refuses to accept the tragedy facing her family and the nation, the film was a reminder of the immense loss caused by World War II, and touched the hearts of the spectators. Having lost her husband and son to war, Tolgonai, the strong mother, mother of the nation, carries the burden of daily struggle for survival with dignity. The scenes where Tolgonai carries a dialogue with the picture of her dead husband, even asking him for tobacco, were filled with pathos.

Bazarov made nine feature films before Independence, but has not been able to make a film ever since. The following interview took place in Nantes during *festival des 3 continents*, on 17 November 2001, which, incidentally, was the 60th birthday of Kyrgyz cinema.

A CULTURE TO SHARE WITH THE YOUNG

We watched your film, *The Mother's Field* (1968), as part of the Kyrgyz cinema retrospective here in Nantes. Few years ago, Bakty Karakulov also made a film on the same story, which is based on an Aitmatov novel. His film is called *Boranly Beket/The Snowstormy Station.*

This is a re-make. I am not comfortable saying it, but I do not think that the film was a success.

Karakulov concentrates on mother-in-law/daughter-in-law relations. Your film has a global view of war and how it affects society.

I did not see Karakulov's film but, in my film, I wanted to show how the bloody war changed the Kyrgyz society. When Aitmatov wrote his novel, he had a real woman as a model for the character of Tolgonai, a woman who always believed that her husband and her children were not dead and one day they would return. When he met her later in the1960s, she said, 'Chingiz, you are a writer, why don't you write a new novel in which my husband and children come back to me'? There was a documentary made about the meeting between Aitmatov and this woman. She was saying, 'please write this novel to bring them to life or do much better, write a novel in which all dead kids come back to life'. She is still hoping that some miracle will happen. There is a Russian expression, which says hope dies last.

Kydykeeva, who plays Tolgonai, was trained in theatre, I believe.

Initially, she was a theatre actress and was very well known. After she began to make films, she gave up the theatre. She died ten years ago. I have a story about her that is very important for me. In the late 1950s, she played in a film shot in Moscow, which was shown in Paris. When Gerard Philippe, who loved horses, watched this film and saw her riding the horse, he invited her and the others to his place and promised her that in his next film, they would be riding together. Six months later, he was dead. So, she never played in a French film, but I am very happy to bring her image to France now.

How about the other actors? Are they all professionals? Now the trend is to use non-professionals. Those days, did you get extras?

Half of them were professionals and half non-professionals. When I was making the film in 1968, I was 26 years old. Many people among the old had seen the war. When they heard that a film about the war was to be made, they came themselves. I did not need to invite them. They acted as consultants. We helped each other. They said, 'you film us as you want, we'll do it free' because it was important for them.

Who wrote the script?

Three people: Chingiz Aitmatov, a well-known Russian director, Talankine, and screenwriter Boris Dobrodeev.

The photography is very striking.
That is Vilenski. We changed nothing, and used only natural lights and natural sets.

The scene when the trains keep passing and the woman is running after them, crying her son's name, touches the heart.
When she sees her son?

When she is looking for him.
While I was shooting those scenes, the people who came to participate were helping me, telling me where the train was and where they were standing to meet the train. In the Soviet Union, you cannot find one family that did not suffer from the war. In each family, at least one member died – brother, son or husband – everyone experienced the war.

How many films have you made?
Nine feature films. *The Mother's Field* was my first film, made at the end of my studies at the VGIK. Attending film school in Moscow was a wonderful experience. I discovered foreign directors such as Kurosawa and Fellini, as well as important Russians such as Tarkovsky. As a student in Moscow, I made a short film called *Molitva/The Prayer* (1963) based on a story I wrote myself about the *basmati* rebellion. When Aitmatov saw the film, he called me and said, 'I [will] give you my novel. Make a film with it at the end of your studies'. I was so honoured. Chingiz Aitmatov founded the Kyrgyz cinema, but he was not a dictator. He let the director do his film the way he wanted.

What about your co-operation with Larisa Shepit'ko?
After finishing school, I worked at the Kyrgyz Film Studio doing all sorts of jobs, as director's assistant, photographer, etc. I was Shepit'ko's assistant director in *Znoi/Heat* (1963).

***Heat* was Larisa Shepit'ko's debut film, which was scripted by Iossif Olchanski from a book by Aitmatov. Where was it shot?**
On the border between Kyrgyzstan and the Kazakh steppes.

There was a period when many well-known film-makers from other republics such as Eldar Shengelaya from Georgia came to Kyrgyzstan to make films. Mosfilm studios sent many film-makers to Kyrgyzstan. Vasili Pronin's *Saltanat* was produced by Mosfilm in 1955. Some others from neighbours with more developed cinema also arrived. In 1957, *Leguenda O Ledianom Serdtze/The Legend on the Heart of Ice*, by A. Sakharov and Shengelaya, was produced by Mosfilm with the collaboration of the studios of Frunze, as the capital Bishkek was called then. In 1958, *Daleko V Gorakh*, by A. Karpov, was produced by Kazakhfilm. In 1961, *Pereval/The Collar*, the first experience of Aitmatov as a scriptwriter, was made by Sakharov after Aitmatov's novel *My Small Poplar to the Flipping Red*.

The middle of the 1950s was very active in that respect. Then, in the 1960s, Andrei Mikhalkov-Kontchalovski started his career in Kyrgyzstan with *Pervyi ucitel/The First Teacher* (1965), a black-and-white film made from a script by Aitmatov and Boris Dobrodeev.

Russian film-makers built a link between cinema and cultural tradition and helped the new wave of Kyrgyz cinema. They were all friends in the same school (VGIK) and helped each other. Just like Andrei Mikhalkov-Kontchalovski, several important Soviet film-makers made their first works in Central Asia.

When Aitmatov appeared, there was already a cultural and creative atmosphere. People wanted to come to Kyrgyzstan to be part of what was happening there. I remember it very well; I was at school at the time.

What about your other films?

After *The Mother's Field*, I began to search for a theme of my own rather than continue to make films based on others' scripts and soon started to make films based on my own scripts that focused on people living in the moment and in their own interior world. I always chose protagonists who were in a quest to find the truth for themselves – criminals, prostitutes or artists in a stressful state – not knowing where to go or how to act. One is never born a criminal or a prostitute. The situation makes them that.

Or the society?

The society. When such characters are locked in a vicious circle, they try to find a way out. I try to understand their point of view because each one of them has his/her dignity and each one has something to defend. My films are mostly psychological dramas.

But in a socialist system, the criminal or the prostitute is not supposed to exist, not officially, that is.

Officially, they did not exist. It was all hidden. That is why I had to fight a long time before I could make my films because they were not supposed to exist. When I showed my scripts, they said, 'you want to make a film about the alcoholics or prostitutes'? 'No, you can't'. I had to make films based on scripts written by other people. Things started to change with *perestroika*. The system was more open. I could begin to make my films. But these were the stories I was thinking about for ten years. Sometimes I had to publish a novel first and then adapt it to screen. I published two novels and then made films on them.

Was that a test to see if they would be accepted?

It was to make the nomenclature understand that if it was published, then it was not that bad – not that 'anti-Sovietic' – and that it could be made into a film.

Was the censorship worse for literature than for cinema?

The censorship was very strong in all parts in the Soviet Union. Everything was dictated: how to dress, to think, what to say. Everything was controlled.

But cinema can find ways to say what it wants to say through other means.
Of course, we tried to tell what we want through metaphor or allegory to get around the censors but many things were cut off from the films of many directors, for instance, Tolomush Okeev.

When did you make your last feature film? What is the title?
I made *Anomaly* in 1989. It is about prostitutes. It was the end of the Soviet Union. Then we became independent and poor without any money to make films. I did not shoot a film for over ten years because there is no money.

Do you work on television?
For five years, I have a contract with the television, my own show where I speak about the problems of art and spirituality. I invite artists to come and discuss issues. I also make short video films and publicity films, etc. I continue to write scripts and novels, but I cannot publish them because it costs too much money. They stay home and are not read by other people.

Your government has recently decided to allot 1% of its budget to cinema. But for the moment, the only films that are made in Kyrgyzstan are made with foreign aid. According to the Kyrgyz Studio head, 'There is a big problem of commercial persuasion to focus on national topics when the money comes from abroad. They want to tell you how your film should end. The relationship between the film and spectator and the one who gives the money and the censorship is difficult'. What do you think about the films made with foreign money? Are they really 'Kyrgyz films'? Do they represent the national cinema?
Only Aktan has made films with foreign aid and, yes, of course, this is Kyrgyz cinema. It is a new point of view of the same problems tackled by the new generation. Aktan is a very talented film-maker. He was the set painter in two of my films. One already sensed in his way of work his curiosity and his artistic creativity. Artists must not be ashamed of learning from each other. The younger film-makers say that they learn from the older generation but the older generation learns from the younger one too. We are not trying to be proud in Kyrgyzstan; we are happy to learn from each other and I am happy when I see the others succeed.

I enjoy the films of Aktan Abdikalikov. I have seen all of them. He already had a name in Kyrgyzstan with his documentary films, but it was really his medium-length film, *Swing*, which opened international doors for him. *The Adopted Son* (1998) is said to have received 28 awards. The industry must have profited from its success.

Ernest is also very talented. He admits he owes all he knows to Aktan, and Aktan admits he owes to you and Okeev.

Aktan and Ernest carry our hopes for Kyrgyz cinema.

The film they made together, *Bus Station*, is very good.

They did not learn cinema at school. They learnt it by doing it. You add to this their talent.

With a simple story, *Bus Station* conveys the situation of the country after Independence.

They know how to make an image represent the whole philosophy.

Tajik directors I met in Cottbus last year told me that they have formed schools to teach the young. Do you have such programmes?

We have just created the National Cinema Academy and established the Cinema Development Fund. An association of young film-makers, *Jebe*, has been established under the Union. We can no longer send the young to VGIK. It costs dollars now. So we thought we have all the people we need in Kyrgyzstan – directors, screenwriters, painters… Even if many of us do not make films anymore, we still know our job. If we can produce one talented director a year, it would be good for us.

During the round-table discussion yesterday, Okeev claimed that in Kyrgyzstan, there is no interest in cinema, but he does not live there anymore. Aktan Abdikalikov did not think it was so catastrophic. He said that there are seven cinemas working in Bishkek and a number of others in other regions. His film, *The Chimp*, was shown for 15 days with two screenings each day and the ticket price was two times higher than before. What do you think is the general attitude towards cinema these days?

Some people want to see Kyrgyz films, but there are many problems. The cinemas are very old. In the cinemas that work, Hollywood films, action and pornography are shown, and the third problem is that people don't even go to see these Hollywood films because they are so poor that if they have to choose between buying a ticket for the cinema and buying bread, they would buy bread. A new law has just been signed by the president about aiding national cinema – it is small but symbolically significant. I hope this will grow into a policy of supporting national cinema. I would call it ideological help to make people understand that spiritual issues are important, art is important and that they will go back to art.

In the context of the recent turbulence in the region regarding Afghanistan, what is the opinion or stand of Kyrgyz film-makers/intellectuals?

Afghanistan is always at war, so it is not new for us. There was war with the Soviet Union and before the Soviet Union. I would like the people to stop fighting and ask themselves what they are fighting for. The earth is one for everybody. I ask the Afghan refugees in Kyrgyzstan why they are fighting; they do not know. Of course, there is the important fact that Bin Laden is hiding in Afghanistan. America should look for Bin Laden and not just kill the innocent population by bombs. It does not help. My idea is every conflict in the world can be solved around the table. The influence should be one of argument and not force. I remember a sentence by Timur Lenk, 'Courage is to be patient when you are in danger'. When you are in danger, it is not very clever to rush and say I will kill you. It is better to wait and think.

Do you think that religious revivalism in Central Asia can eventually be a threat to stability in your country? According to reports, Hizb ut-Tahrir activists who seek to restore an Islamic caliphate, although by peaceful means, are also active in Kyrgyzstan targeting impoverished citizens with a promise of bringing social and economic justice.

Kyrgyz people have traditionally been very far from religion and religious fanaticism. They have always respected religious traditions, but they are not really believers.

One final question: I am curious why you have a Russian name, Gennadi.

During the war, my father had a very good friend, a Russian, called Gennadi. The day I was born, this man received a letter announcing the death of his son, who was a pilot, so my father called me Gennadi.

– Nantes, November 2001

BIO/FILMOGRAPHY

Gennadi Bazarov was born on 14 May 1942 in a village called At-Bachi in the Tian Shan Mountains. Between 1959 and 1961, he worked as an assistant before entering VGIK to study under Seguel. In 1963, he made *Molitva/The Prayer* about a conflict in the 1920s between two *basmati* brothers. His first fiction film *Samancynyn Zolu/Materinskoe Pole/ The Mother's Field* was a big success. *Asylum for those of Age* (1967) was about patients of a drug clinic. In 1969, he made *Zassada/The Ambush*, which combined documentary with fiction. His career as a feature film-maker came to a halt after Independence.

Feature films:
1968 *Samancynyn Zolu/Materinskoe Pole/The Mother's Field*
1969 *Zassada/The Ambush*
1972 *Oulitza/The Road*
1976 *Zenitza Oka/Apple of the Eye*
1978 *Kanybek*
1980 *The Writer*
1984 *The First*
1987 *Refuge for the Miners*
1989 *Anomaly*

TOLOMUSH OKEEV

Tolomush Okeev, one of the most important film-makers of contemporary Kyrgyz cinema, started his career with a ten-minute documentary, *Attar/Eto Loshadi/Horses* (1965), made as he was graduating from Mosfilm apprenticeship creating a beautiful visual poem with simply the images and sounds of horses in motion. His first feature, *Bakajdyn Zajyty/Nebo Nachego Detsiva/The Sky of Our Childhood* (1967), was a requiem to the world of ancestors, a world that has been vanishing rapidly with the arrival of modernity. In this spectacular film, when his children begin to move to the city, a horse-groomer tries to keep the last son in the mountains to teach him the old ways, but a new road has already been built and constructions are in progress to connect the railroad to the newly discovered mine. He has no choice but to send his son to the city for his education. *The Sky of Our Childhood* is considered Okeev's most autobiographical film and a seminal work for Kyrgyz cinema. *Lyuty/The Ferocious One* (1973), which is considered his masterpiece, is an unsentimental and unromantic picture of nature, which can be very cruel to man. Traditional education of the boys to make a man out of them is also questioned. However, Okeev does not create black-and-white characters. The cruel uncle can be a fascinating character from a different point of view. The world presented in the film is so 'ferocious' that, at times, the viewer can easily take his side.

Tolomush Okeev passed away in December 2001, few days after our last meeting. He was 66. He was one of the greatest outdoor film-makers. He knew the Kyrgyz steppes and the mountains well. Kyrgyz Film Studio is now named in his honour.

The following interview includes our first meeting in Istanbul in 1993 and the last in Nantes, during the *festival des 3 continents*, 2001.

SEARCHING FOR LOST IDENTITY

You belong to the first generation of Kyrgyz film-makers. There was no one before to influence or lead you.

I grew up during World War II, which was a very difficult period for everyone. Our influences were classical Soviet cinema such as Yurkevich and Reisman. Chingiz Aitmatov's *The Spirit of Rebellion* influenced my first film although it contains a certain amount of propaganda and certain arriviste elements, of which I am not proud.

I have read that you were born in a tent in Bokanbaevo in the Issik-Koul.

I was born in 1935, the year when Stalin was working hard to bring forced collectivization to the nomadic people of Kyrgyzstan. My father was a herdsman. I recreated this era in *Urkui/The Worship of the Fire* about Urkui Salieva, the first

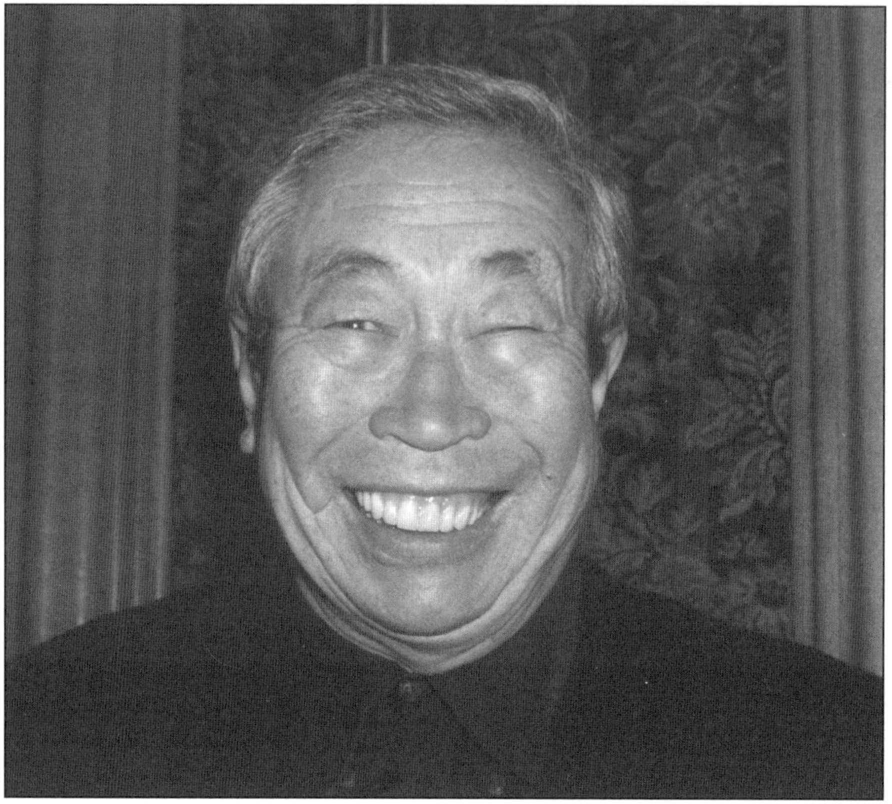

Tolomush Okeev

woman communist of the republic and her murder at the hands of the religious fundamentalists.

The Worship of the Fire has a common element with all your other work. Your focus is on the environment and the search for a balance between the inescapable modernization and nostalgia for eroding traditions.

One cannot separate the history of Kyrgyz cinema from the history of the country. In a period when our world was rapidly changing, through our films, we tried to understand the present without losing sight of the traditions of the past, which are embedded in the daily lives of the people.

What is noteworthy is that you do not glorify traditional values or misrepresent the outcome of modernization, but rather focus on the effects of change upon individuals. You exercise a non-judgemental objectivism.

The officials at Goskino were not so happy with my 'non-judgemental objectivism'. They would rather have didacticism and social rhetoric. *The Sky of Our Childhood* was shelved for many years. The powers were alarmed by the way the film showed the erosion of traditions and rituals in the name of progress.

The shots of the mountain peaks are breathtaking in that film. One can feel them lamenting the disappearance of the national culture. I can imagine that ecological and ethnic issues were not subjects for consideration in that period although you have never given up voicing your concerns.

I developed this theme further in *Potomok Belogo Barssa/The Descent of the Snow Leopard* (1984).

Your messages often come across through metaphors. For instance, in *The Sky of Our Childhood*, when Bakai's sons want to move to the city, he refuses. He has a tamed golden eagle that he is forced to set free, but the eagle has forgotten how to fly.

In the end, the eagle is stuffed and placed on top of a nomad stone idol by the construction workers!

Tell me about your relationship with Chingiz Aitmatov.

We met in 1956 in Leningrad. Aitmatov was studying literature at a higher level. (He used to be a veterinarian before.) I was studying with his sister. One day, he came to visit his sister and we were introduced. When his first novel, *Dzamilja/Cemila*, came out, he was 28 years old and I was 26. He was not famous then. Once he stayed in the room I was sharing with three others and the director of the school was not happy when he found out. We have known each other for several decades.

When did you start working together?

In the 1960s, we met again at the Union of Cinema Producers and Actors of Soviet Union. We were the first members from Kyrgyzstan. Aitmatov was the chief of this union. At first, I went to Moscow to study direction and screenwriting and made my first film, a short film called *Horses*. *The Sky of Our Childhood* was my first feature, as you know. What we discovered about each other was that our point of view, our soul was the same. *Cemila* was against the formal rules, the rules of morality. It was a novelty. While the woman's husband has gone to war, she takes a lover. And there is no communist ideology in the film. I was criticized for my first film, *Horses*, because the horses were killed and sent to the meat factory. The critics said why should the horses be killed? Why is this allegoric? Why is this a tragedy? *The Sky of Our Childhood*, which is about Kyrgyz life, the problems of the old, ecology, culture, language, land, received the same reaction.

I made a film about the conquest of our land by the Russians and everyone criticized me. The media was totally against me. If the media is against you, there is no money. With Aitmatov, our ideological fight was the same. To defend is to offend. When the government offends, we must defend.

Aitmatov wrote a story about the relationship of a man to his horse, *Goodbye Gulsari*.
I made *Horses* in 1965. Perhaps he was influenced by my film. Until 1986, we worked together. Then he went to the Union of Writers and I became the chief of the Union of Cinematographers.

Another collaboration was *Al Alma/Krasnoye Yabloko/The Red Apple*, I believe. Aitmatov wrote the script.
Before *The Red Apple*, I made *The Ferocious One* at the Kazakh Film Studio. It was a very difficult shoot. The weather conditions were terrible. *The Red Apple* was finished in 1975. I was 45 and Aitmatov 47. We were getting old. Our youth was passing by. We decided to make a film about love and we discussed about it. At this point, other film-makers – Russian and Kyrgyz – also wanted to make films on Aitmatov's stories: *Cemila, Goodbye Gulsari, The White Boat*. Aitmatov said to me, 'other film-makers want to make films about my stories. Let us make a film together'. I said, 'they make so-and-so films of your classics, which scares me. I want to take one of your works that is not a classic and turn it into a classic film. I do not want to damage our relationship. And I do not want to adapt *The Red Apple* 100% but rather extract the meaning and add my own point of view to it. I will give you credit as a screenwriter but it will be my script'. We made a gentlemen's agreement.

Aitmatov's works have been adapted to screen by Russians as well as Kyrgyz. Which one was able to give the spirit? Were the Russians able to understand and project the Kyrgyz essence and the spirit?
I want to tell the truth. On the works of Aitmatov, Russian or Kyrgyz, no one has made a better classic than Aitmatov. Two Kyrgyz film-makers adapted Aitmatov books: Bazarov made *The Mother's Field* in 1968 and Bolatbek Shamshiev made *Ak Keme/The White Boat* in 1975 and *Voshozdenie na Fudzijamu/The Ascent of Mount Fuji Yama*. *The White Boat* is the best, but even that film has a tendency to recount the story, at least 70% if not 100; so it looks like an illustration.

I have read that Shamshiev changed the ending because in the novel, the end is very tragic.
The film ends as a tragedy but it has two meanings: it is not clear whether the boy actually dies. There are some very good moments but the parts dealing with the traditions are confused and confusing. In my opinion, the film has its own structure and form and when you adapt from a literary work, you must follow the rules of cinema. When you read *Kafka* and then see the films of Orson Welles, these are two different things. For

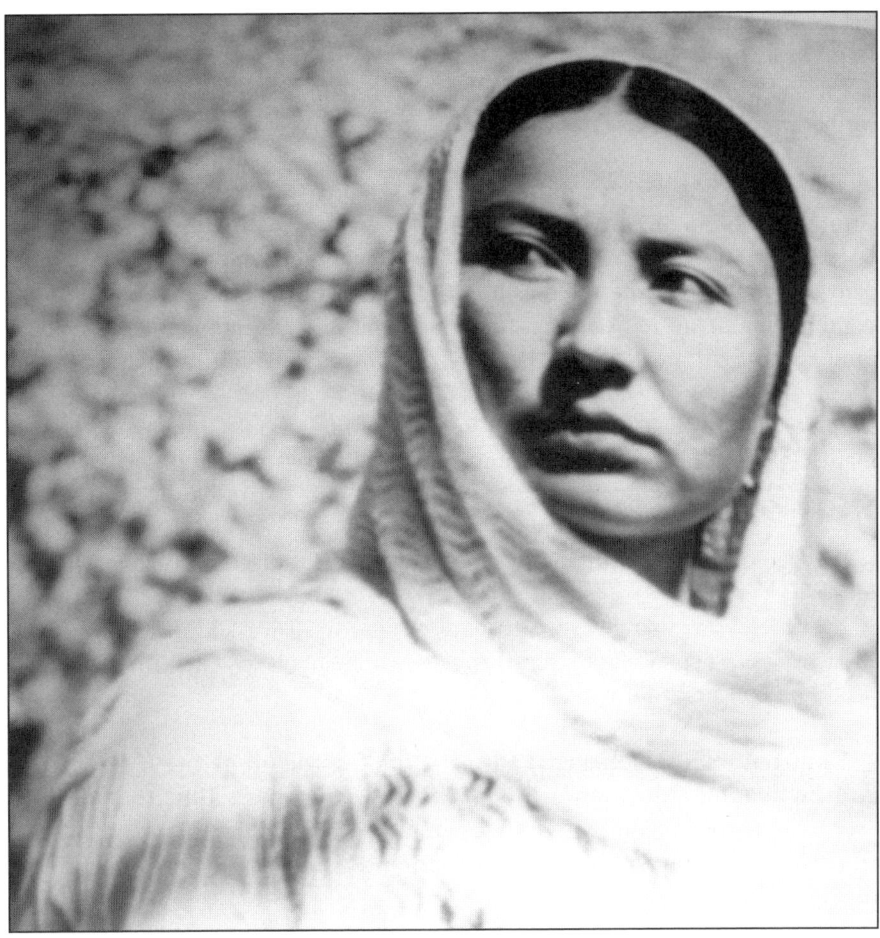

Worship of the Fire

instance, *Gone With the Wind* is a good piece of work, both as a film and as a novel. Or take Kurosawa, the films he made on literary classics are also classics. This is my understanding of making films. It is not necessary to translate the book 100% onto the screen.

Some non-Kyrgyz film-makers also adapted Aitmatov's works to cinema.
There are three: Larisa Shepit'ko, who was Ukrainian, made *Heat*, which is based on the short story *The Eye of the Camel*; Andrei Mikhalkov Konchalovksy, who is Russian,

made *The First Teacher* and Karen Gevorkian, an Armenian, made *A Piebald Dog Running on the Edge of the Sea* (1990). I worked on the script of the third one. Gevorkian is a friend of mine from Moscow. I was planning to make this film myself, but he said, 'you are very busy. I have nothing to do. Let me do it'.

What were the Kyrgyz doing in the Sakhalin Island, with the Nivkh, a fishing community of no more than 4000 people?
It is a serious matter. Vladimir Sangi is a Nivk writer, who told this story to Aitmatov, who was very much interested as he was looking for material on the philosophy of the continuation of life. When Sangi told him about this subject, Aitmatov decided to work on it because for great film-makers or great writers, it is not satisfying to create works about one nation only. For instance, Bertolucci has made a film about the Chinese Emperor; Podovkin is Russian, but he made a film about Chinghiz Khan; Mikhalkov made *Urga* about the Mongolians and I am looking for material in Turkey. The meaning of all this is that, you love your partner but from time to time you go elsewhere!

Andrei Mikhalkov Kontchalovski wrote the script of *The Ferocious One* along with others.
Kontchalovski, Shengelaya, Shepit'ko, Sakharov all worked in Kyrgyz Film Studios. Bazarov was Shepit'ko's assistant director in *Heat* (1963), her first film, which was produced by Kyrgyz Film.

Kontchalovski was engaged to make his film debut at the Kyrgyz Film Studio and he adapted Aitmatov's *First Teacher* to screen, a film that deals with the establishment of Soviet rule in Kyrgyzstan in 1923. Some historians consider this film the beginning of independent cinema. However, he was criticized for his infidelity to the novel.
I must say that Kontchalovski's *First Teacher* showed the point of view of the colonizer. It was made for the colonizer and not for the Kyrgyz people.

Larisa Shepit'ko's *The Heat* is also based on an Aitmatov work, *The Eye of the Camel*.
I was the assistant soundman for that film, which was made four years before I made my first feature, *The Sky of Our Childhood*. One of our important film-makers, Bolatbek Shamshiev, acted in the film.

What were some of the difficulties of working under the Soviet rule?
Sovexport controlled the export of our films and exercised chauvinism. Soviet films were shown only after the Russian films. It was a case of big brother and little brother. That is why a wonderful film, Bazarov's *Samancynyn Zolu/Materinskoe Pole/The Mother's Field*, did not get the publicity it deserved. My career during the Soviet Union was a long struggle with each film I made, except, *The Red Apple*. Moscow manipulated distribution

by making very few copies of the films that did not make them happy. *The Sky of Our Childhood* received international fame thanks to a festival in Frankfurt in 1967. Those days, the interest of the West made a big impact. This was also good from the point of view of bringing in money for Sovexport. If a film could make money, they did not care about its ideology. They made a compromise. The advocates of the official ideology were encouraging us to make films that would make money.

Aitmatov's books include elements opposing the Soviet ideology and, yet, in 1963, he was awarded the Lenin Prize for literature.

The first reason is what I just mentioned. Aitmatov was already famous then. Aragon and other western artists supported him. It was difficult to stop someone with international reputation. The second is that for the Soviet system, it was convenient to show to the West that they were not totalitarian but on the contrary, they supported artists like me, or Aitmatov. It was a democratic country! In comparison to Russian writers and artists, our job was somewhat easier because they could ignore certain things saying 'it is the Kyrgyz who write these things; they don't really understand our politics'. For us it was better to be in a situation of ignorance under their big brother politics. We had a goal to get out of it. We must not forget that Aitmatov is also a very diplomatic person. He is not only a genius, but also very smart.

Do you think that Kyrgyz cinema, literature and art have a certain peculiarity different from the other Central Asian republics such as Kazakhstan or Turkmenistan?

It certainly does, otherwise it would not be very interesting. One characteristic is the epic works. With *Manas* leading the way, there are more than 20 epic works. Most of these epics are written in poetic form. Aitmatov's works are written in prose but you can hear the rhythm of poetry in the words. This is the most important issue. Kyrgyz and Georgian films occupy a large space in the 1960–1970 Soviet cinema. Both became famous with films that tried to reflect real life. Those years, we were the first ones to hear the voice of Independence.

What is the language of Kyrgyz films after Independence?

Kyrgyz and Russian. The old films, all the adaptations from Aitmatov works, had been in Russian.

Aitmatov told me that except one or two, he is not very happy with the adaptations from his works. Do you think it is because they were not in the Kyrgyz language that they could not give the essence of the story?

You are right. This is the reason these films could not reflect Kyrgyz character or spirit very well. Right after Independence, we took up the issue of national language in the parliament. For instance, Bolatbek Shamshiev does not speak much Kyrgyz. I made my films in the Kyrgyz language. In *The Sky of Our Childhood*, the grandmother laments the fact that her children speak Russian. I even got into trouble because of that scene. I was accused of being against the Russian language.

Is there any action taken to preserve the national language?

In 1991, Kyrgyz was accepted as the official language. This was not very easy as the Russians wanted Russian to be official as well. After the law was passed, we started to publish books in Kyrgyz and teach Kyrgyz language in the schools. Until World War II, we used the Latin alphabet, so it was important to return to it, as the Cyrillic alphabet does not have some of the Kyrgyz letters. But the nationalists do not understand the main purpose and try to turn it into a revolution. The changes come slowly and money is needed. Extremist nationalists want to change everything overnight. After Independence, we have had two enemies: Russian chauvinism and extreme patriotism.

What are some of the major developments after Independence and what are the ramifications of Independence for Kyrgyz cinema?

Our political situation is stable in comparison to our neighbours but the economic situation is very bad and there is no support from the government. The cinemas do not want to show our films. Uzbeks receive money to make their films, but they have always been in a better situation than us. Cinema is not only art; it has to be financially stable as well. Before Independence, we received everything from Moscow. They also took care of distribution. Kyrgyzstan has a population of 4.5million. If you make films with only Kyrgyz money and even if they all go to see it, you would not recover your money. Marx, Engels, Lenin wrote about how to move from a capitalist system to a socialist system, but no one wrote the opposite. Therefore, it is a very difficult period for us. In times of economic crisis, people do not have the time to think of cinema. Today we can continue to make films, thanks to outside funds.

You have served as Kyrgyz ambassador to Turkey and lived in Ankara. Are you still involved with Kyrgyz film-making?

I was Aktan's teacher and I produced his first film, *Where Is Your Home, Snail?* I am involved in a project for a series with participation of all former Soviet republics.

(translated from Turkish by the author)

– Istanbul, April 1993 and Nantes, November 2001

BIO/FILMOGRAPHY

Tolomush Okeev was born in the Issik-Koul region of Kyrgyzstan on 11 September 1935. In 1958, he graduated as a sound technician from the Faculty of Electronics at the Leningrad School of Cinema Engineers (LIKI). He worked at the Kyrgyz Film Studios as a sound engineer, but resumed his studies at the VGIK between 1964 and 1965 and graduated in scriptwriting and directing in 1966. He wrote scripts, acted in films, staged plays and made documentaries before becoming a feature film-maker alongside Bazarov, Ubukeyev and Shamshiev. He also wrote a book called *Art With Wings*. A deputy and an ambassador to Turkey, he was also the founder of *Keletchek/The Future*, a private company that produced the multi-national super production *Chingiz Khan*. He died in December 2001 in Ankara where he had been living for several years, shortly after receiving his lifetime achievement award at the *festival des 3 continents – Nantes*.

Feature films:
1967 *Bakajdyn Zajyty/Nebo Nachego Detsiva/The Sky of Our Childhood*
1970 *Heritage*
1971 *Urkui/The Worship of the Fire (semi-doc)*
1973 *Lyuty/The Ferocious One*
1975 *Al Alma/Krasnoye Yabloko/The Red Apple*
1977 *Ulan (semi-documentary)*
1980 *Altin Guz/Zolotaya Osen/Golden Autumn*
1984 *Potomok Belogo Barsa/The Descent of the Snow Leopard*
1987 *Mirazi Lioubvi/Mirages of Love*
1991 *Chingiz Khan*

TAJIKISTAN

TACHIR MUKHAROVICH SABIROV

Tachir Mukharovich Sabirov belongs to a generation of Tajik film-makers who appeared on the scene in the latter part of the 1950s to a climate of moderation following the Twentieth Party Congress's critique of the cult personality, survived the repression of the Soviet censorship but reached an artistic stalemate with Independence and the economic crisis that followed. He is known for works of epic dimension imbued with the colours of the 1001 Nights, a good example of which is *Ashk va Samshed/Tears and Sword* (1991), his last film, which was shelved after Independence and never screened until invited to Cottbus Film Festival in the former East Germany. This was the first and only screening of the film. Sabirov sat through the film with the audience and watched it with tears in his eyes. He did not make another film until he passed away in 2003.

The following interview took place in Cottbus, October 2001, following this historical screening.

MORE THAN A GENERATION GAP

I have noticed that this morning you watched your film *Tears and Sword* with the audience. May I ask how you felt?

I felt like a student having an examination in front of a teacher. I was happy to have this experience in front of the audience and was comparing my film with the film we saw the opening night, Jol/The Road, by the Kazakh director Darejan Omirbaev. I noticed some people in the audience leaving that film, but in my film, some people cried during the touching moments. I am happy about this. I hope that you understand the film in the correct way because you are familiar with Islam. German audiences may have some difficulties. This morning a German woman interviewer asked me if I was endorsing Bin Laden by showing the reading of the Koran. She did not understand the film at all. There is war. People are dying. The country is broken to pieces and the young voice comes to put it all together. This is my way of speaking about it and I hope that you understand it that way.

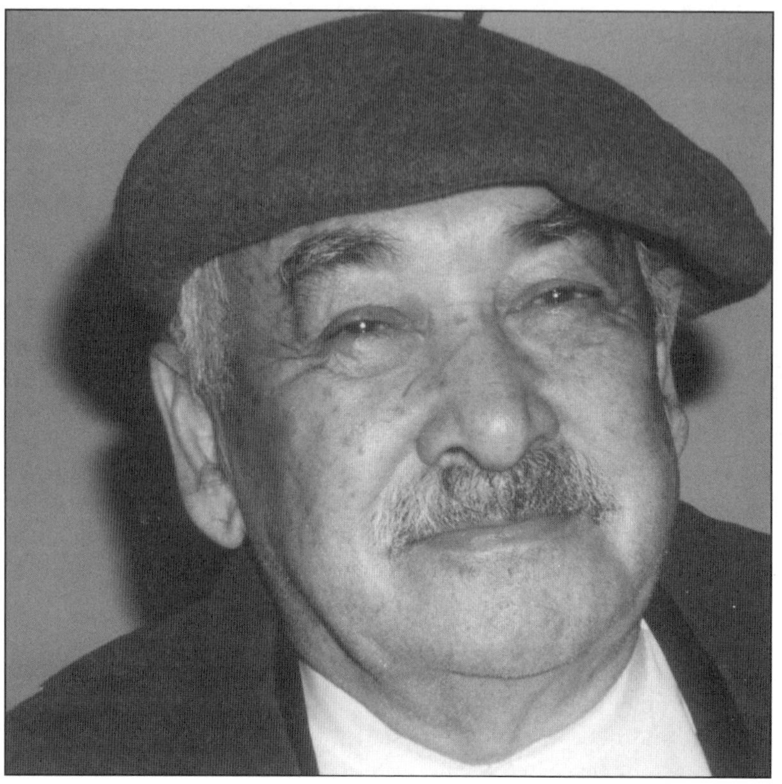

Tachir Mukharovich Sabirov

You made this film ten years ago. If you were to make it today, would you change anything?

Nothing! Imagine this: There is a book, and there are the lines and then there is the subtext. I am working very much with the subtext in this film. When I was visualizing the film, I was reflecting on some concrete problems such as the death of my protagonists. How am I going to kill them? It is not by chance that Gulisor says she is a widow without being married. The problem was to show how they die in concrete terms. Before dying, she closes her eyes and sees her wedding. Greso had to die in a heroic fashion – on his horse.

I liked the balance. A war film or simple melodrama can be tedious. In your film, when the mood is down, you somehow lift it up again.

I wish you had the possibility to see the whole film with its four parts. For instance, there is a story about Mirso and his daughter. He steals his daughter from his first wife to give her to someone to receive something in return. This is in the longer version.

I did not know that there was a longer version.

It is a series. There are four parts. I tried to extract some parts to make one film. In the series, I have some interesting scenes about how Mirso kills his two wives and how his hands are smeared in blood.

How long is the whole film?

Each part is one hour and ten minutes. Unfortunately, several important issues, such as how a person can do anything to achieve what he wants, are lost. For instance, there is a subplot about a character placed in jail owing to mistaken identity. The breakdown of the Soviet Union influenced the film and it was not shown anywhere. The screening here in Cottbus is the first time. I am deeply sorry that I lost so many things such as the issues about women – women who are married when they are 16 years old, women from the lowest social strata.

Who is the screenwriter?

I wrote the script and then we worked on it with Semen Lungin.

Did you make another film after this one?

When I started this film, we planned a series of ten episodes, but we stopped after four for lack of money.

How many films have you made all together?

Too many! You can sit in a cinema for two months without a break to watch them.

When did you start making films? What kind of a background do you have?

Each man born on this earth has to become something. Sometimes it is wisdom and sometimes it is written up here (pointing to his forehead) – film-maker, thief, communist… It is inside. It moves in yourself and you learn.

Did you study film-making or did you have an apprenticeship with another director? At what age did you make your first film?

I was 13 years old when I began and I am still learning.

What type of films did you make when you were 13?

At that age, I was hanging around film sets with friends. I decided to become an actor, so I took acting classes in Tajikistan. I began as an actor for main parts in the period after World War II, which was, basically, a dead period. I played special parts about national feelings, etc. Then I went to Moscow to study film direction under Zavadski. I studied and worked there. In 1958, I was the youngest film-maker who directed his own film and made many films at the Mosfilm Studios.

Historians look at Tajik cinema in terms of three periods: The first period from the post-revolutionary to 1955, the most significant film made in the republic being *Pochetnoe Pravo/Emigrant* **(1934) by Kamil Yarmatov, which he dedicated to the Red Army. Kamil Yarmatov was the first Tajik film-maker who created a new expression for silent cinema with** *Emigrant* **about the fight for a new life and the difficulties encountered by** *serdniak* **(the middle peasants). He plays the protagonist Kamil from the Kolkhoz in that film.**

Yarmatov is the beginning of silent cinema and the first for talkies. Some sources cite Nikolai Dostal's *Syn Dzhigita/The Garden* as the first talkie, but this is not correct. Dostal's film was made in 1939.

You began to work during a period of oppression when many films and projects were shelved and many film-makers were persecuted. One of the founders of Tajik cinema, Gouliamriza was one of the first victims of Stalinism. Kamil Yarmatov had to leave for Uzbekistan. Until 1955, no significant feature film was produced. But even later, a collaboration of Shamsij Kiamov with Nikolai Litus, *Moi Drug Navrusov/ My Friend Navrusov* **(1957), was stopped from screening because it told the story of an innovative agronomist who had to suffer the obstacles of conservatism and bureaucracy. The second period is from 1955 to the 1970s with the Twentieth Party Congress's critique of the cult personality, when Tajik cinema recovered from the harmful effects of negligible production, propagandist documentaries and persecution of directors and artists. This is when you came in along with Boris Kimiagarov and Shamsij Kiamov. The landmark of this period, I believe, was the epic** *Dohounda* **(1956) by Boris Kimiagarov about the Revolution.**

In the 1960s, it was as if a man had been hungry for a long time and finally he could eat. But things did not ease up at all. It was a period of persecution of film-makers. We could make some films, but then we were hit on the head and this went on until perestorika (reconstruction).

What about after the thaw when a new vitality emerged following the examples of Georgia and Kyrgyzstan, marked by a diversity of styles and themes? The pioneer was *Dohounda* **(1956).**

I played the part of peasant Edgor in that film opposite Zoukhra Karmova, who played Gulnor.

Shamsi Kiyamov, Abdussalom Rakhimov, Mukaddas Makhmudov moved from documentary to fiction and, in 1966, you made a very important film, *Margi Sudhur/ Death of an Extortionist* (1966), from the novel of A. Aïni. In the beginning of the 1970s, young talents, such as Marat Aripov (*Nisso*), Sukhbat Khamidov (*The Legend of the Paviak Prissn*), Margarita Kazimova (*The Summer of '43* and *Djura Sarkor*) and Anvar Turayev (*The Third Girl*), arrived searching a new form of expression. In 1978, you made *The Woman Who Came from Far* about the search for spiritual and moral values. Would you consider this period the new wave of Tajik cinema?

In Europe, you are always talking about waves! We do not have any waves in Tajikistan. We have some talented film-makers so we can make films. With two or three directors, there is no wave!

The third period began with a new group of film-makers such as Davlat Khudonazarov, Bako Sadikov and Oleg Tulayev and continued until *perestroika* and Independence. Davlat Khudonazarov is considered the 'shining star' of the third period.

He was just a cameraman. He worked with Boris Kimiagarov.

Even in his earlier work as a cameraman for Kazimova in *Djura Sarkor* on the series that Kimiagarov was making about *Shahnama*, the talent of Khudonazarov and certain lyricism and a poetic language are in evidence. His films are a sharp departure from the dramatic heroic cinema of Boris Kimiagarov whose *Skazanie o Rustam/Legend of Rustam* (1971), *Rustam va Sukhrab*/Rustam and Sukhrab (1972) and *Shah Nama Firdausi/Firdausi's Shahnama* (1977) are important testimonies to the history of Tajik cinema.

Khudonazarov was in the party, a KGB man. Now he lives in America! No one wants to see the films of Davlat Khudonazarov.

I beg to disagree with you. In my opinion, the features and documentaries of Davlat Khudonazarov, most of which deal with life in the Pamirs, present history and tradition lyrically. For instance, his best-known feature film, *Vlatom snege zvon ruchya mardi roh/Murmur of a Brook in the Melting Snow* (1982), still in the tradition of realist genre, is a poignant portrayal of an old shepherd, a veteran of the Great War, in search of a comrade who had saved his life. There is the inevitable clash of the old and new, of age and youth and of town and country amid a quest that we know will remain forever unrealized. *Ustad/Master* (1988) on the revolutionary national poet Abulkosim Lakhuty uses archival material not only to present the life of the writer, but also to comment on the events he lived through such as the Civil War. Khudonazarov was the Chairman of the Confederation of the Autonomous Unions of the Cinematographers of the CIS, and one of the leading figures of the democratic opposition to the communists. Don't you think that his active involvement in the

process of democracy in Tajikistan is what forced him to leave his country to live in the US?

We have some other directors who touch the heart of people, of women. For instance, Bakhtiyar Khudoynazarov, who is very talented.

Bakhtiyar is definitely a very talented young man. He is not political, but he also cannot survive in his own country. He lives in Europe and makes his films with foreign money. When he tried to shoot *Kosh Ba Kosh/Odds and Events* (1993) in Dushanbe amidst the civil war, his equipment was stolen and he was kidnapped. Are his films shown on Tajik television?

Yes.

What is the situation with the film studios? Does Tajik Kino, which was established in 1930, still exist?

When we talk about Central Asia, our republic is at the margin of this region. We had a very difficult period when we could not make any films. During this period, our film-makers chronicled everything between war and peace. For the present, we exclusively work on video. We have established a film school to pass our experiences to the young generations. Our distinguished film-maker Munavar Mansurchodjaev, who made several films that moved us on the issues of the water, Lake Aral and the return of the migrants from Afghanistan, namely the problems of our daily lives, is one of the teachers. We do not have enough money to make feature films today but we still have important films from the past. For the moment, Festival Kinoshock is the only venue for us to show our films, except for Cottbus Film Festival, which has lifted our veil. The film I brought here, Tears and Sword, is ten years old but it is still as topical as it was then.

In the beginning of our conversation, you mentioned your dislike for the film *Jol* by Darejan Omirbaev. Could you tell me why?

Who is this guy with long hair?

One of the young talented film-makers of your country, Jamseed Usmanov.

He is another one who lives in the US.[1] A hero has to be handsome, someone I would like to talk to. Would you fall in love with a man who looks like that?

Everyone is not beautiful in real life.

In a film, you have the possibility to show an actress not too pretty in a very feminine way. For instance, for my film, Sheherazade, I took a young girl and made her look beautiful. People were running from one theatre to the next just to see her!

– Cottbus, October 2001

Notes

1. Usmanov lives in Paris, France. His first feature, Parvaz-e Zanbur/The Flight of the Bee (1998), which he directed with Byong Hun-Min, won international acclaim. His second film, Farishtay Kifti Rost/The Angel on My Right Shoulder (2002), also won several awards. In 2005, when I met him in Tehran he was working on a new feature, To Go to Heaven, You Have to Die First. All three films are shot in his native village, Asht, in Tajikistan. I learned from him that Tacir Saburov passed away in 2003. Speaking of Saburov, he said that he was an eccentric who liked only his own films.

BIO/FILMOGRAPHY

Tachir Mukharovich Sabirov was born in Stalinabad (present Dushanbe) on 21 December 1929 and died in 2003. He completed his studies in acting at the Theatre Academy in Tashkent in 1951 and direction under I. Zavadski at the GITIS State Institute of Theatre Art in Moscow in 1956. He began working in cinema in 1955, first as an actor in *The Road* (1955) by Alexandr Stolper and *Dohounda* by Kimiagarov and, then, some commercial films. His first film, *It Is Time to Marry the Son* (1959), was a comedy. He often chose commercial genres such as comedy, sentimental adventures and oriental legends. *Margi Sudhur/Death of an Extortionist* is considered a classic comedy of Central Asia. He was also the President of the Association of Tajik Film-Makers.

Feature films:
1959 *It Is Time to Marry the Son*
1960 *The Possessed*
1963 *Chakhsanem and Garib*
1966 *Margi Sudhur/The Death of an Extortionist*
1967 *Treason*
1968 *The Revelation*
1973 *We Are Nothing* (three episodes)
1976 *A Chest for the Betrothed*
1978 *The Woman Who Came from Far*
1984 *And again One Night of Sheherazade*
       New Tales of Sheherazade
       The Last Night of Sheherazade
1991 *Ashk va Samshed/Tears and Sword*

TURKMENISTAN

HALMAMMET KAKABAEV

One of the important film-makers of Turkmenistan, Halmammet Kakabaev made *Ogul/ Syn/The Son* (1988) during perestroika. In fact, *The Son* is the last Turkmenian feature film of the Soviet period. A poetic film with a fair dose of healthy folk humour, *Ogul* is a parable on the value of creativity and its connection to life. The script, written by well-known Russian film-maker, Sergei Bodrov, focuses on a boy whose father, a celebrated local musician, goes to war and does not return. The latest film of Kakabayev, *Toba/ Raskayanie/Repentance* (1997) recounts a traumatic mother and son relationship as a metaphor for the loss of human values during the social changes after Independence, particularly, the arrival of the market economy and the western style values of material profits. Jagmur, a successful businessman, who has benefited from the new economy, lives in the big town among other successful young men like himself. He is embarrassed of his humble origins and particularly of his ailing old mother. But his greed eventually leads him to a dead end. When his mother dies alone in the village, while he is on holiday abroad, he is burdened by feelings of guilt. He gives up his career and becomes a shepherd; however, repentance does not come easily.

Kakabaev insists on the non-political nature of his work, but does not hide his nostalgic sentiments about the previous regime. 'I don't believe in blaming the former Soviet period', he reiterates, '70 years was a huge period of our lives'.

The following interview took place during Cottbus Film Festival 2000, where a retrospective of Turkmenian cinema was held.

HUMAN VALUES IN A WORLD IN TRANSITION

Ogul/Syn/The Son **and** *Toba/Raskayanie/Repentance* **are both explorations on a psychological level.** *The Son* **is a coming of age film, a boy reaching adulthood in a hostile environment.** *Repentance* **deals with the issue of guilt for not doing the right thing for one's parents, which I think is more relevant to the East than the West**

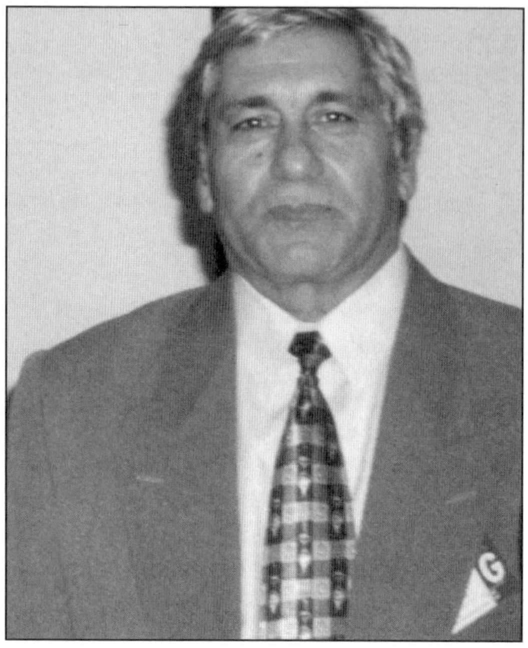

Halmammet Kakabaev

and more so, in countries where the difference between the country and the city is greater.

The guilt feelings for not doing the right thing for one's parents may be more relative to the East but people like my protagonist who live their lives the wrong way exist everywhere. As I was writing the script, I was thinking it might happen in South America.

When the mother visits her son in his posh city flat and his friends ask who the old peasant in the kitchen is, he says, the neighbour. I do not think he would be ashamed of her in front of his friends, if the mother were a sophisticated lady from the city dressed accordingly.

This is also true but I did not want to base the film on the city and country issue. The same thing could have happened in the village also. The man is not a bad man, he is a scientist but he does a bad thing.

With the market economy, the gap between generations and the alienation of each seem to be increasing. Do you think that the scene when children are left alone to watch television while the parents go to a party would have happened a decade or two ago?

I am trying not to be a politician. I do not believe in blaming the former Soviet period. Seventy years was a huge period of our lives. These things are probably new but there were things happening at that time also.

In both films, you switch from black and white to colour at certain moments. I think, in general, the happier moments are in colour and sad moments are in black and white.

It was a special decision for me. In *The Son*, after the letter arrives from the front, there is sadness. The world of the young boy could not be in colour. It is the black-and-white side of his world. The second letter is like a new beginning so I chose colour. At the end, when the father dies, I wanted to keep the reality of death, as well as the strong presence of life. When the boy plays the *dutar*, it is like a new life. His decision is symbolic. The film is about how life should go on no matter what.

The absence of the father and the search for a substitute (the father's master in this case) is a recurring trope in Soviet films for not belonging or being different from one's society, but perhaps, this particular story has autobiographical elements for you.

My father also did not return from the war. In that sense, some autobiographical elements are evident, but I would say that two other films I shot about the post-war generation, *The Boy with the Donkey* and *Papa Comes Back* are much more autobiographical. The three make the trilogy about children whose fathers went to war. These children had to grow up fast. I began to work as a mailman when I was only seven. Instead of playing with toys, we had to assume the responsibility of our families.

You have collaborated with Sergei Bodrov on the script of *The Son*.

The script was written with Bodrov. I have another film called *The Bird of Paradise*, also written with Bodrov. Out of the ten fiction films that I have made, two were written with him. I cannot work with him anymore because now he lives in the US. I have collaborated with others as well, but written the script myself for the last five films.

Although a Russian, Bodrov was also born in Central Asia. During an interview, he told me that the affinity he feels to Central Asia is in his blood.

He made two films in Kazakhstan.

***Son* is a very sensitive film that narrates the pains of the loss of a parent with music and poetry. Central Asian legends recount that in the *dutar* sounds, a keen ear and a fine soul would hear a peaceful step of time, fast race of a herd of Akhaltekin horses, plaintive song of the winter wind and the mother's tender tune. The lyrics often mix**

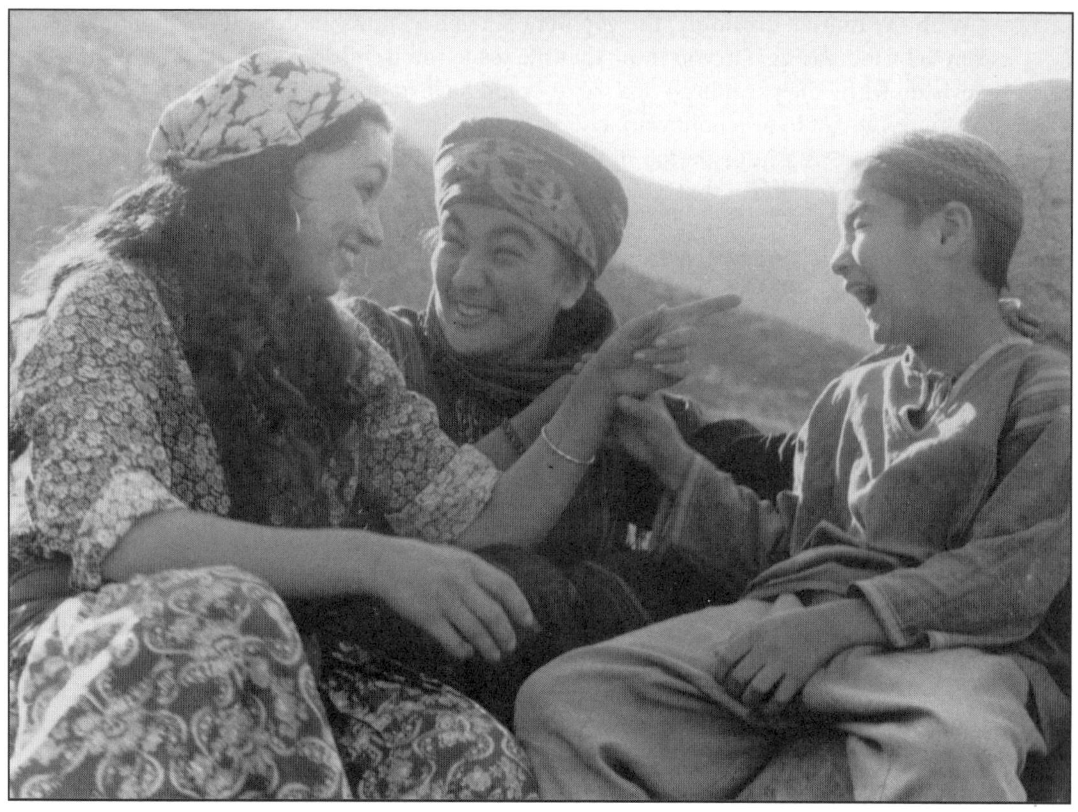

The Son

high poetry with down-to-earth spicy folk humour. Do you call the *dutar* musicians *akynd*, as do the Kazakhs?

The player is *dutarci* and the singer is called *bahshi*. There are so many legends about these wonderful musicians. People could not manage without a *dutarci* at their feasts. In the past, this folk art was handed down from father to son. That is why in *The Son*, Nuri, a well-known and accomplished musician, is very disappointed when his son, Batyr, is not interested in playing the *dutar*. When the Great Patriotic War begins, just like the other men of his village, he leaves for the front taking his *dutar* with him as no one is interested in playing it at home. But all of a sudden, his son feels a strong desire to play the instrument and with perseverance and the help of his father's teacher, he makes the first step towards mastering the art.

Such a twist of fate that when the son earns his first fee – a slice of bread – playing the *dutar*, his father dies at the front with a stray bullet.

I intended the film as a parable for the value of creativity, which is tightly connected to life.

Do you have an audience for your films in your country?

Our films focus on our culture. Even if we wanted to, we could not surprise someone else. But when we make a film, we do not think of the target audience, and this goes back to the Soviet Union. The film-maker has an artistic idea and he makes his film for himself. My film *Repentance* is about a man who forgot his mother. Don't you have that in your country?

Do you sell your films anywhere else?

We sell our films to the Russian television. I was able to finish *Repentance* because my previous films were sold to Turkey, Iran and Germany. But the major client is the Russian television.

Do you venture into co-productions? What are the problems?

Every artist is responsible for himself. The relationship is between the artist and his work. In the 1970s, when I was a student, Georgi Danelia, my teacher at the Moscow Film School, began a co-production with Italy, but when a proposal was made to change things, he put the script on the table. You are responsible for your own conscience. When I shoot a film in Turkmenistan and show people something they do not understand, this is a crime.

Do young people want to become film-makers?

Our Academy of Fine Arts will have its first graduates in artistic film this year. Cameramen, directors for television production and actors are trained at the Cultural Institute, but after graduation, they follow the same route as our neighbours – they make video clips.

Turkmenian cinema experienced a golden period in the 1970s. Khodzakuli Narliev's *Nevestka/Daughter-in-Law* (1972), *When a Woman Saddles a Horse* (1975), *You Must Dare to Say 'No'* (1977) and *Derevo Dzamal/Jamal's Tree* (1981), all of which incidentally have female protagonists, are prominent examples of high achievement. What is the present situation?

The 1970s was the peak of Turkmenian cinema when the graduates of VGIK returned home and started to make films. About 20 feature film-makers are active today, but for the moment, we do not have the possibility of shooting 35-mm films.

In 1976, Narliev was unanimously elected the First Secretary of the Board of Film-Makers' Union of Turkmenistan and, in 1986, he was chosen as the People's Artist of the Republic. Despite such high visibility as a popular public figure, he seems to

have retreated to the shadows. The same for Biul-Biul Mamedov, whose first feature *Iashlygymyn Destany/The Legend of My Youth* (1992) and *Archaly Adam/Man with the Fir Tree* (1995) were pioneering works of Turkmenian cinema. Rumours circulate that they are in conflict with the regime of your president for life, Saparmurat Niyazov, who has proclaimed himself *turkmenbashi,* the father of all Turkmens?

Narliev and Mamedov follow different paths. Mamedov is working in the theatre.

According to Sergei Shugarev, a film-maker from the younger generation, who made *Ham Hyyal/Aromat Dzhelany/Fragrance of Wishes* (1996), Turkmenistan is a closed system that persecutes people who think differently and dissidence is not allowed.

Shugarev is not a dissident. He was my assistant. He was given the opportunity to practice his trade in Turkmenistan; he chose to go to Moscow. He can come and work in Turkmenistan whenever he wants. He should not be spreading lies.

Why do we not see political films interrogating the recent past or the present changes?

In Turkmenistan, we have had political stability for nine years. We have not had a single political conflict with any party. Why create an artificial situation?

– Cottbus, November 2000

BIO/FILMOGRAPHY

Halmammet Kakabaev was born on 1 June 1939 in the Turkmenian village Kochuchut. He studied at the conservatory of the capital Ashkabad and the philological faculty of the Turkmen State University. Between 1958 and 1961, he worked as assistant director at the Theatre Opera and Ballet of Ashkabad and between 1971 and 1973, he attended the Higher Courses of Film Directing and Scriptwriting in Moscow under Georgi Danelia and became a director for Turkmenfilm Studio in 1973.

Feature films:
1980 *Vot Vernutsa Papa/Papa Comes Back*
1988 *Ogul/Syn/The Son*
1991 *Gennet Gusi/Rajskaja Ptischka/Bird of Paradise*
1994 *Takdyr/Karma*
1998 *Toba/Raskajanuje/Repentance*

UZBEKISTAN

KAMARA KAMALOVA

How does one describe Kamara Kamalova? The 'Grande Dame of Central Asian cinema', who is as fresh and as energetic as a young girl. Perhaps that is the secret behind her special bond with the youth. The pains and joys of being young come alive in her films from *Atrof Qorga Burkandi/All Around Was Covered by Snow* (1995) about the emotions and insecurities of a young girl to *Dikar/The Savage* (1988), which speaks of the injustices of the Soviet system through the story of young lovers. *Yol Bulsin/Dorogapod Nebesami/ The Road Under the Skies* (2006) also has that special element, which addresses the young people directly, hence its immense success with young audiences from India to Uzbekistan.

During the wrap-up session at the X. Forum of the National Cinematographies of the ex-Soviet Union (21–27 April 2006), Kazakh film scholar Gulnara Abikeyeva divided the historical evolution of post-Soviet cinema into three stages: the resolution of the post-colonial issues in terms of their relationship to the Soviet hegemony; the return to the ethnic–folkloric creativity and the most recent trend of promoting national pride. Whereas she placed films such as those of Sergei Bodrov, Ivan Passer, and Talgat Temenov's box-office hit, *The Nomads* (Kazakhstan, 2005) in the last category, she thought Kamalova's *The Road Under the Skies,* with its highly decorative style, belonged to the second category. A close reading of this beautiful film, however, shows elements from all of these stages, since the revival of the folkloric culture is another way of showing national pride, which also involves a certain coming to terms with the colonial past.

Kamara Kamalova is the most celebrated woman film-maker of Central Asia. But the road to the top has been a thorny one. To enter the prestigious VIGK (All-Union State Institute of Cinematography in Moscow) in the early 1960s was far from easy for a woman. However, graduation was not the end of her worries. She had to make cartoons and work for television before she could make her first film. Circumstances are different today but each epoch brings with it its own problems. With relative freedom gained after Independence, Uzbek cinema, just as other national cinemas of Central Asia, is battling with lack of funds on the one hand and the hegemony of Hollywood on the other.

The following interview with Kamara Kamalova began in Moscow in April, 2006 and continued six months later in Thiruvananthapuram in Kerala, India, where *The Road Under the Skies* was in the competition section of the Kerala International Film Festival.

THE 'GRANDE DAME' OF CENTRAL ASIAN CINEMA

The Road Under the Skies has all the elements of a classic melodrama. A boy and a girl fall in love. Immersed in the euphoria of their emotions, they forget customs and traditions. Whereas the boy can walk away from his responsibilities, the girl pays the high price of being the subject of malicious gossip and mothering an unwanted child. And just like in the classic melodramas about the deceived and deserted maidens, before she is ready to end her life, another man arrives and by accepting her as she is, saves both her and her child. Despite this melodramatic structure, far from sponging the emotions of the audience, your film exudes life and hope exalting the audience to a world of dreams, where life can be beautiful despite its pains.

The film is inspired by a legend, which is familiar to the Uzbek people, but I was not interested in a narrative-driven film. I chose a style that was not realistic, but rather naturalistic and surrealistic. What I mean stylistically naturalistic is reflecting national customs and traditions and most importantly, the rituals. For this purpose, I used our national poetry and music. The subject motivated me because I had never done anything in the naturalistic style before. I believe that a good subject is necessary to create a good arrangement, but that is only the starting point.

The film begins with the red train car planted on the sand with a wide ocean in the background and the story unfolds as the blind father spins the colourful yarn. At the end, we return to the train car as the man who marries the girl helps her and her baby to step inside while he sings a beautiful love song. What does the train signify for you?

The literal translation of the Uzbek title of the film is 'Have a Nice Journey'. The train and the road belong together. Just like the road, which you may perceive as signifying life, the train also goes towards eternity.

The way you present the love story with the Biblical references to Adam and Eve, the apple and the snake and the Paradise that eventually is lost to the lovers because of their 'sin', is very poetic. You also use several erotic symbols (such as the chalice), all of which are a visual feast. At a time when the screens are inundated with sex scenes that turn lovemaking into gymnastics, your approach is very fresh. The scene when the shadow of the girl's playful hand falls on the naked body of her lover was subtly suggestive. But some references escape those not familiar with the customs of the area. For instance, when the man sends a leaf with a blue stone on it down the stream to the girl, I understood this to be a premonition that their love would be endangered

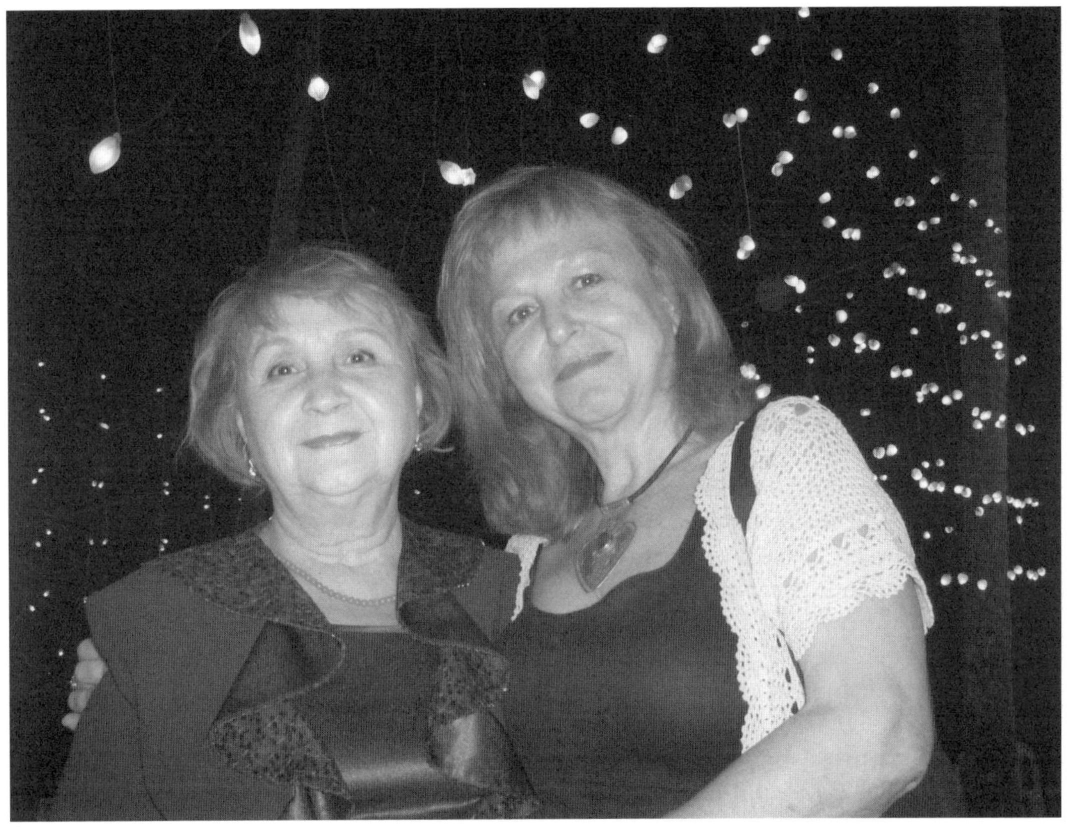

Kamara Kamalova (left) with the author at the Kerala International Film Festival.

one day; for the Middle Eastern cultures, the blue stone signifies protection against the evil eye, *nazar*. But I did not understand why after the marriage, her husband takes a piece of wood from the family's garden, wraps it with a rug and brings it to his house to place it between the two walls of the entrance.

The wood is her trousseau. The man hangs it at the entrance to tell the village that now his house has a woman. It is not empty any more.

The old women turning around, singing and dancing reminded me of the chorus in Greek tragedies, as well as the sirens of the Greek mythology.

I did not intend to draw a parallel. These women spread rumours about the girl's illicit love affair.

In certain scenes, we move away from the legend and the folkloric costumes to contemporary settings, such as the school playground and see the girls in uniform. But this does not change much of the story. How important is virginity today?

It is still very important.

A mature woman in white appears several times and gives the impression of somehow directing the characters. I was not sure exactly what she represented.

The woman in white represents humanity. She appears right at the beginning, in the prologue, which aims to attract the interest of the audience and to give a clue as to what will happen at the end. A premonition, one might say.

What about the burning of the effigy?

The effigy is the symbol of gossip. The gossip also burns with the burning of the effigy.

Let's talk about your background. Where does the passion come from? Are you from a family related to cinema?

I was born in Bukhara, which was a small town then. I did not come from a cinematic family. My father was a professor of philosophy and my mother, a schoolteacher. We moved to Moscow when I was very young. I saw my first film when I was six, in Moscow, where we lived next door to a movie house. My passion for cinema goes back to those days. I originally studied physics at the Moscow State University, but I had friends attending the VGIK and I began to envy them. That is how I took the decision to switch from physics to cinema. I made documentaries at the VGIK and after graduation I joined the Uzbekfilm Studio and started to make films. I have made 25 animation films and 10 fiction films.

Having worked within both systems, the Soviet and the independent Uzbek, what is your feeling about the Uzbek national cinema?

After Independence, we had no money to make films. For the last two years, the government has been giving us money. But there is a financial crisis, which makes it very difficult for a national film industry to grow. I worked on this film for eight years. The hardest was to find the finance. In Uzbekistan, films are generally made with government funds. Fifteen fiction films are made each year, out of which five are 35 mm. We also make 40 documentaries annually. There are some private studios such as mine. But even if you have a private studio, the government can fund your film.

What kind of films receive government funding?

The State supports nationalistic films. About me, they have been saying, 'She makes Russian films'!! So, here I made a film that was purely Uzbek, based on Uzbek culture and traditions!

What form of State censorship, if any, is exercised?
The screenplay goes through the government competition system. Violent films are refused.

There have been incidents reported in the West pointing to the control exercised by the State on the artists.
They don't control me! If they give me money, I proceed. I do not have the concern of some private companies that make movies with private money and then are obliged to ensure that the investors get their returns.

What is the present relationship with Russia in terms of cinema?
In the past, we studied in Moscow and made Soviet movies. Today former actors make movies, but they lack the experience.

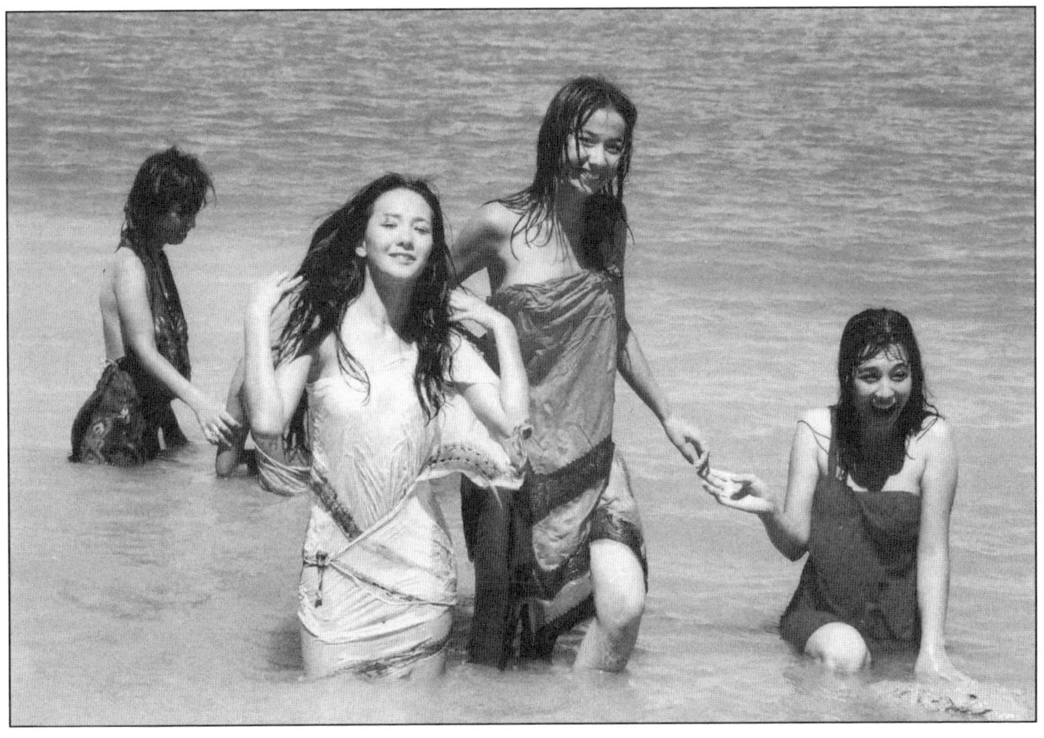

The Road Under the Skies

What about cinema halls? Are they privately owned?

Cinemas are owned both by the State and the private companies. But there are very few cinema halls in the capital Tashkent and none in the rural areas. Television replaces what is missing.

Around the world, the audiences are drawn to American culture and the Hollywood movies. What is the reaction to your films in your country?

My films are for the youth; they are dedicated to young people. The reception is very good.

Some years ago, Uzbek films used to draw more crowds than Hollywood films.

This is no longer the case. American movies dominate the market. In the old days, good films from different parts of the world were shown, but today, there is no money. Cheap Hollywood movies are bought and shown in theatres. Most of these films are very violent. We also show Indian (*Bollywood*) movies.

In some other countries such as Turkey, local film-makers have been resorting to Hollywood-style potential blockbusters to gain back the audience alienated by art films. Is this the case in Uzbekistan?

Very much so. They try to imitate Hollywood to win back the audience. But to imitate Hollywood, you have to have good technology and good actors, which we do not have.

I hope we do not have to wait another ten years for another film from Kamara Kamalova.

I am ready but it depends on financing, which may take very long.

BIO/FILMOGRAPHY

Kamara (Shadmanovna) Kamalova was born in Bukhara, Uzbekistan in 1938. After graduation from the All Union State Institute in Moscow in 1964, she began to make animation films until the early 1970s when she plunged into feature film-making. She worked as a film-maker at the Uzbekfilm studio until 1992 and then established her own studio.

Feature films:

1975 *Gorkaya yagoda/Bitter Barry*
1978 *Somebody Else's Happiness*
1986 *O tom, chego ne bylo/My Grandson Working in Police*
1988 *Dikar/The Savage*
1995 *Atrof Qorga Burkandi /All Around Was Covered by Snow*
2006 *Dorogapod Nebesami /The Road Under the Skies*

ZULFIKAR MUSSAKOV

Zulfikar Mussakov is one of the most productive film-makers in Uzbekistan, where, unlike neighbouring Central Asian Republics, national cinema is alive and well. Mussakov's first feature film, *Askar Ertagi/Soldatskaja Skazka/A Soldier's Story* (1989), was about life in the country barracks, where Uzbek and Russian soldiers, who are divided according to their nationality, help or reject each other and harass the weaker ones. The tragic end does not come from hate, but rather boredom, ignorance and an inability to communicate in a world full of tension.

Bomba/The Bomb (1995), shot in the Uzbek language, is a slapstick comedy in the style of a television sitcom. A family discovers a bomb in their garden and tries to use the unfortunate situation to benefit. The neighbour, who hears that he can get a flat in Tashkent as a replacement if the bomb explodes on his property, steals the bomb and places it in his garden. Parallel to this is a love story where the traditional arranged marriage and modern freedom of choice are in a contraposition. Fascinatingly, in all the mayhem at the centre of the film, the only ones who make some sense are the young.

Yaratganga Shukur/Ja Chotschu/I Wish (1997) follows the same genre. An average white-collar worker one day discovers that he has magic powers. Initially, he is happy to impress his privileged friends with his new talent, but his magic powers begin to threaten his peace of mind when he is coerced to choose between good and bad wishes.

National feelings and return to roots in a search for identity are current subjects worldwide and Zulfikar Musakov's *Vatan/Motherland* (2006), which I had a chance to see during the X. Forum of the National Cinematographies of the ex-Soviet Union (21–27 April 2006) is a good example. A young man who has a comfortable life in the US and considers himself American experiences vicariously his father's long journey back home to come to terms with his own identity, and at the end of the film utters the long expected statement: 'I am Uzbek'. Critics at the Forum were somewhat divided over the naïveté of this deliverance and some even went further and called it 'a propaganda film' advocating 'correct' behaviour although the film was not without its tender moments.

A film-maker from a country little known in the West except for its magnificent monuments of Samarkand and Bukhara, Zulfikar Mussakov believes that, one day, Uzbek films may reach beyond their borders. For the moment, he is content making films for his 'own people'. I met Zulfikar Mussakov during Cottbus Film Festival in November 2000, where his films were shown as part of the Uzbek Panorama.

HUMOUR IN THE ABSENCE OF HOPE AND LAUGHTER

The Bomb and *I Wish* are both about society and social issues revealed through the medium of comedy. What drew you to this mode of expression?
This is because of my personal character. I make films that I would like to see.

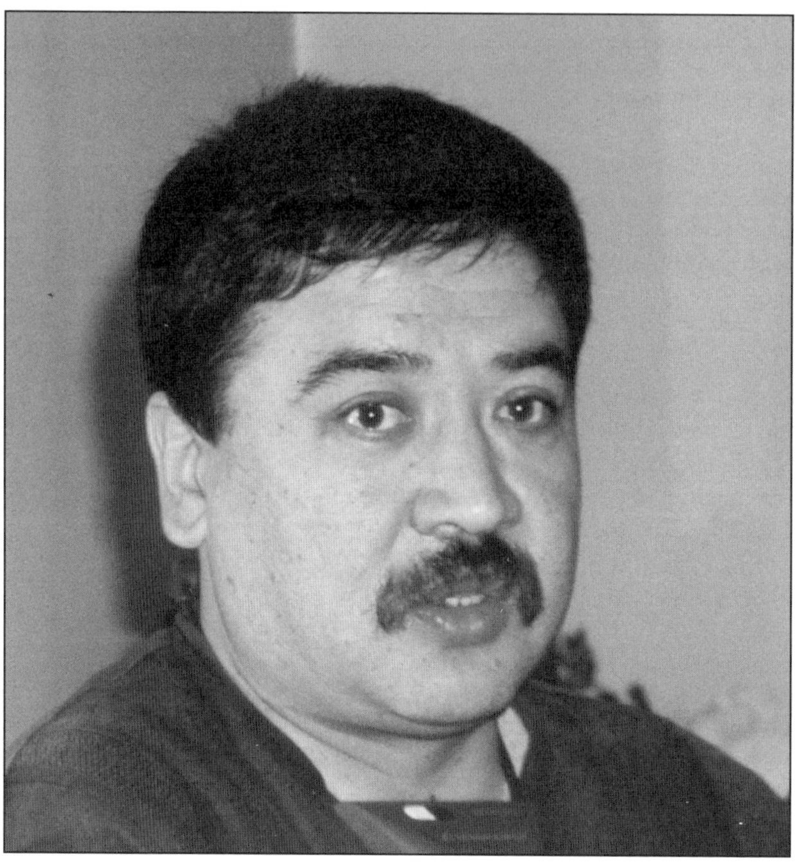

Zulfikar Mussakov

Could you tell me about your background?

I completed two years of High Courses at the Moscow Film Academy – not the VGIK – to become a director. My first film was made in 1989. I made six fiction feature films in ten years. I also wrote ten screenplays for such films as Yuri Sobitov's *Bir Qadam O'ngga, Bir Qadam Chapga/Left March, Right March* (1991) and his latest, *Price of Happiness, Go Ask a Woman*; Bahadir Adilov's *Birinchi Bo'sa/First Kiss* (1991) and *Dallol Makler/The Broker* (1993); Changir Kasimov's *Bechoralar/Poor Guys* (1991) and Nazim Tulahoyaev's *Face*, an animation film. I have also worked with Shakleva.

How did it feel to become a film-maker during the transition period from the Soviet regime to Independence?

We lost something – contacts with friends and teachers. In return, we gained the freedom to travel to foreign countries without asking permission. I lived a big part of my life in the Soviet Union. No one asked me whether I agreed with the changes. This was done by forces outside my control. Therefore, my relationship to the break-up is a philosophical question and my reaction is to make comedies with some humour because smile and hope are not present in our lives at this moment.

According to the western media, despite economic stability in Uzbekistan, lack of freedom is still an important issue. Amnesty International reports allege that people tried on charges of terrorism or attempting to overthrow the constitutional order are tortured while in detention to force them to confess.

I did not have restrictions to make my films. Perhaps that is why I do not deal with politics. I make movies and people like them. Independent of political changes, the real film will be loved by people. I make films about people I love. I think films should give people the feeling of love. If after the screening, people have a nice feeling about our country, I succeeded.

Uzbek cinema has a long history. The national cinema produced its first films in the 1930s – *The Upsurge, Ramazan, Before the Dawn, Klych* ... The arrival of sound with *The Oath* in 1937 was an important event. The same year, a documentary, *Tashkent Textile Factory*, directed by M. Kayumov, received a golden medal at the World Exhibition in New York. During World War II, when some of the film studios of other republics were evacuated to Uzbekistan, the creative collaboration with masters like Romm, Kozintsev, Lukov was very fruitful in producing milestone films such as *Takhir and Zukhra* (1944) and *Adventures of Nasreddin* of Ganiev and *Alisher Navoi* of Yarmatov. Ganiev's films are very much in the epic form, or *dastan* (legends) that keep the oral traditions alive. Yarmatov's *Alisher Navoi* stresses the natural and historical originality of the Uzbek people. In the 1960s–1980s, some of the landmarks of Uzbek cinema were made such as *Tashkent, Gorod hlebnyj/Tashkent, the City of Bread* (1968) by Shukrat Abbosov in the tradition of Italian neo-realism. What are the prevalent themes and genres of the Uzbek films today?

Different themes. Historical films, documentaries, fiction. My aim is not to make films for festivals but for people. Uzbek film-makers shoot films for the 23 million Uzbek people.

Why do we not see political films that delve into the issue of coming to terms with the Soviet period even a decade after Independence?

We do not make only children's films or comedies. Naturally, there are political films, but these are essentially historical. Everything that happened in our country until the 1930s has made itself to the celluloid. During the Soviet period, we shot films about the 1930s and 1940s. Now we are reconsidering these topics and trying to understand what happened at that time. Presently, Uzbek Film is shooting a film about *jadids*[1] who brought history to our people. They even went to Germany to study. There is another film about the February 16th explosion in Tashkent, the attack on the President.[2] We got the script and the theme. I do not think there are taboos. This applies to politics. Of course, we have censorship. Violence and sex are not allowed. We do not need them.

Are you referring to *Bo-Ba-Bu*, Ali Khamraev's controversial latest work, which is not released in your country?[3] He is one of your best film-makers, although he left Uzbekistan to live in Italy and then Moscow. He is also the name behind the most popular film that has been topping the charts in Uzbekistan for 40 years, the comedy *Yer-Yer/Where Are You, My Zulfiya*.

About *Bo-Ba-Bu*, I want to make it clear. In the film history of any country, there must be moments when national feelings of the people were hurt or when people left the theatre because they did not want their sons to see the film. I do not want my children to see this film. Why should we have a film that 23 million Uzbek people do not want to see? Don't forget where we are! Our national feelings are very strong, so are our traditions. Violence and sex are not allowed because they offend the feelings of mothers and fathers. Every director is a human being with a wife and children. Does he want to see this film?

How does one finance films in Uzbekistan?

The government gives the full budget to six films a year. Private studios exist but lack funds. They cannot make more than one or two films.

Since the government finances your projects, is there a script approval by the government? Are there any restrictions?

I have written many screenplays, if the authorities do not like some, I always have others.

What about co-productions?

The possibility is there, but I am not running after anyone. *I wish* was fully financed by Japan. I also participated in the *Womankind* series of America. For my new film, which is called *Mother*, I won a grant from the Japanese Foundation for Arts. It was a competition open to all film-makers from the former Soviet Union and the Eastern European countries. Conditions were to have a common element with Japan. I won for a script that I wrote with Bahadir Adilov, and we will direct it together. The grant will be paid after the completion of the production. Japanese actress Akio is coming to Uzbekistan for the shoot. She will play a dual role – a Japanese woman and an Uzbek one. The story is simple and funny. There is a car accident, in which the mother of an Uzbek girl dies. Then the girl meets a Japanese woman in Samarkand and tells her she is her daughter.

Do you feel a commercial pressure to focus on national topics when you receive money from abroad?

As far as such pressure is concerned, the medallion has two sides. It depends on the cultural level of the director and the morals of the people giving the money. The risk of having nationalistic films is there.

Who is in charge of distribution in Uzbekistan?
The government is in charge of distribution. *Bomba* was sold to Russia and it did very well within the country. As you saw this morning, the copy is completely worn out.

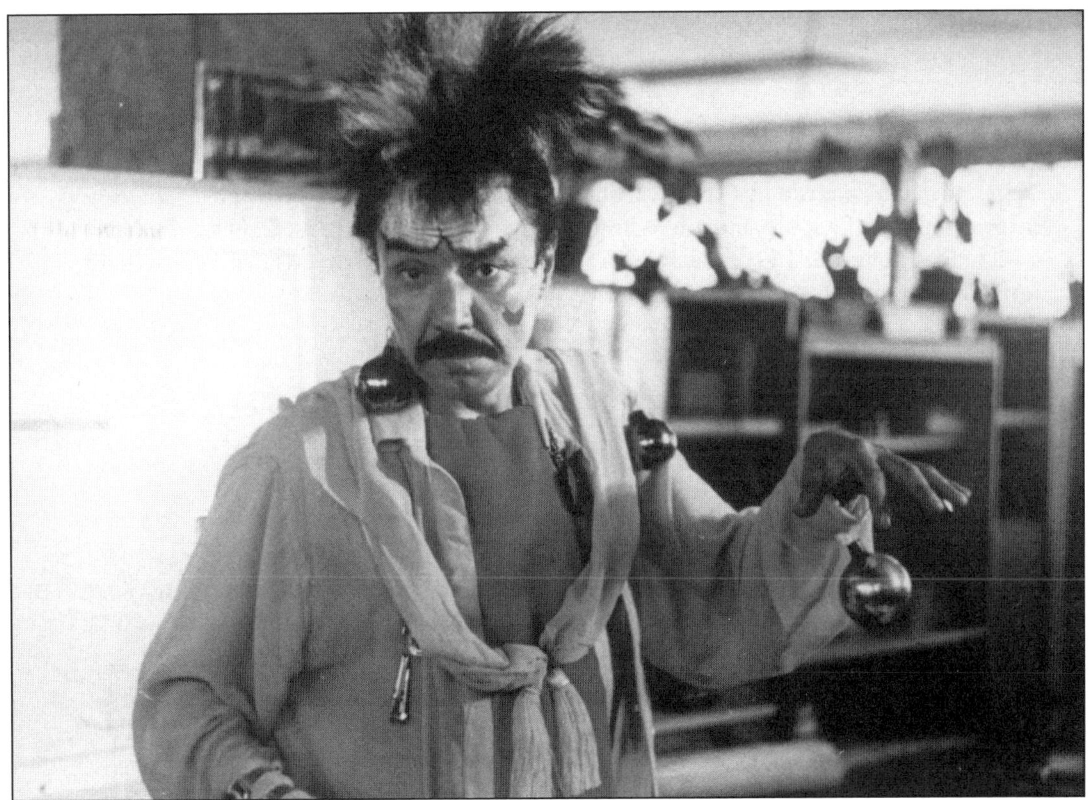

I Wish

To protect the national film industry, does the government establish a quota as to how many foreign and national films can be screened each year?
I am not familiar.

Uzbekistan's national film industry had to survive under the Soviet censorship. After Independence, a new menace has arrived, the western films, so much so that advise has been sought from a foreign development agency (Swiss) to help rebuild Uzbek cinema in an effort to create a new sense of national identity. Which are the most popular films today?
Uzbek films are the most popular. Hollywood is second.

I have heard that there is also a tradition of watching Hindi films and that people still remember Raj Kapoor. Unfortunately, video piracy, which is a threat to all film industries as well as the national one, seems to have seduced your audience as well. I have been told that pirated DVDs of films like yours are sold simultaneously as they are screened in the theatres.
At least they are interested in watching them!

Kamara Kamalova, one of your finest film-makers was once asked if she had encountered difficulties in becoming a director because of her gender. She said that being a director was not just creative, but it also involved working with and organizing large numbers of people, most of whom are men and they have an Uzbek mentality, which does not readily accept having a woman in a position of authority.[4] Are there any other women directors besides her?
This is not an occupation for a woman. It is not because of discrimination; you need hard nerves.

Kamara Kamalova is doing fine.
Kamara is an exception. Many women directors lose a part of being a woman when they become directors.

Do young people want to become film-makers?
We have the Academy of Fine Arts, which will give its first graduates in artistic film this year. Cameramen, directors, film and television producers and actors are trained at the Cultural Institute. But after graduation, they follow the same route as in Kyrgyzstan or Turkmenistan; they prefer to make video clips. In Europe also only two out of three graduates become directors. Directors cannot be made artificially. When I come to Europe, some people ask me if we have Mercedes Benz or high buildings in Tashkent. We have a whole department of film school. We also have television antennas. We see the same films that you see and listen to the same music. Maybe more! Space is not inaccessible. Of course, we have problems, but you have too. Central Asian cinema does not need alms from anyone.

Our cinema has 90 years of history. The first Lumiere film was screened in Tashkent two years after its premiere in France. Of course, our technical equipment is not at par with yours. But from the artistic side, we never ask for mercy. We have the tradition.

– Cottbus, November 2000

Notes

1. The short-lived (1913–1916) *Jadid* or Reformist movement sought closer ties with the rest of the Islamic world. In their schools, they taught classical Arabic to facilitate the reading of Koran. Fearing they were breeding grounds for opposition, the Russians began shutting down the schools and newspapers as early as 1910. Jadid theatre, as an art form previously nonexistent in Central Asia, more effectively thwarted censors to spread the reformist Islamic message. Of the only 20 or so plays remaining from the six-year life of the Jadid theatre, a common theme – the fear of the end of the Muslim community via loss of spirituality – endures. *The Patricide*, by Mahmud Khoja Behbudig, is one of the most well known. Behbudig is only one of many artists who helped establish an Uzbek identity based on traditional values during the heavily censored era of the early 1900s.
2. A series of explosions hit the capital Tashkent on 16th February 1999 for which President Islam Karimov blamed the 'Islamic extremists' and others who wished to undermine the government.
3. A co-production between Uzbekistan, Italy and France, *Bo-Ba-Bu* (1999) takes place in an unspecified time somewhere in Central Asia. A young woman played by Arielle Dombasle (Pauline of Eric Rohmer) loses her memory after a fall and remains mute. Two herdsmen capture and abuse her, forcing her to pray to their god. She becomes their possession but her presence marks a rupture in a delicate equilibrium as the stronger of the two claims her, although the lines of allegiance keep shifting. Shot in the deserts of Afghanistan, *Bo-Ba-Bu* reflects an imaginary wasteland where the harsh desert dominates life. It is all supposed to be a parable, which, incidentally is undermined by the voyeuristic nude scenes and the graphic cruelty.
4. Attwood, L. (ed.) (1993) *Red Women on the Silver Screen*, London, Pandora Press. For Kamalova, also read: Dönmez-Colin, G. (2004) *Women, Islam and Cinema*, London, Reaktion Books.

BIO/FILMOGRAPHY

Zulfikar Mussakov was born in Akkurgan near Tashkent in 1958. During his secondary school years, he participated in amateur theatre troupes and made 8-mm films. After studying theatre in Tashkent, he worked as a director for the experimental theatre Ilkhom. His first short film, shot in 16 mm, received a prize in Brno. He worked for television, made videos, wrote and painted. In 1987, he entered the Superior Courses of Directing in Moscow where he made *The Sparrow*, which is based on a novel by Astafiev. He has been a film director at the Uzbekfilm studio since 1989. His *Boys in the Sky* (2002) and *Boys in the Sky II* (2004) have been box-office hits. An Uzbek variation on Fellini's *Amarcord* (including the boys' first encounter with porn), the two films also display national elements and the precarious feelings of youth of Independence who are at odds with their present.

A Selection of Feature Films:

1989 *Askar Ertagi/Soldatskaja Skazka/A Soldier's Story*

1991 *Abdullajon/Abduladshan Ili Posvjastschaetsa Stiveny Spilbergy/Abdullazhan, the UFO Kid*

1995 *Bomba/The Bomb*

1997 *Yaratganga Shukur/Ja Chotschu/I Wish*

1998 *Kichkina Tabib/Malenkij Lekar/Tabib, the Little Faith-Healer*

2002 *Boys in the Sky*

2004 *Boys in the Sky II*

2006 *Vatan/The Homeland*

2011 *The Lead*

YUSUF RAZIKOV

One of the prominent figures of contemporary Uzbek cinema, Yusuf Razikov uses the genre of comedy to reflect on social, moral and psychological issues. *Voiz/Orator* (1999), which he wrote and produced as well as directed, is a gentle satire on the battle of the sexes layered with subtle nuances about totalitarian regimes. In a fairy-tale style, the film narrates the fortunes and misfortunes of a middle-aged cart driver who inherits his brother's two wives, when he already has a wife. Then he draws the attention of the Bolsheviks with his oratory skills and mastery of the Russian language, and a young revolutionary activist falls in love with him. Razikov maintains a humorous tone in projecting the efforts of ordinary citizens caught between the traditional values of the Islamic culture and the new ideology to keep pace with the regime changes, although, the tragic end is ineluctable. *Orator* was the first Uzbek film to be shown in the Panorama section of the Berlinale (2000).

Ayollar Saltanati/Shenskoje Zarstvo/Women's Paradise (2000), also written, directed and produced by Razikov, is, again, a comedy about the battle of the sexes, at least on the surface. Olim is a middle-aged artist in an existential crisis. Not only that he is suffering from writer's block, but managing several relationships with several free-spirited women is giving him headaches. The fundamental question that faces him is whether to love one woman who stands for all women, or to love all women. The film uses magic, fantasy and a good dose of humour in searching an answer to this question.

I met Yusuf Razikov for the first time during the Mannheim International Film Festival in October 2000. Our next meeting was in Tehran in 2005 during the Fajr International Film Festival, which was followed by several e-mails.

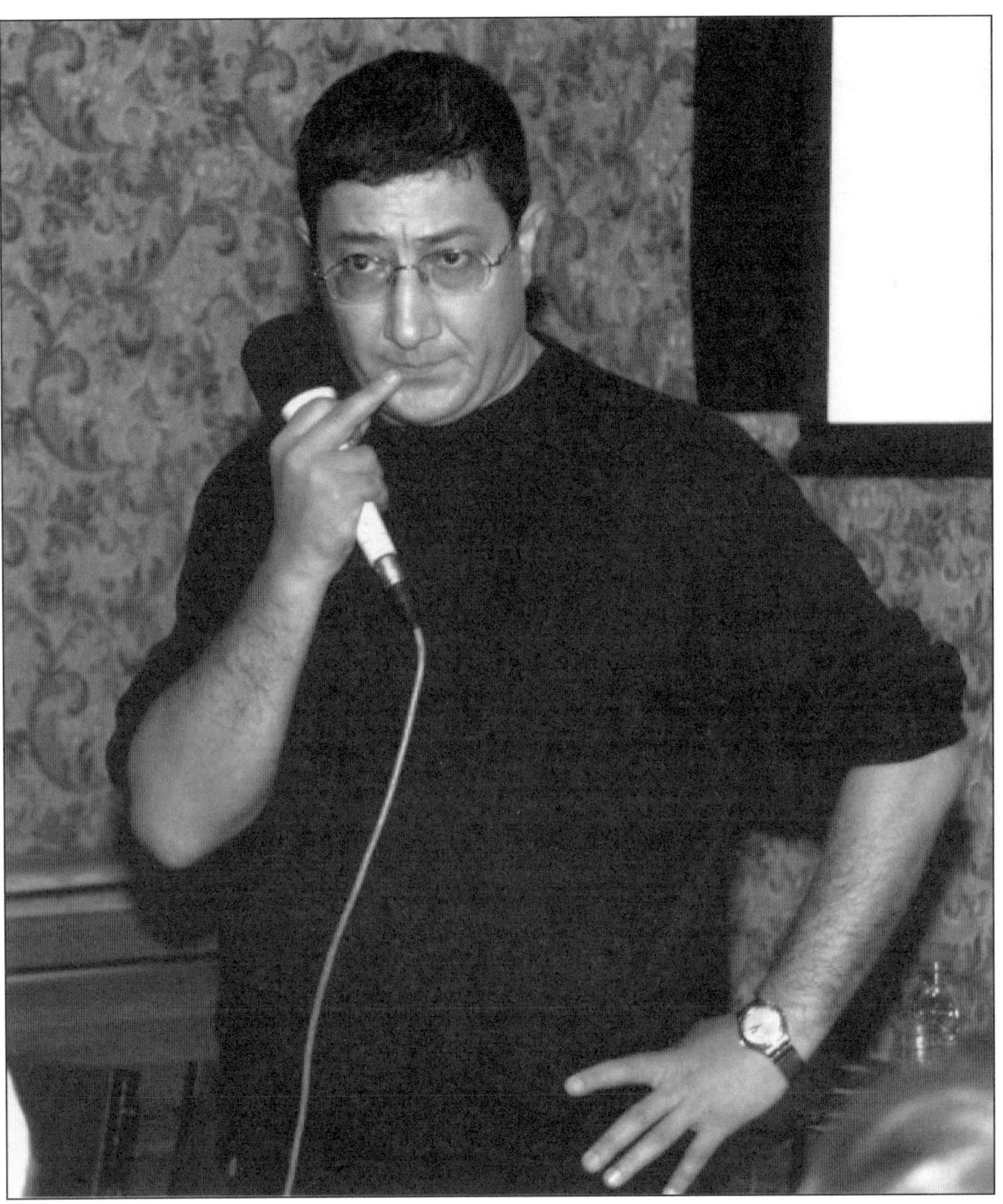

Yusuf Razikov

THE UNFAIR BATTLE OF THE SEXES

In *Women's Paradise*, using mythology, magic, humour and fantastical images, you ask a million-dollar question: To love one woman who stands for all women, or to love all women instead of a single one? When his terminally ill friend and mentor Ismail entrusts his pretty wife Zebo to him, Olim, the writer, sets on a long journey in search of the young woman, but he is lost in a surreal dream journey that lands him at a market surrounded with all the women of his life. What does this false paradise signify?

That scene is in his imagination, which is a part of his art. The women expect to marry him, but for him there are some borders. He is not free for relationships. He is in a personal and artistic crisis. The women serve as a metaphor for his art and at the same time his inability to be successful in his art. There are two levels: emotional and creative. Neither one is perfect.

I did not quite understand the episode with the girl who killed herself.

This episode is connected to the main theme of the film. Olim, the writer, is not able to love. The girl is able to love, but her love is not needed.

What about the scene when the protagonist extends his hands to be cemented in a wall? Does this show his willingness to escape to another world?

I tried to build the film on externally illogical actions to elaborate on the internal life of the main character. This episode is one of them. When he wakes up, his hands are bandaged, which indicates the sense of transition. The relationship of the protagonist to his doctor is similar to that of the writer to his characters; at the core of it is dependence. He needs his doctor the way a writer needs his characters.

Why does Olim take off his glasses and immerse his head in the water at the end of the film?

He takes off his glasses because he wants to change his view and to look and love like a child.

Both *Orator* and *Women's Paradise* depict women as level-headed and independent. Centuries-old Central Asian legends also portray women as strong characters. And under the Soviet regime, they were supposed to be equal to men; however, self-immolation, particularly in the rural areas, was and perhaps still is, an alarming phenomenon in Uzbekistan. Some sources cite religious pressure of a patriarchal society as a determining factor in addition to the harshness of daily life. I have seen Shuhrat Mahmudor's 1988 documentary, *Hudium/Offensive*, referring to the Soviet fight against female oppression in Central Asia in the 1920s. Women throw off their veils and fight for their rights despite assassination of hundreds by their husbands

and brothers for disgracing the family. That film focuses on the fact that despite such a movement, the phenomenon of self-immolation among Central Asian women grew at an alarming rate in the ensuing years. Some of the women interviewed reiterate that they do not want equal rights. The narrator's conclusion is that they have accepted their oppression believing in their inferiority. To unveil their minds would need another *hudium*.[1] Has the status of women changed after Independence? How does the rise of fundamentalism in your country affect the modern Uzbek woman? After all, Uzbekistan is an androcentric society.

The tradition of strong women has cultural roots. According to a popular story, mother and father stand at the end of the courtyard and ask the baby to come forward. He/she makes the first step towards the mother. The community of men adores the face of the mother.

But Islam has always been a strong force in Uzbekistan, even during the Soviet regime. Tashkent was the headquarters of the Muslim Spiritual Directorate of Central Asia and Kazakhstan, which supervised 230 mosques, nearly half of the USSR total. Two-thirds of these mosques were in Uzbekistan. In the mid-1960s, the quest of young intellectuals for a national and religious identity led to an 'unofficial' or 'parallel' Islam. Brezhnev reversed the anti-religious propaganda of Khrushchev and authorized the restoration of religious monuments. During the last few years of the communist regime, Islam was clearly thriving in the cities. From the beginning of *glasnost* (openness), the official Soviet policy of tolerance had far-reaching effects. In 1990 alone, the number of mosques in Uzbekistan tripled. There must be some changes to the family situation, especially with the recent rise of fundamentalism.

The free women movement started during the Soviet period and it cannot stop now. Of course, there is the danger of Islam.

What about women film-makers in Uzbekistan? The West only knows of Kamara Kamalova.

Beside Kamara Kamalova, we have Rano Kubayarev who made *Kenja/Mladschaja/ The Youngest* in 1994 and Svetlana Murathaciayava.

Another Uzbek director told me that, when women become directors, they lose something from being a woman. What do you think?

This is not my opinion. What I do not like is the subject becoming an emancipation issue. We have presently three female students studying direction. They got prizes in Almaty in the 'Look in a New Way' Film Festival. To think that film direction is ugly should be ugly for men.

I understand you make your films with State money. What are some of the ramifications?

In comparison to the other Central Asian states, we are happy to make films. We have State money to find foreign money. Twenty per cent of box-office profit is for Uzbek films. The main idea is that cinema is part of culture, which should be supported by the State.

Uzbek cinema's struggles with censorship go a long way. Nurchon, one of the first Uzbek actresses, was assassinated in 1929, accused of having violated the interdiction for a woman to show herself in public and in 1933, director Soleiman Khodjaev disappeared in a gulag because of his film *Before Sunrise*, which dealt with the theme of the revolt of Bukhara against the Russian power in 1916. What is the situation with censorship today? Although your president, Islam Karimov, has invited the film-makers to be bold in choosing their subjects, we do not see any burning issues depicted in your films.

I call it 'inner censorship'! But there are films. For instance, a film was released recently, which shows violence against women.

Apart from sex and violence, what other 'inner censorship' exists? We have read about writers being harassed or even exiled.

I have never had any problems. The opinion of censorship is more on the outside. This is part of the culture. State gives money for a film; the least they would expect is a film that the audience would like to see.

Is there a movement of independent cinema?

I Wish by Zulfikar Mussakov was made with private sources. My films are made with State money.

You are also the head of the Uzbek Film Studio. Is it totally State owned?

Fifty per cent of the action belongs to the State; the rest is private.

The period from 1986 to 1991, *perestroika*, the transparency policy introduced by Gorbachev, was a golden period for Uzbek cinema. Using the government funding, the film-makers tackled previously taboo subjects such as drug abuse and prostitution in several documentaries. But Independence meant freedom to open the door to Hollywood, which is perhaps the biggest menace to your film industry, not to mention video and DVD piracy.

In the beginning, our society became infatuated with all things western, and the video pirating, which is still flourishing, caused loss of jobs in the industry. From another point of view, one may say that the arrival of western values had the positive effect of slowing down Islamization. Now, people are getting tired of the western styles. Novelty has faded. They want to see their own stories on screen.

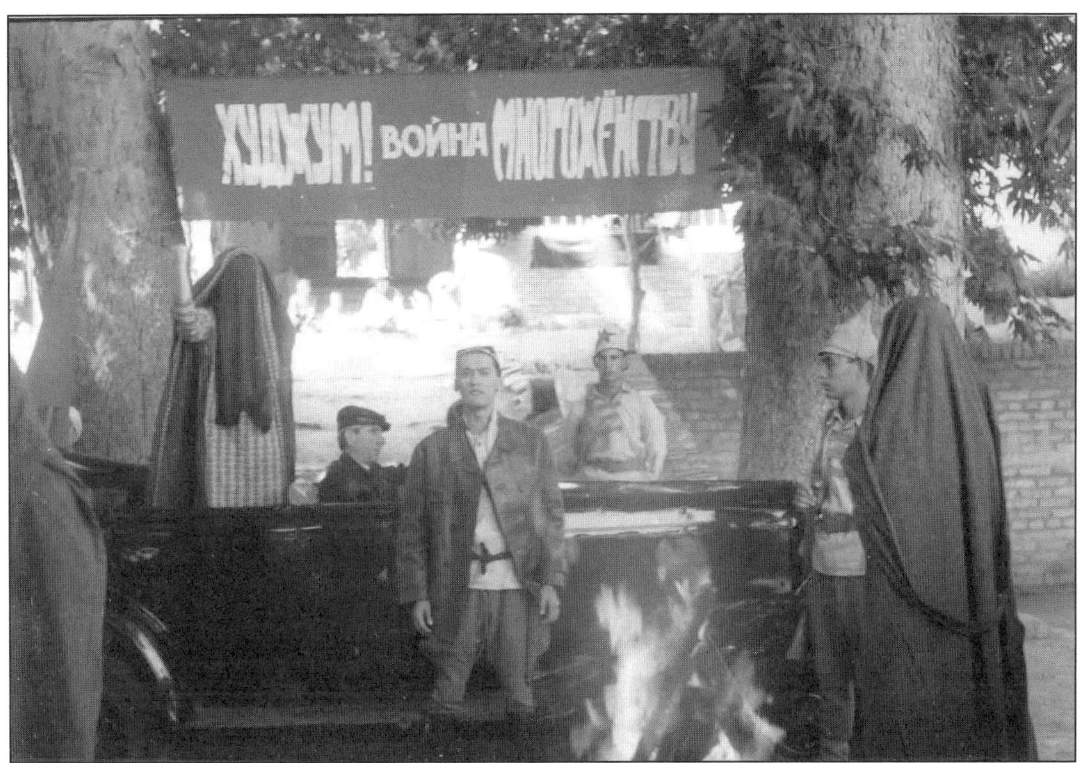

Orator

What is the language of cinema after Independence? And do you use the Latin alphabet?

Uzbek and Russian are both used. During the Soviet period, we used to shoot in Russian and then dub to Uzbek language for national release. We use the Latin alphabet.

What is your next project?

I have several projects. One project is as a director with David Sefarian; another one as a scriptwriter for Rano Kubayarev for a co-production with Russia and possibly Netherlands. As a director, alone, I am working on a video film that will be called *Dilxiro/ The Man's Dance*, taking its name from the national Uzbek dance, which is only for men. The narrative follows the entry of a young man into the adult world in Islamic Uzbekistan. He endures physical pain as his bride-to-be undergoes her own rite of passage. Such conflicts that abound in our culture will be viewed from the traditional point of view as well as contemporary. The theme is the meeting point of the two.

– Mannheim, October 2000

* * *

When we met last night, and I told you about my recently published book, *Women, Islam and Cinema*, which includes some of your work, you mentioned you were working on a new film, again about women. What is your motivation for choosing stories that foreground women?

I do not think I make films only about women. Actually, *Women's Paradise* is not about women but about a writer and film; and *Orator* is not about women. The storyline touches

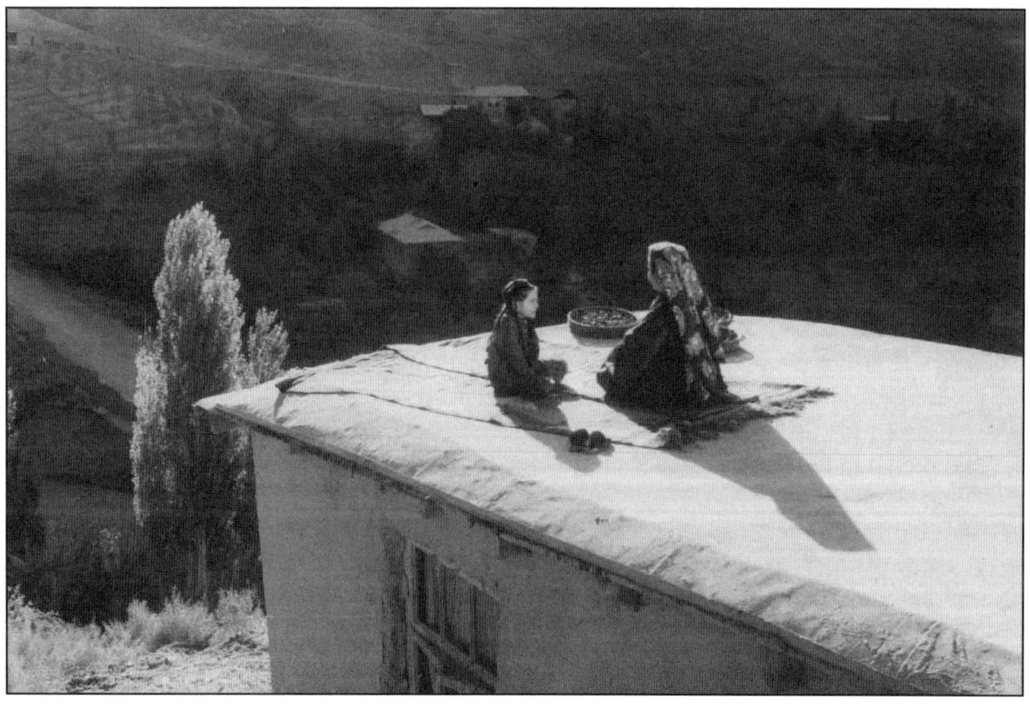

The Man's Dance

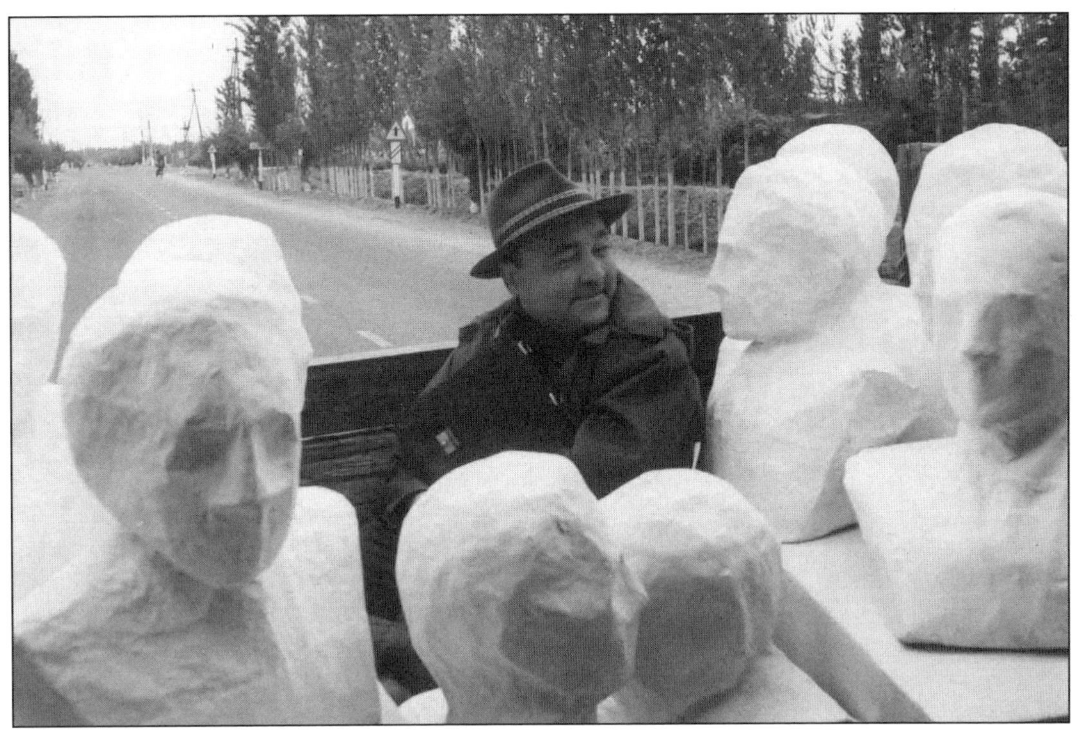

Comrade Boykenjayev

upon the subject of women's issues. If you consider the numbers of heroines in painting, literature and poetry, you can understand my motivation. Artistically, I think that the character of women is more interesting for dramaturgic development. On a personal level, I grew up in the company of women – grandmother, mother and four younger sisters.

Unlike other Central Asian republics, in Uzbekistan Uzbek films attract a wide audience, perhaps more than Hollywood films. Can you explain why?

This is a matter of social psychology. Moslems are traditionally more closed and, hence, they try to preserve cultural contents (not as an obligatory result of religion), which are based on respect for elders, traditions and family relations. All these elements are very strong in Uzbekistan.

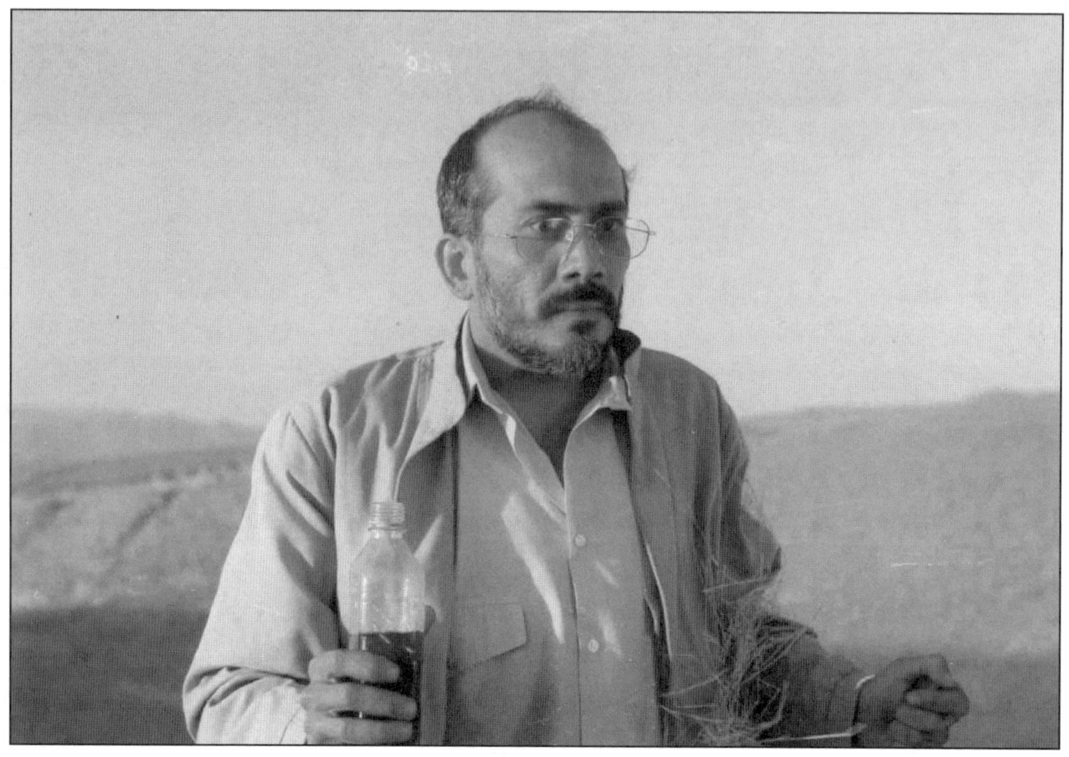

Women's Paradise

Are you still the Head of the Studio?
I was the head of Uzbekfilm studio for five years. Now I am the Art Director.

Besides yourself and Zulfikar Mussakov, who are the other prominent working directors today?
I think soon you will be hearing such names as Yolkin Tuychiyev, Ayup Shakhobiddinov, Khilol Nasimov, Fattykh Djalalov, Sobir Nazarmukhammedov and Turaniyaz Kalimbetov.

What are the most important subjects in Uzbek cinema today – contemporary issues or the revival of culture and tradition?

Uzbek cinema is not obliged to follow a political doctrine. Each film-maker is free to choose a theme. Everything else depends on his taste/mind and talent/abilities. Certainly, all subjects you mention are explored.

What is the main difference of Uzbek cinema from other Central Asian cinemas?
It is completely financed by the State.

Are there any women directors beside Kamara Kamalova? What are the issues they deal with?
We have a young film-maker, Saodat Ismailova. She has shot several short films. At present, she is in Berlin as part of the programme Artists in Residence working on a big project.

How many films are made in Uzbekistan each year? How many of these are commercial films?
Together with video films (which have a small budget), Uzbekistan produces about 20 films a year – 2 or 3 of these are commercial. Commercial films are mainly produced by private studios.

What is the major influence on Uzbek cinema today? Hollywood? Old Russian/ Soviet masters? Europe?
I think Asian cinema and partly French.

What is your latest project?
A contemporary rural story with elements of a road movie about a relationship between a 14-year-old boy and the wife of his elder brother, who has left to search for a job.

– Tehran, February 2005

Notes

1.	Attwood, L. (ed.) (1993) *Red Women on the Silver Screen*, London, Pandora Press.

BIO/FILMOGRAPHY:
Yusuf Razikov was born in Tashkent in 1957. He started his career in the film industry as a light technician at the Uzbekfilm Studio while studying philology at the Tashkent State University. Following his military service, he was employed by Uzbek TV as assistant director and then director and the author of art programmes. In 1981, he was accepted to the scripting department of the VGIK in Moscow. In 1983, his film *The Ladder in the House with a Lift* was awarded the Grand Prix for Best Script of a short film

at the Moscow Festival of Youth Films. After majoring in screenwriting in 1986, he did an internship at the Mosfilm Studio in Moscow for two years and began writing scripts for Uzbekfilm, Mosfilm, Gruziyafilm (Georgia) and other similar studios. In addition to the feature films that he has directed, Razikov has written screenplays for more than 10 feature films and around 100 television episodes that he directed. Between 1999 and 2004, he was the president of the Uzbekfilm Studio.

Feature films:
1992 *Olovdagi Farishta/Angel in the Fire*
1998 *Voiz/Orator*
2000 *Ayollar Saltanati/Shenskoje Zarstvo/Women's Paradise*
2002 *Ortok Boykenjayev/Comrade Boykenjaev*
   Dilxiroj/The Dance of Men
2003 *Dard/Healer*
2004 *Erkak/Girl's keeper*
2007 *Beglyanki/Runaways*
2009 *Gastarbeiter/Migrant Worker*

FILM CREDITS

1997 – Sapisi Rustema S Risunkami/1997 – Rustem's Notes with Drawings
1998, 75 mins, colour
Director: Ardak Amirkulov
Producer: Ard-film
Cinematographer: Renat Kusayev and Nariman Turebaev
Screenwriters: Erzhan Rustembekov and Nariman Turebaev
Art Director: Larisa Reshetova and Gaziz Tleulin
Leading Players: Erzhan Rustembekov

At the end of the 1990s, aimless youth in modern Almaty run in circles. Rustem is lazy and indifferent in comparison to his hard-working sister. When his boss at the zoo fires him, he begins to wander around the city without a destination. One day he meets Miko, a well-mannered pretty girl, but his feelings for her are confused, as he does not know anything about her. Together they try to discover the world for themselves and record everything in words and drawings. The film shows the city of Almaty shrouded by inertia, similar to the insomnia suffered by the citizens of Makondo in Gabriel Garcia Marquez' novel *One Hundred Years of Solitude* when exhaustion from lack of sleep causes amnesia.

Abai
1995, 135 mins, 2 series, colour
Director: Ardak Amirkulov
Producer: Kazakhfilm
Cinematographer: Khasan Kidiraliev
Screenwriters: Ardak Amirkulov, Layla Akhinzhanova and Alexander Baranov
Art Director: Umirzak Shmanov
Leading Players: Gabiden Turikbaev, Tungushpay Al'-Tarazy, Bolot Beyshinaliev, Farida Zhantelova, Dinmukhamed Akhimov, Umirzak Shmanov, Beken Rimova

Awards:

The film won the Grand-Prize of Tashkent Film Festival (1995) (Uzbekistan) and the Karlovy Vary (1995) (Czech Republic).

The film pictures Abai, an epic character and a historical person, poet and philosopher, whose poetry is regarded as the mirror of the Kazakh soul.

Akcyat/Aksuat
 1997, 94 mins, colour
 Director and Screenwriter: Serik Aprimov
 Production: Kazakhfilm
 Cinematographer: Boris Troshev
 Art Director: Sabit Kurmanbekov
 Music: Kazbek Spanov
 Leading Players: Sabit Kurmanbekov, Erzhan Ashim, Makangali Abdullaev, Nurzhuman Ikhtimbaev, Gulnazit Omarova

Awards:

The film won the Best Director award at the Euresia Film Festival Almaty (1998) and the Grand Prize in the Asian Program at the Tokyo Film Festival (1999).

After the collapse of the Soviet Union, the small village of Aksuat is in a hopeless situation. The economy is bad and injustice and corruption are widespread. The life of a promising man in the village starts to take an unexpected turn when his brother arrives with his girlfriend and their baby. The brother who lives in the village is an honest and upright man, whereas the one from the city is an amoral, irresponsible idler running away from his debtors. Conflict is bound to surface.

Alciz Shurek/Coeur fragile/Tender Heart
 1994, 85 mins, colour
 Director: Ermek Shinarbaev
 Producers: Ken Legargeant and Romaine Legargeant
 Production: Kazakhfilm Studios and ACC Productions
 Cinematographer: Sergei Kosmanev
 Screenwriter: Leila Akhinzhanova
 Art Director: Vladimir Trapeznikov
 Sound: Sergei Lobanov and Thierry Delor
 Editors: Marie-France Poulizac and Khadisha Urmurzina
 Cast: Natal'ya Arinbasarova, Adilkhan Yesenbulato, Saule Suleymenova

Awards:
The film won awards at San-Sebastian (1994) and at Geneva (1994).

An unexpected encounter changes the existence of a 50-year-old woman, disappointed in life after three husbands and two children. Ageing ballerina Aijan gives dance classes in an Alma-Ata theater. Her son is away studying in Paris, and her troubled daughter is about to move out of their apartment. Returning home one evening, Aijan is attacked by young Adik, who tries to rape her. Understanding the loneliness that drove the young man to such an extreme, Aijan does not takes legal action and, one day, when he appears at her doorstep totally drunk, she lets him in and a relationship begins. However, Aijan is tormented by love and fear of humiliation due to their age difference.

Anshi/The Hunter
  2004, 93 mins, colour
  Director and Scriptwriter: Serik Aprimov
  Executive Producer: Gulmira Aprimova
  Producers: East Cinema, Kazakhfilm/NHK/Hubert Bals Fund/Sud Fond/Fondazione
Monte Cinema Verita
  Director of Photography: Hasan Kidiraliev
  Editors: Dina Bergusugurova and Tatiana Suhorukova
  Music: Kazbek Spanov
  Leading players: Dogdurbek Kidiraliev, Alibek Zhuasbaev, Gulnazid Omarova

Brought up by a young, free-spirited and sexually liberated woman, the protagonist suffers from peer incrimination, which augments his adolescence pains in an environment that is cold, cruel and indifferent. He particularly has a certain aversion towards the lover of his surrogate mother, a mysterious hunter. One night, while the couple are together, he vents his anger by stealing the hunter's gun for a target practice at the local bar. The hunter bails him out of jail on the condition that he accompanies him on his journey. Hence begins the initiation of Erken into the world of adults, which brings with it certain emotions such as warmth for the opposite sex or for one's own mother.

Azghyin Ushtykzyn' Azaby/The Place on the Tricone
  1993, 82 mins, colour
  Director: Ermek Shinarbaev
  Production: Alem
  Cinematographer: Sergey Kosmanev
  Screenwriter: Nikita Jelkybaev

Cast: Adil Yesenbulatov, Saulye Suleymenova, Yulia Sukhova, Andrei Melnik, Kasim Jakibayev

Awards:
The film won the Golden Leopard at the Locarno Film Festival (1993).

Divided into 22 episodes, the film is a psychological drama about a young man with a very cynical view of life who decides to kill himself. The suicide attempt fails and causes him to re-evaluate the meaning of life.

Diki vostok/Wild East
   1993, 95 mins, colour
   Director and Screenwriter: Rashid Nugmanov
   Producers: Murat and Rachid Nugmanov
   Production: Studio Kino Almaty
   Cinematographer: Murat Nugmanov
   Art Directors: Rustem Abdrashev and Baurzhan Aldekov
   Music: Alexander Aksyonov
   Editor: Hadisha Urmurzina
   Leading Players: Konstantin Fyodorov, Alexander Aksyonov, Gennadi Shatunov, Konstantin Shamshurin, Zhanna Isina, Pavel Shpakovsky

Awards:
The film won the Prix Special du Jury at the 5th Festival of Action and Adventure Films Valenciennes (1994).

During the civil war in the ex-Soviet Empire, a troupe of midgets, named 'Children of the Sun', escape to the faraway mountains of Tian Shan. When they are threatened by roving bands of evil bikers, they find the Lone Cowboy and convince him to gather a motley crew of unlikely heroes to fight the gangs and save the day.

Ghibel Otrara/Otrar's Death
   1991, 160 mins, colour
   Director: Ardak Amirkulov
   Producer: Kazakhfilm
   Cinematographers: Saparbek Koychumanov and Aubakir Suleev
   Screenwriters: Svetlana Karmalita and Alexei German
   Music: Kuat Shildebaev

Leading Players: Bolat Beyshinaliev, Dogdurbek Kadiraliev, Tungishpay Jamankulov, Sabira Ataeva

Awards:
The film was awarded at the Montreal World Film Festival (1991); Figuera da Foz (1991); Ashgabat (1992); Kinotavr (1992) and Almaty (1993).

The story is based on the Mongol invasion led by Ghingiz Khan of Otrar, a city in Central Asia. A personal drama is revealed through the story of a native Otrar now serving in the Mongol army. His patriotic feelings take over and he decides to save his fatherland from the Golden Horde.

Igla/The Needle
1988, 81 mins, colour
Director: Rachid Nugmanov
Producer: Kazakhfilm Studios
Cinematographer: Murat Nugmanov
Screenwriters: Alexander Baranov and Bakhit Kelebaev
Designer: Murat Mussin
Music: (written and performed by) Victor Tsoi
Leading Players: Victor Tsoi, Marina Smirnova, Petr Mamonov, Alexander Bashirev, Archimed Iskakov, Alexander Konko

Awards:
The film won the Zolotoy dyuk in Odessa (1988) and was awarded at Nuremberg (1990).

Moro (played by Viktor Tsoi, who was the leader of the popular rock band Kino) returns to his hometown Alma Ata to collect money owed to him. He visits his former girlfriend Dina and discovers that she has become a morphine addict. He decides to help her kick the habit and takes her away to the shores of Aral where he finds the woman he once loved. But the dealers are omnipresent. He decides to fight the local drug mafia responsible for her condition and comes face to face with a deadly opponent in 'the doctor', who happens to be the mafia kingpin exploiting Dina.

Konechnaya Ostanovka/Qijan/The Last Stop/The Terminus
1989, 77 mins, colour
Director and Screenwriter: Serik Aprimov
Producer: Kazakhfilm Studio

Cinematographer: Murat Nugmanov
Art Director: Sabit Kurmanbekov
Leading Players: Sabit Kurmanbekov, Murat Akhmetov, Bakhytzhan Alpeisov, Nagimbek Samaev

Awards:
The film won the Grand Prix at the Youth 90 Film Week in Kiev (1990) as well as at Molodost Film Festival (1989).

On completing his military service, Erken returns home in Aksuat, a village in the desolate steppes of Kazakhstan, and discovers that people from his generation have become alcoholics, thieves or corrupt degenerate beings with no respect for any one. His old girlfriend, who is now married, is reprimanded by her tyrannical supervisors for stopping work to talk to him while repairing a building. After a drunken brawl at a wedding, he witnesses an intoxicated man firing at the local police from a rooftop. He realizes that his old friends and relatives are only interested in petty concerns of a daily routine dominated by inertia and indifference. Bitterly disillusioned, he decides to leave this suffocating milieu. The film is shot in the director's native village with non-professional actors – friends and family – giving an authentic look to this examination of a society in crisis.

Karalisulu/Krassavitsa v traure/The Mourning Beauty
1982, 40 mins, black & white
Director: Ermek Shinarbaev
Production: Kazakhfilm
Screenwriter: Ermek Shinarbaev
Cinematographer: Fedor Aranishev
Art Director: Abdrashit Sidikhanov
Music: Edward Artemev
Leading Players: Natal'ya Arinbasarova, Nurmukhan Janturine

When Karagoz, a young nomad woman, loses her husband prematurely, she takes a vow of abstinence for several years, a vow she has difficulty keeping.

Meist/Revenge
1989, 106 mins, colour
Director: Ermek Shinarbaev
Production: Kazakhfilm/Alem Union
Screenwriter: Anatoli Kim

Cinematographer: Sergey Kosmanev
Music: Vladislav Shoot
Set: Elena Elisseeva
Sound: Gulsara Mukateva
Leading Players: Alexander Pan, Valentina Tieu, Kasim Zhakibayev, Lubov Germanova, Oleg Lee, Yuzas Budraitis, Zinaida Em, Maxim Munzuk

Awards:
The film won awards at Podolsk (1991) and Tour (1992).

The film starts with a brief prologue set in the court of a young king during the eighteenth century. Flash forward to Korea at the end of the last century where a teacher murders a child in a fit of rage and flees the village. The parents seek revenge and the father spends ten years tracking the teacher but is unsuccessful. The mother lets her husband take a second wife so that she can give birth to a son who would take over the task when he grows up. The boy becomes a poet and asks the god to let him commit the murder, accepting the fate of a murderer instead of a poet. Destiny, though, keeps him from fulfilling his sinful duty.

Sergelden/A Dream in A Dream
1993, 90 mins, colour
Producer: Kazakhfilm
Director and Screenwriter: Serik Aprimov
Cinematographer: Fyodor Aranishev
Art Director: Umirzak Shmanov
Music: Kuat Shildebayev
Leading Players: Baurzhan Ibragimov, Gulnara Dosmatova, Bakhitzhan Alpeesov, Dana Zhamanbalina

Awards:
The film won awards at Almaty (Kazakhstan,1993).

A young theatre director is preparing a new play inspired by Dostoevsky's story *The Meek*. All events in the film are free translation of this story and the destiny of the protagonist Erken who kills his girlfriend and then tries to reconstruct the events leading up to the murder. His diary, the only evidence of the crime, contains four subjects: theatre, dreams, love and friends. The police investigator studying the diary explores the psyche of the director. The film has the same theme as *The Last Stop* except that instead of focusing on the disintegration of society, this one focuses on the individual. The protagonist is in a void; his only aim is to flee into imaginary worlds.

Sestra moia Liussia/My Sister Lucy
1985, 94 mins, black & white
Director: Ermek Shinarbaev
Production: Kazakhfilm Studio
Cinematographer: Georgi Guidt
Screenwriter: Anatoli Kim
Art Director: Vladimir Trapeznikov
Music: Nikolai Karetnikov
Sound: Gulsara Mukateva
Leading Players: Khamar Adambeva, Olga Ostrumova, Nikolai Grinko, Anuar Moldabekov, Larissa Velikotskaya

Awards:
The film won the Special Prize at Minsk Film Festival and Special Mention of the Jury and the Public Prize at the Amiens International Film Festival (1987).

The narrative focuses on two women in a Kazakh village, one Kazakh and the other Russian, and their struggles to survive as widows after World War II. The Russian, Klava, lives with her 12-year-old daughter Liussia next door to Kazakh Aigul, who lives with her 7-year-old son. The story is told by the boy as a grown-up man.

Tri Brata/Three Brothers
2000, 80 mins, colour
Director: Serik Aprimov
Executive Producer: Gulmira Aprimova
Producers: Serik Aprimov and Sano Sinju
Production: East-Cinema Production and NPC
Cinematographer: Fedor Aranishev
Screenwriters: Serik Aprimov and Meirman Karbozov
Art Directors: Sabit Kurmanbekov and Svetlana Chigrinova
Music: Manas Karakulov
Sound: Alia Mirzasheva
Editor: Dina Bersugurova
Leading Players: Aibar Temenov, Shakir Vilyamov, Yura Dankov, Baurzhan Syetbayev, Bakhtiyar Kuatbayev

Three brothers live in a little village near a military airbase and a cemetery of old locomotives, where the old man, Klein, works. He tells the children about a wonderful lake behind the mountains where beautiful women live. That is where, he says, he drives the officers from the military airbase. Obsessed with the idea of seeing the lake, the boys steal an old locomotive that can still work, little knowing that the officers use the old trains for target practice.

KYRGYZSTAN

Bakajdyn zajyty/Nebo nachego detsiva/Bakay's Summer Pasture/The Sky of Our Childhood
  1967, 78 mins, black & white
  Director: Tolomush Okeev
  Cinematographer: Kadirjan Kidiraliev
  Screenwriters: Tolomush Okeev and Kadirkoul Omurkulov
  Music: Tachtan Ermatov
  Set: S. Ichenov
  Leading Players: Aliman Djankorozova, Mouratbek Ryskoulov, Nasret Doubachev, Sovietbek Djoumadylov, B. Ryskoulova, Samak Alymkoulov

Kalika, who studies in the city, returns to his native village and to his herdsman father, Bakai. The old grazing grounds are soon to be replaced by the construction of a new road. Bakai is forced to move his herd to a new pasture. After trying his best to keep his youngest son in the mountains, the patriarch reluctantly accepts his son's departure for the town.

Beket/Bus Station
  1995–2000, 22 mins, black & white
  Directors and Screenwriters: Aktan Arymkubat (Abdikalikov) and Ernest Abdishaparov
  Production: Kyrgyzfilm Studio
  Cinematographer: Hassan Kidiraliev
  Editor: Rosa Umuralieva
  Sound: Bakitt Nijasaliev
  Leading Players: Mirlan Abdikalikov, Ernest Abdishaparov, Taalajkan Abazova, Emil Ibragimov

Awards:
  The film won the Grand Prize at Kinoshock Film Festival of CIS and Baltic Countries (2000) and the Second Prize at the Cottbus Film Festival (2001).

It is almost dark on a winter day. The ground is covered with snow. Few people are waiting for the bus at a stop in the middle of nowhere. They wait. The light fades and the cold becomes more unbearable. A drunken intruder bothers the woman but is chased away by a man in a fur coat. The woman almost intervenes to protect the drunken intruder, who begins to cry. Everyone huddles around him protectively. There is no sign of the bus although the traffic keeps moving, mostly in the other direction.

Beshkempir/The Adopted Son
  1998, 81 mins, black & white/colour
  Director: Aktan Arymkubat (Abdikalikov)
  Producers: Irizbai Alibaev, Cedomir Kolar, Marc Bashet and Frederique Dumas
  Production Company: Kyrgyz Film and Noé Productions
  Cinematographer: Hassan Kidiraliev
  Screenwriters: Aktan Abdikalikov, Avtandil Adikulov and Marat Sarulu
  Editor and Set Designer: Tilck Mambetova
  Music: Nurlan Nishanov
  Leading Players: Mirlan Abdikalikov, Albina Imasheva, Adir Abilkassimov, Bakit Zilkiejiev

Awards:
The film won the Silver Leopard for Best Director at the Locarno Film Festival (1998); the Don Quixote Prize of the International Association of Cinema Clubs; Grand Prize at the Eurasia International Film Festival, Almaty (1998); Viewer's choice and jury's choice awards at the Vienna Film Festival (1998); Asian Film Juries Award at the Tokyo Film Festival (1999); Grand Prize and Students' Choice at Cottbus (1999); Jury Award for Artistic Contribution at the Buenos Aires Film Festival (1999) and the Silver Film Can and FIPRESCI awards at the Singapore Film Festival (1999).

Little Azate's parents follow an old Kyrgyz tradition and give him away to a childless couple as their family is already big enough. When he learns the truth, Azate is upset, but his feelings are quickly resolved when a bigger calamity befalls him – his adoptive grandmother dies. With maturity, he declares that he will repay her debts if there are any, as according to Kyrgyz customs, a person who owes to people cannot be buried. The film is the second part of Abdikalikov's trilogy about growing up, which he started with his short film *Selkinchek/Swing*.

Lyuty/The Ferocious One
  1973, 90 mins, colour
  Director: Tolomush Okeev
  Screenwriters: Andrei Mikhalkov Kontchalovski and Ernest Tropinine
  Cinematographer: Kadirjan Kidiraliev
  Set: Victor Lednev

Music: D. Botbaev
Leading Players: Kambar Valiev, Suimenkul Chokmorov, Aliman Djangorozova

In pre-revolutionary Kazakhstan, a young boy, Kurmash, is trusted to the care of his uncle and grandmother. His uncle is a brutal man; however, he justifies his cruelty to the boy as a process of education to prepare him for a cruel world. Kurmash raises a wild wolf cub that he saves from death at the hands of his brutal uncle and becomes attached to the animal.

Maimyl/The Chimp
2001, 98 mins, colour
Director: Aktan Arymkubat (Abdikalikov)
Production: Noe Productions, Beshkempir Studio and Bitters End
Director: Aktan Abdikalikov
Cinematographer: Hassan Kidiraliev
Scriptwriters: Aktan Abdikalikov, Aftandil Adikulov and Tonino Guerra
Editors: Tilek Mambetova and Natalia Vavilkina
Sound: Bakit Nijazaliev and Dominique Warnier
Music: Alexander Ortaev
Leading Players: Mirlan Abdikalikov, Ajnagul Essenkoeva, Jylkychy Jakypov, Aleksandra Mitrohina, Sergei Golovkin

Awards:
The film won the FIPRESCI award at the Bratislava Film Festival and the Jury Special Prize at the Festroia-Troia Film Festival (2002).

In a desolate Kyrgyz village, a young man called 'chimp' by his friends because of his slightly protruding ears waits to be called for military service. The youth of the village pass the time fighting, partying and trying to have their first sexual experience while waiting to be drafted. The chimp experiences his first fears and his first wounds. His father's addiction to alcohol puts a heavy burden on the family's everyday life and causes his mother and his little sister's departure. The film is the third part of Arymkubat's trilogy about growing up, which he started with his short film *Selkinchek/Swing*.

Samancynyn Zolu/ Materinskoe Pole/The Mother's Field
1968, 72 mins, black & white
Director: Gennadi Bazarov
Production: Kyrgyz Film
Cinematographer: V. Vilenski

Screenwriters: Chingiz Aitmatov, B. Dobrodeev and I. Talankine
Set: K. Yusupov
Music: You Chein
Leading Players: B. Kydykeeva, A. Douicheeva, M. Assanbaev, G. Alieva, L. Abdoukarimova, S. Djoumadylov, N. Kitaev

Tolgonai's husband and sons are killed in the war and her daughter-in-law prefers to die also, but Tolgonai does not accept defeat. She talks to her dead husband's picture and teaches her grandson to work in the fields.

Saratan/Village Authorities
2005, 84 mins, colour
Director and Screenwriter: Ernest Abdishaparov
Producers: Tinai Ibragimov, Kanat Sartov, Herbert Schwering and Hans-Erich Viet
Production: Kyrgyzfilm Studio, Icon Film and Viet Filmproduktion
Cinematographers: Jorzsh Hamitski and Talant Akyubekov
Editor: Saida Sadykova
Music: Ernest Abdishaparov
Sound: Bakyt Niazaliev
Leading Players: Abylov Kumondor, Aktanov Tabyldy, Sulaimanov Askat

Awards:
The film won the Special Mention at FIPRESCI Fribourg International Film Festival (2005).

A small Kyrgyz town serves as a metaphor for the condition of the country ten years after independence. Village people have not changed much from before: diehard communists; the cattle thief Tashmat, who still carries on with his business; the policeman Salamat, who is busy chasing after him; and village administrator Kabylbek, who has to listen to all the grievances. There is a serious lack of money; pensions are not paid and everyone is determined to do what is necessary to survive, even resorting to dubious dealings if need be. To the villagers, nothing seems to be fair or right any more. Losing their faith in a better future or a just God, the villagers decide to devote themselves to earthly pleasures. However, in spite of all their bitterness, life seems to go on as usual; some manage to take great advantage of the situation and others less so. Then comes the surprising and shocking news that the cattle thief has finally been captured by the village policeman; moreover, unable to bear the humiliation, he has committed suicide. Community spirit is put to the test as the headman struggles to keep his village in one piece.

Selkinchek/The Swing

1993, 48 mins, black & white
Director: Aktan Arymkubat (Abdikalikov)
Producers: M. Abakirova and P. Eliferenko
Production: Maek Film
Cinematographer: Hassan Kidiraliev
Screenwriters: AktanAbdikalikov, Ernest Abdizhaparov and Talgat Asirankulov
Editor: Hadicha Urmurzina
Sound/Music: Sergei Lobanov
Sets: Talgat Asirankulov
Leading Players: Mirlan Abdikalikov, Bakit Toktokojoev, Ainur Tolokabilova

Awards:

The film won the Grand Prize at the Locarno Film Festival (1993); the FIPRESCI at the Turin Film Festival (1993) and the Grand Prize at the Potsdam Film Festival (1994).

A young boy and a retarded man love pushing a beautiful girl on a swing. These are the happiest moments of their lives. But their joy is suddenly stifled by the arrival of a marine coming home from service and taking the girl far away with him. Whereas the retarded man dies of boredom, the young boy makes drawings of the girl on the swing to help him bear his grief.

Svet-Ake/The Light Thief

2010, 80 mins, colour
Director: Aktan Arymkubat
Producers: Altynai Koichumanova, Cedomir Kolar, Thanassis Karathanos, Marc Baschet, Karl Baumgartner, Denis Vaslin
Production: A.s.p.a. Films, Volya Films, Oy Art Film, Pallas Film
Cinematographer: Khasan Kydyraliyev
Screenwriters: Talip Ibrahimov, Aktan Arymkubat
Editor: Petar Markovic
Music: Andre Matthias
Leading Players: Aktan Arymkubat, Taalaikan Abazova, Askat Sulaimanov, Asan Amanov

Awards:

The film won the Best Film and FIPRESCI prizes at the Eurasia International Film Festival (Almaty-Kazakhstan).

A kind hearted electrician, called Mr Light (Svet-Ake) by his friends, brings light to the inhabitants of a small city who have not lost the ability to love and laugh despite desperation in their daily lives. Naïvely, he strikes a bargain with a rich developer running for the local office to supply wind-generated electricity to the whole valley. But he is faced with corruption.

Urkui/The Worship of the Fire
1971, 91 mins, colour
Director: Tolomush Okeev
Production: Kyrgyzfilm
Cinematographer: Kadirjan Kidiraliev
Screenwriters: N. Baitemirov, G. Orlov and Tolomush Okeev
Set: Syganbek Ichenov
Music: T. Ermatov
Leading Players: Tattabubu Tursunbaeva, Isken Riskulov, Suratbek Mumushaliev

In the 1930s, collectivization is in full force on the Fergana valley. Ali proposes to vote for a young peasant mother to be the head of the Kolkhoz, but the rich Koulak are sure that she cannot do the job. But she may have a chance because the construction of a canal will change life in the village. The village chief is a wise man who is counting on the strength of tradition, but one night a man enters the house of the woman and kills her and her husband.

TAJIKISTAN

Ashk va Samshed/Tears and a Sword
1991, 129 mins, colour
Director: Tachir M. Sabirov
Producer: Munavar Mansurchodaev
Production: Tajikfilm
Cinematographer: Vladimir Saposhnikov
Screenwriters: Tachir M. Sabirov and Semen Lungin
Music: Abdilfatach Odinaev
Leading Players: Muhammadsaid Pririon, Buchon Radshabov, Chotam Nurov, Madina Machmudova

The subjects of the emir of Bukhara are suffering. Grain prices are low and taxes are exorbitant. Then a son finds out that he is to be held responsible for the debts of his deceased father, who had mortgaged his lost plot of land and sold his horse. He decides to rise up against this injustice.

Margi sudhur/Death of an Extortionist
  1966, 90 mins, black and white
  Director: Tachir Sabirov
  Cinematographer: Anvar Mansurov
  Screenwriters: Igor Lukovski and Tachir Sabirov
  Décor: David Iliabaev
  Music: Ziodullo Shakhidi
  Leading Players: Zokir Dusmatov, Khabibullo Abdurazzakov, Ato Mukhamedjanov,
Zulfia Assanova

In Bukhara, before the revolution, a young man who arrives in the city is attacked and
robbed of the little money he has. He has to fight the rich merchants to find his fiancée.
The gang leader of the thieves agrees to help him and they kill the moneylender.

TURKMENISTAN

Ogul/Syn/The Son
  1988, colour
  Director: Halmammet Kakabayev
  Production: Turkmenfilm
  Cinematographers: Sergei Shugarov and Alexander Udashev
  Screenwriters: Sergei Bodrov and Halmammet Kakabayev
  Set: Salim Amangeldiev
  Music: Aman Agadikov
  Leading Players: Salih Bairmarov, Bekmurad Kutlimuradov, Tamara Shakirova

After the departure of his musician father for the war front, Batyr stays behind in a
village that is populated mostly by women. Although he is not willing to learn to play the
dutar (a traditional cord instrument) in the beginning, he changes his attitude after the
death of his father and decides to become a great *dutar* player.

Toba/Repentance
  1996, 90 mins, colour
  Director and screenwriter: Halmammet Kakabayev
  Producer: Turkmenfilm
  Cinematographer: Batir Atayev
  Music: Igor Pinkhasov
  Leading players: Chari Ishankuliyev, Salikh Batramov, Aisaltan Berdiyava, Kerim
Annanov

Awards:
The film won the Jury Award at the Eurasia Film Festival, Almaty (1998).

A new-capitalist son living in the city is ashamed of his humble mother but learns a lesson when it is too late. He decides to settle back in his village to repent his sins.

UZBEKISTAN

Askar Ertagi/Soldatskaja Skazka/A Soldier's Story
1989, 60 mins, colour
Director: Zulfikar Mussakov
Production: Uzbekfilm, Cooperative EKVIS and Superior Directing Classess
Cinematographer: Talgat Mansurov
Screenwriters: Zulfikar Mussakov and Nikolai Gueiko
Leading Players: Nikolai Gueiko, Aleksandr Zavialov, Pavel Egorov, Abduljamil Mamedov, Bekzad Mukhamedkarimov, Elena Lopatko

Life in the barracks has its ups and downs when young men from different corners of the Soviet Union are gathered under the same roof. Conflict arises not because of hate or enmity, but boredom and ignorance in an atmosphere that is conducive to tension.

Ayollar Saltanati/Shenskoje Zarstvo/Women's Paradise
2002, 75 mins, colour
Director: Yusuf Razikov
Production: State Joint Stock Company and Uzbekfilm
Cinematographer: Chotam Fayziev
Screenwriters: Yusuf Razikov and Mahmud Tucev
Editor: Olga Morova
Music: Dzamsid Izamov
Leading Players: Bachtiar Zakirov, Mokhira Nurmetova, Fatihh Jalolov, Nigora Rachimova, Zakir Ismailov

A middle-aged writer, Olim, is having a mid-life crisis as well as a writer's block. While his wife is trying to give birth, he is visiting his lover. He escapes through the window not to be caught at his mistress' house by his pregnant wife, and spends the night on the window ledge as the baby is born to the sound of high (western) opera. At his deathbed, his best friend hands down his beautiful wife (according to custom) to him and divulges the secret of the magical root, part of which is a woman. Obsessed by the thoughts of this root, Olim begins his holy quest, encountering various male comic buffoons and beautiful women on the way, his journey culminating in a women's market, a paradise on earth.

Dilxiro/Men's Dance

2002, 77 mins, colour
Director: Yusuf Razikov
Production: Uzbekfilm
Screenwriters: Erkin Azam, Yusuf Razikov
Music: Jamshed Izomov
Leading Players: Totu Yusupova, Zikir Mukhammedzhanov, Seving Muminova, Alisher Khamraev

With the titled dance serving as a sign of the communal joy taken in the cyclic events of social life, director Razikov creates an observational narrative that follows a young manís entry into the adult world of Islamic Uzbekistan. The boy endures physical pain as his bride-to-be undergoes her own rite of passage. The complications that impede the marriage of this young couple not only suggest the actual conflicts that abound in the culture, but also give the work spiritual and philosophical dimensions.

Genosse Boykendschajew/Comrade Boykenjayev

2002, 78 mins, colour
Director: Yusuf Razikov
Producers: Murad Mukhammad Dost and Yusuf Razikov
Production: Uzbekkino/Uzbekfilm Studios
Screenwriters: Yusuf Razikov and Abdukhalik Abdurrazakov (from a novel by Abdukhalik Abdurrazakov)
Cinematographer: Khotam Fayziyev and Bobur Ismailov
Editor: Olga Morova
Sound/Music: Djamshid Izamov
Leading Players: Farkhad Abdullayev, Matluba Alimov

During the last years of the Soviet Union, a humble party servant Boykenjayev is entrusted with the task of setting up a graveyard for the mortal remains of Uzbek people, regardless of their ethnic or religious background. But Boykenjayev's mission is thwarted by ethnic conflicts, religious quarrels and mafia manipulations. The film satirizes the Soviet regime before its demise at the same time evoking a sense of nostalgia. 'After all, why did we make a revolution'? is the last sentence spoken by the high-ranking official.

Osmondagi Bolabar/*Malchiki V Nebe/Boys in the Sky*
2002, 86 mins, colour
Director Zulfikar Mussakov
Producer: Yusuf Razikov
Production: Uzbekfilm
Cinematographer: Abduralhim Ismailov
Screenwriters: Zulfikar Mussakov and Risivoy Muhammadonov
Leading Players: Timur Mussakov, Muzaffar Sagdullev, Davron Gulyamov, Aziz Sultanov, Kristina Taipova, Malika Alimova

A gentle comedy about four boys growing up in Tashkent (modelled after Fellini's *Amarcord*), the film combines a series of loosely connected episodes to convey the pains and pleasures of adolescence. Some of the scenes, such as the Michael Jackson homage or watching a pirated copy of *Emmanuelle*, are hilarious.

Yol bulsin/ Dorogapod Nebesami /The Road Under the Skies
2006, 77mins, colour
Director and Producer: Kamara Kamalova
Production: SHOD Film Studio
Screenwriter: Shomirza Turdimov
Cinematographer: Rifkat Ibragimov
Editor: Olga Morova
Music: Mustafa Boboev
Leading Players: Aziz Rametov, Zarina Nazanetdinova, Mukhabat Iso Abdukhairov

Awards:
The film won the Best Director award at the Eurasia International Film Festival and the State Prize of Uzbekistan (2007).

A classic love story of adolescent passion and desertion is told using Uzbek folklore. When the young man who gets the girl pregnant leaves choosing his freedom over his love, to cleanse her damaged honour, the girl marries a good-hearted man she does not love.

Voiz/Orator
1998, 83 mins, colour with black & white inserts
Director and Screenwriter: Yusuf Razikov
Production: Uzbekfilm Studio
Cinematographers: Ulugbek Khamrayev and Daniar Abdurakhmanov
Editor: Olga Morova

Music: Dmitri Yanov-Yanovsky and Nariman Chadiev

Leading Players: Bakhodir Adilov, Asal Alikhodzhayeva, Javokhir Zakirov, Lola Altoyeva, N. Rakhmonova, Sh. Khamrakulova

Awards:

The film won the Grand prize of Kinoshok (1999) and the Grand Prize at the Moscow Film Festival (2000).

In 1915, just before the Bolshevik revolution, Iskander, a cart driver in his 40s, lives happily with his three wives, one he married by choice and two that he inherited after the death of his brother. The arrangement is permitted under the Islamic law of sharia, but not tolerated by the Bolsheviks. He provides refuge to a wounded revolutionary fighter and, after the revolution, receives the honorary title of 'national cadre'. His life becomes complicated when his oratory skills attract the love interest of a revolutionary activist. He ends up marrying her as well, but she gives birth to their son in jail (arrested for the distortion of the policies of the Communist Party) and dies. Iskender does not claim his son; the boy is brought up by the three wives. The story is told by his grandson.

SELECTED BIBLIOGRAPHY

GENERAL WORKS

Ahmed, Leila. (1992) *Women and Gender in Islam: Historical Roots of a Modern Debate.* New Haven, Conn: Yale University Press.

Appadurai, Arjun (1996) *Modernity at Large: Cultural Dimensions of Globalization.* Minneapolis: University of Minnesota Press.

Armbrust, W. (ed.). (2000) *Mass Mediations: New Approaches to Popular Culture in the Middle East and Beyond.* Berkeley: University of California Press.

Armes, Roy. (1987) *Third World Film Making and the West.* Berkeley: University of California Press.

Bernstein, Matthew and Gaylyn Studlar (eds). (1997) *Visions of the East: Orientalism in Film.* London & New York: I.B. Tauris.

Bhabha, Homi K. (1992) 'The World and the Home', *Social Text*, 31/32, 141–153.

———. (1994). *The Location of Culture.* London: Routledge.

Chomsky, Noam (2003) *Middle East Illusions; Peace, Security and Terror.* New Delhi: Penguin Books.

Davies, Miranda (ed.). (1983) *Third World – Second Sex.* London: Zed.

Downing, John D. H. (ed.). (1987) *Film and Politics in the Third World.* New York: Praeger.

Dönmez-Colin, Gönül. (2004) *Women, Islam and Cinema.* London: Reaktion Books.

————. (2007) *The Cinema of North Africa and the Middle East* (ed.). London & New York: Wallflower Press.

Gabriel, Teshom H. (1982) *Third Cinema in the Third World: The Aesthetics of Liberation.* Ann Arbor, Mich.: UMI Research Press.

Gresh, Alain and Dominique Vidal. (2004) *The New A–Z of the Middle East.* London: I.B. Tauris.

Jameson, Fredric. (1986) 'Third World Literature in the Era of Multinational Capitalism', *Social Text*, 15, 65–88.

————. (1992) *The Geopolitical Aesthetic: Cinema and Space in the World System.* Bloomington & London: Indiana University Press and BFI.

Jayawardena, Kumari. (1986) *Feminism and Nationalism in The Third World.* London: Zed.

Leaman, Oliver (ed.). (2001) *The Companion Encyclopaedia of Middle Eastern and North African Film.* London: Routledge.

Mayne, Judith. (1990) *The Woman at the Keyhole. Feminism and Women's Cinema.* Bloomington: Indiana University Press.

Mernissi, F. (1996) *Women's Rebellion and Islamic Memory.* London : Zed Books.

Mir-Hosseini, Ziba. (1999) *Islam and Gender, The Religious Debate in Contemporary Iran.* Princeton: Princeton University Press.

Moore-Gilbert, Bart. (1997) *Postcolonial Theory, Context, Practices, Politics.* London: Verso.

Naficy, Hamid (ed.). (1999) *Home, Exile, Homeland: Film, Media and the Politics of Place.* London & New York: Routledge.

————. (2000) 'Self Othering: A Postcolonial Discourse on Cinematic First Contact' in F. Afzal-Khan and K. Seshadri-Crooks (eds.) *The Pre-Occupation of Post Colonial Studies.* Durham: Duke University Press.

————. (2001) *An Accented Cinema: Diasporic and Exilic Filmmaking.* Princeton & Oxford: Princeton University Press.

———— and Teshome H. Gabriel (eds). (1993) *Otherness and the Media: The Ethnography of the Imagined and the Imaged*. Langhorne, PA: Harwood Academic Publishers.

Nichols, Bill. (1991) *Representing Reality*. Bloomington: Indiana University Press.

Nichols, Peter M. (2001) 'Middle East, Elusive on Film', *New York Times*, Oct 12, E28.

Pines, Jim and Paul Willemen (eds). (1989) *Questions of Third Cinema*. London: BFI.

Rony, Fatimah Tobing. (1996) *Third Eye: Race, Cinema and Ethnographic Spectacle*. Durham: Duke University Press.

Russell, Catherine. (1999) *Experimental Ethnography: The Work of Film in the Age of Video*. Durham: Duke University Press.

Said, E. W. (1978) *Orientalism*. New York: Vintage Books.

————. (1981) *Covering Islam: How the Media and the Experts Determine How We See the Rest of the World*. New York: Pantheon Books.

————. (1983) *The World, the Text and the Critic*. Cambridge, MA: Harvard University Press.

————. (1992) *Culture and Imperialism*. New York: Knopf.

————. (2001) *Reflections on Exile and Other Literary and Cultural Essays*. London: Penguin Books.

Shohat, Ella. (1985) 'The Cinema After Babel: Language, Difference, Power' in *Screen* (London), 26, 3–4.

————. (1997) 'Gender and Culture of Empire: Toward a Feminist Ethnography of the Cinema', in M. Bernstein and G. Studlar (eds) *Visions of the East: Orientalism in Film*. London: I.B. Tauris, 19–66.

———— and Robert Stam. (1994) *Unthinking Eurocentrism; Multiculturalism and the Media*. London: Routledge.

Slemon, Stephen. (1988) 'Magic Realism as Post-Colonial Discourse' in *Canadian Literature*, 116, 9–24.

Spivak, Gayatri Chakravorty. (1999) *A Critique of Postcolonial Reason, Toward a History of the Vanishing Present*. Cambridge & London: Harvard University Press.

Thoraval, Yves. (1998) 'West Asia: Wars and Much More', *Cinemaya*, 41, 30–35.

———. (2000) *Les cinémas du Orient, Iran, Egypte, Turquie*. Paris: Séquier.

Vasudev, Aruna et al. (eds). (2002) *Being and Becoming, the Cinemas of Asia*. New Delhi: Macmillan India Limited.

CENTRAL ASIA

Abdizhaparov, Ernest. (2000) *Das Kirgisische Kino*. Katalog des Film Festivals, Cottbus.

Abikeyeva, Gulnara. (2001) 'Women in the Kazakh Film Industry' in *Aus dem Herzen Der Welt*. Vienna: Oesterreichisches Filmmuseum, 52–53.

———. (2003) *The Heart of the World: Films from Central Asia*. Almaty.

Attwood, Lynne. (1991) *The New Soviet Men and Women: Sex Role Socialization in the USSR*. Bloomington: Indiana University Press.

——— (ed.). (1993) *Red Women of the Silver Screen*. London: Pandora Press.

Binder, Eva. (2001) 'Film in den Mittelasiatischen Sowjet-Republiken: Brüche und Kontinuitaten' in *Aus dem Herzen Der Welt*. Vienna: Oesterreichisches Filmmuseum, 21–26.

Birkos, Alexander S. (1976) *Soviet Cinema: Directors and Films*. Hamden, Conn: Archon Books.

Ciesol, Forrest. (1989–1990) 'Kazakhstan Wave', *Sight and Sound*, 59, 56–58.

———. (1990) 'After a Twenty-five Year Struggle with Censors, Uzbek Hero Tamerlane Rides Again', *Variety*, 13, 6.

———. (1990) 'Many Hollywoods of Central Asia', *World Monitor*, 2, 66–70.

Doraiswamy, Rashmi. (2009) *Cultural Histories of Central Asia*. New Delhi: Aakar Books.

Dönmez-Colin, Gönül. (1997) 'Kazakh New-Wave: Post Perestroika, Post Soviet Union', *Central Asian Survey*, 16, 1, 115–118.

———. (2001a) 'Turkmen and Uzbek Filmmaking' in *Aus dem Herzen Der Welt*. Vienna: Oesterreichisches Filmmuseum, 60–65.

———. (2001b) 'Central Asian Cinema' in *Companion Encyclopedia of Middle Eastern and North African Film*. London: Routledge Ltd.

———. (2001c) 'They Do Make Films in Central Asia', *Blimp*. Graz, 44, 99–132.

———. (2002) 'Central Asia Redefining Its Cultural Roots' in *Kinema*, Waterloo, Can: University of Waterloo, 43–54.

———. (2005) '*The Hunter* by Serik Aprimov', *Cinemaya*, 65, 1, 25.

Golownja, Jekaterina and Jewgenija. (2001) 'Sergei Solowjows Meisterklasse und die Kasachische Neue Welle' in *Aus dem Herzen Der Welt*. Vienna: Oesterreichisches Filmmuseum, 43.

Goulding, Daniel J. (ed.) (1989) *Post New Wave Cinema in the Soviet Union and Europe*. Bloomington and Indianapolis: Indiana University Press.

Horton, Andrew. (1990) 'Nomad from Kazakhstan: An Interview with Rashid Nugmanov', *Film Criticism*, 14, 2, 33–38.

——— and M. Brashinsky. (1992) *The Zero Hour: Glasnost and Soviet Cinema in Transition*. Princeton, New Jersey: Princeton University Press.

Karow, Willi. (2001) 'Tschingis Ajtmatow und Das Kirgisische Kino' in *Aus dem Herzen Der Welt*. Vienna: Oesterreichisches Filmmuseum, 27–31.

Krill, Herbert. (2001) 'Zentralasien und Seine Filme' in *Aus dem Herzen Der Welt*. Vienna: Oesterreichisches Filmmuseum, 15–17.

Lawton, A. (1990) 'Soviet Cinema Four Years Later' in *Wide Angle*, 12, 4, 9–22.

———. (1992) *Kinoglasnost: Soviet Cinema in Our Time*. Cambridge: Cambridge University Press.

Nogerbek, Bauyrzhan (trans. by Vladimir Padunov). (2004) 'Demythologizing and Reconstructing National Space in the Kazakh "New Wave" in *Kinocultura'. www. bris.ac.uk/kinocultura.*

Nugmanov, Rachid. (2001) 'Die Kazachische neue Welle: Ein Blick von Innen' in *Aus dem Herzen Der Welt.* Vienna: Oesterreichisches Filmmuseum, 44–45.

Passek, Jean Loup (ed.). (1981) *Le Cinéma Russe and Soviétique.* Paris: L'équerre, Centre Georges Pompidou.

Rumer, Boris and Stanislav Zhukov (eds). (1998) *Central Asia: The Challenges of Independence.* New York and London: M. E. Sharpe.

Vorontsov, Lu. (1980) *The Phenomenon of the Soviet Cinema.* Moscow: Progress Publishers.

Vronskaya, Jeanne. (1972) *Young Soviet Filmmakers.* London: George Allen and Unwin Ltd.